The Palestinians

The Palestinians

Jonathan Dimbleby
The Palestinians

Photographs by
Donald McCullin

Quartet Books Inc.
Distributed by Horizon Press

TITLE IV B
ES

Acknowledgements

I am grateful for the help of many individuals, some of whom are
named in this book, some of whom preferred to remain
anonymous. All of them have given me their time and hospitality
in abundance; many of them in the last few years have offered me
their friendship. Although all of them have contributed—
occasionally unwittingly—to the judgements and views reflected in
The Palestinians, the responsibility for its conclusions is mine.

I owe a special debt to the staff at the Institute of Palestinian
Studies in Beirut; to Professor Walid al-Khalidi who gave me
early guidance, and whose *From Haven to Conquest*, a collection
of the most important documents relating to the period up to
1948, is invaluable; and to David Hirst, whose rare understanding
of the Middle East is reflected in his excellent *The Gun and the
Olive Branch* which has helped clarify my own perception.

Heather Laughton transcribed almost incomprehensible tapes and
typed the manuscript with astonishing speed and accuracy. The
staff at Quartet bore my elusiveness with patience, and Bel
advised and sustained me from start to finish.

Published in the United States of America by Quartet Books Inc. 1980
A member of the Namara Group
156 Fifth Avenue, New York N Y 10010

First published in Great Britain by Quartet Books Limited 1979
A member of the Namara Group
27/29 Goodge Street, London W1P 1FD

Design by Mike Jarvis

Historical illustration research by Angela Murphy

ISBN 0 7043 2256 0

Library of Congress Catalog Card Number 79-48038

Origination by Culver Graphics Group,
Printed and bound by Hazell Watson and Viney Ltd, Bucks, England

For the victims

Contents

Introduction

Some Palestinians will find the image on the cover of this book heroic. I find it tragic. The old man was a child when the Balfour Declaration sanctioned the future of Zionism in Palestine, and for the last thirty years he has lived in a refugee camp. He is proud of his grandson, who carries the gun which is now the Palestinian birthright, expecting him soon to join the fedayeen to fight Israel. And he will do so, if not with a gun, then with a bomb. Israeli soldiers will seek to kill him. If they succeed, which is not unlikely, they will report that another 'terrorist' has been eliminated. And the PLO will announce that another 'martyr' has been born.

It is impossible to approach the tragedy of the Middle East without recognizing the long agony to which the Jews of the Western world have been subjected; without respecting the vision which inspired the original Zionist movement; without recoiling from the images of the Holocaust; without weeping to the lamentations in the music of Bloch; or without honouring the history of a people whose genius has so enriched Western civilization.

It should not be necessary to reiterate this – but it is. The reporter is an advocate in the court of public opinion. His client is that amorphous chameleon, Reality, upon which he occasionally, if foolishly, confers the title Truth.

In the case of the 'Palestinian problem', it is particularly difficult to represent reality, even if it may be more than dimly perceived. Merely to describe the Palestinians as a people with a past, a present and a future is to call into question some of the popular assumptions from which the prevailing strategies of the state of Israel derive their justification. To go further – to pay attention to Palestinian accounts of their own history, to record the impact upon them of the rise of Zionism, to relate their stories of the exodus, the exile and the resurgence – is for the reporter to risk finding himself in the dock, charged by an articulate lobby with being an enemy of the people of Israel, if not an anti-Semitic racist.

The charge is pressed with a noisy vehemence, reinforced – for lack of evidence – by a particularly virulent form of moral blackmail which invites public opinion to perceive Zionism in terms of the Holocaust, filtering the facts of the Middle East through the tears of disgust, outrage and guilt which the bestialities of Nazism arouse in all civilized men.

Yet the reporter is obliged to resist such obloquy if he is to report the other side of the case. And to report that other side is crucial to the understanding of a crisis which not only endangers its chief protagonists but, in a world which can be destroyed by a single act of nuclear madness, poses a persistent threat to all mankind.

It is now generally agreed that the conflict in the Middle East is, at root, a territorial dispute between two peoples: the Israelis and the Palestinians. It is further acknowledged that the conflict has a history and even, lurking in the past, that there is a Palestinian case to be answered. Yet the struggle is still presented in a woefully lop-sided fashion: a small embattled, occasionally obstinate, but usually admirable democratic state (Israel) under challenge from a despicable, occasionally pathetic, but usually brutal gang of desperados (the PLO). The Zionist case for Palestine is well known and remains the point of departure for all Western policy towards the conflict. The Palestinian case is equally powerful, though it is still referred to, in terms which reflect the imbalance of our Western perception, as the Palestinian 'problem'.

It is not surprising that Western statesmen should regard this 'problem' with that combination of amorality and pragmatism upon which the martial art of diplomacy depends. In international relations, the concept of justice which is so movingly enshrined in so many noble constitutions is but a diplomatic coda, a rhetorical flourish, written into the script in the hope of convincing public opinion that the most venal political decision is always inspired by the highest moral principle.

In this political quagmire, it is customary for a

sceptical public opinion to be invited to challenge the distortions which statesmen carve out of the facts. In the case of Palestine, however, the distortions have endured to become myths, unshakeably established in the public mind. The distinguished Palestinian historian, Walid al-Khalidi, has described the consequences of this process.

This Western purblindness is itself a hallmark of the Palestinian problem. The Palestinians are not the first and will probably not be the last to be dispossessed and banished; but so far they are, perhaps, in the unique position where not only is their Catastrophe ruled out of the Western Court as being irrelevant to their reactions against its perpetrators, but where these very reactions are held to incriminate them.[1]

This book is neither a hymn to terrorism nor an apologia for the PLO. It is, however, an attempt to redress our balance of perception. For too long – with rare and distinguished exceptions – those who mould Western public opinion have cravenly failed to extricate themselves from the political and moral framework which has been bequeathed to today's statesmen by their predecessors. Much of the relevant history has been persistently ignored, and most of the relevant facts have been sedulously reconstructed in the image of Zionism. The fathers of Zionism may have initiated an epic and even heroic struggle for Jewish emancipation, but the impact of this struggle upon the Palestinian people has been cruel and catastrophic – a fact which, unforgivably, the Western media have rarely sought to understand or explain.

Instead, they have persistently delivered themselves of portentous and superficial moral judgements, which serve only to establish and confirm the distortions which underpin and legitimize Western policy in the Middle East.

The most obvious symbol of this distortion is the use of the term 'terrorist' to distinguish Palestinian from Israeli atrocities. 'Terrorists' do not have jet planes to mutilate innocents from a distance; they do it with bombs in markets. Is the former less heinous than the latter because it is sanctioned by an Israeli Cabinet? Reason and morality answer 'No', but again and again the Israeli authorities emerge morally inviolate from their military adventures while the PLO is compared to the Nazis or the Ku-Klux-Klan for refusing to give up guerrilla war.

To tolerate this imbalance is to beg the central question to which all others lead: to whom does Palestine belong? This is a reporter's book. It does not argue a case, nor does it propose a solution. It merely attempts to give an account of their 'problem' as it is perceived and experienced by the Palestinian people.

It was once said by President Wilson that, 'Peoples and Provinces are not to be bartered about from sovereignty to sovereignty as if they were mere chattels or pawns in a great game.' Unhappily his wisdom has been systematically neglected by the great – and the not so great – powers whose strategic manoeuvres have brought the Middle East into ever more dangerous confrontation.

Even now, the West persists in the belief that a solution can be imposed upon the Middle East which ignores the origins of the conflict and the aspirations of *both* its principal protagonists. For how much longer can the PLO – by any yardstick, the legitimate representative of the Palestinian people – be excluded from the negotiations which will depend for their success upon Palestinian involvement? Depressingly, the answer appears to be: for as long as statesmen are free to pursue the narrow-minded and shortsighted policies which have already led the world to the brink of nuclear war, unchallenged by those who elect them into office.

To acknowledge the Palestinian cause is not to deny the cause of Israel, but to elevate the Palestinians to their proper place in the debate, and to recognize that their will cannot easily be sidestepped.

In this book I have focused particularly upon the Palestinians who are in exile in the Lebanon, in the belief that they are the spearhead of the Palestinian Resistance to which the overwhelming majority of Palestinians in the diaspora and under occupation owe their allegiance.

The conflict in the Middle East will be solved only when Palestinians and Israelis are able to work out their joint salvation with each other. The minimum condition for this is an environment – which has to be created by the rest of the world – in which both peoples are obliged to recognize that each has an equal but reconcilable claim upon Palestine. *The Palestinians* is a modest attempt to help promote such an environment by demonstrating what it means when Palestinians say: 'We are a people.' Mrs Golda Meir once stated:

There was no such thing as a Palestinian people . . . it is not as though there was a Palestinian people and we came and threw them out and took their country away from them. They did not exist.[2]

The Palestinians is written in the conviction that there can only be peace in the Middle East when it is universally recognized that the Palestinians did exist, do exist and will exist.

One
The Camp

At first glance the camp seems like any other Arab village: a sprawl of white houses, a main street in pot-holed tarmac, and a spider-web of alleyways, echoing to the shouts of young children. There is a huddle of shops: a cobbler's, a tailor's, a black-smith's, half-hidden behind smoke and sparks; a baker, filling a cavernous dark oven with flat rounds of fresh bread. Stringy meat from shins and shanks is hung on hooks and tormented by flies. Men stand gossiping and women move slowly from one counter to another, comparing prices and making careful meagre selections.

Bicycles weave through indifferent pedestrians; ancient Mercedes taxis, held together with wire and ingenuity and belching black fumes, force a passage, laden so heavily with passengers and their belongings that the wheels splay outwards and the axles groan. Ignoring the crush and the noise, a wrinkled old man rests at a café table with his small cup of black coffee, smoking a hookah, staring at nothing. Others talk and argue, gesticulating fiercely, or play a solemn and incomprehensible game of cards with no money changing hands.

In the back alleys it is suddenly quiet. In a doorway an old lady sits sewing; behind her, a younger woman sweeps the small courtyard, already clean. Whitewashed walls surround her, overhead a green vine shuts out the sun, except for a few spots which shimmer on the wet smooth concrete where she works. Shirts and pants and a row of tiny infant smocks are hung dripping from a rusty wire line. A baby sits in the corner, her hair tightly curled, teasing the tail of a sleeping dog.

A deceptive camera could make this street as inviting as a Tuscany village in summer, confirming the first impression that here is a settled community, impoverished but not discontented.

But this is not an ordinary village. It is a Palestinian refugee camp in south Lebanon – and gradually the abnormalities impress themselves upon the stranger. Among the hoardings and bill-boards advertising the stars who will soon appear at the local cinema are other posters; peeling portraits of young men and women. Their faces stare out at the passer-by, usually unsmiling, but often gentle and handsome: long dark hair, brown eyes, unblemished skin. Sometimes they are in jeans, sometimes in military fatigues. A few have posed with a rifle; others look resolutely ahead, expressionless like blow-ups from a passport, time-less, without age or life. Beneath each portrait is a name and around them on the walls there are written slogans about Israel or Sadat or Carter; the hammer and sickle of the Communist ideal is daubed on doors and walls, along with demands to crush Imperialism or support the PLO or the PFLP or Fatah. And plastered on telegraph poles and windows, and behind shop counters in protective

glass frames, is the ubiquitous face of Yasser Arafat – Abu Ammar, as he is called by those millions for whom he is an inspiration, the symbol of their dreams, the voice of their redemption. It was at his behest that the young men and women who linger now as memories on the peeling posters went off to fight the enemy and died; who are now 'martyrs' for Palestine, 'terrorists' for Israel.

Among the old taxis there are open Land-Rovers with machine-gun mountings instead of seats at the back, and Fiats and BMWs driven by fierce young men with that air of easy authority which brooks no disrespect. Their hair is long and they sport rifles and pistols. In any other village, their arrival, at speed with horns blaring, would scatter the people in fear. Here they are ignored, unless they call out in greeting to friends or smiling girls. Here they are at home, and expected.

The young men congregate around a few buildings which are indistinguishable from the rest,

except that they are without windows. On those thick walls the posters and slogans compete incomprehensibly, slapped one upon the other so that all meaning is obliterated in a wildly militant mosaic. It is to this place – the local headquarters of the Palestine Liberation Organization (PLO) – that any stranger must come. In no normal village would he need permission to look, and walk, and talk. But here, in Palestinian territory on Lebanese soil, he must seek authority and carry a pass; he must explain why he has come, and to whom he would speak. He sits inside the headquarters where the young fighters gather, to drink coffee and to be appraised. The courtesy with which he is met is casual but meticulous; the distrust which he sees in the questioning eyes is absolute.

This camp has been shelled from the sea and bombed from the air; there is a house a little way off which has been sheared in half. It looks grotesquely like a stage set for a domestic drama, a

13

A refugee for thirty years

The ubiquitous face of Yasser Arafat

A backyard in the camp

The camp has been 'shelled from the sea and bombed from the air'

bed with its ruined mattress half on the floor, an old electric cooker, a broken armchair, a child's doll without arms, some old newspapers and tin cans – all covered with bits of fallen plaster and ash from the fire that broke out when the shell burst into the living room, fortunately (and for once) when the family was not at home.

So the PLO officials are always suspicious. No one can be trusted: the stranger may be an agent for Israel, or Western Imperialism, or even, though it is rarely expressed so bluntly, for one of the Arab powers which compete with each other to control the destiny of the Palestinian people by provoking internal dissension among them.

It takes time to explain, for a decision to be made. So the room becomes familiar: the desk, the telephone, the upright chairs around the wall, the PLO calendar with its illustration of Haifa. On the wall is a painting by Ibrahim Ghannan. It shows three women dressed in black, with water-pots on

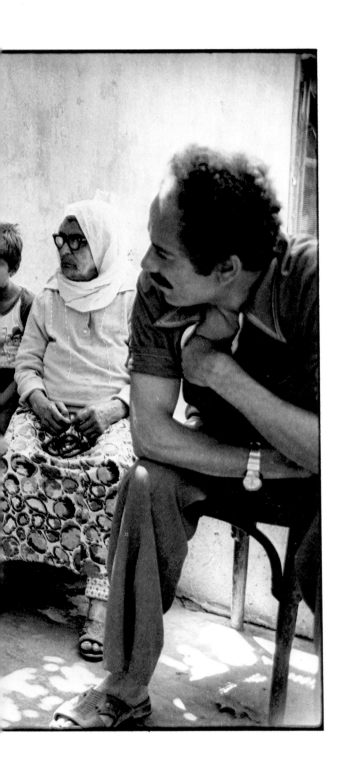

their heads. They are standing together in a lane, gossiping, one of them leaning on a low stone wall. The sun is rising over an orange grove. They could be discussing their children, or their husbands, or a marriage, or a scandal, or a rumour. In the ripe fields behind, men and women are stooping to cut the corn by hand. They work in tranquillity. In the background are the white houses of their small village, built on the top of a low hill, surrounded by olive groves. It is a simple, romantic memory of Palestine. Ghannan is the most popular painter in the Palestinian camps. His images – the scenes, the ceremonies, the rituals, the customs and habits which form the framework of a living culture – evoke a sense of loss and offer a moment of escape. For the young men who have never seen Palestine, they are vivid as a recurring dream, a passionate statement of how it might have been. They nourish a love for the homeland, and nurture the will to return.

The newest refugees. Their parents fled from Palestine,
they are victims of war in Lebanon

Elders from Galilee

One of Ibrahim Ghannan's paintings – the night before the wedding

The formalities end. The outsider is permitted to wander freely through the camp, and to listen to its voices.

The elders need no images from the past. They live with their memories – intense and private, and not easily to be shared. They wait for the visitor without trust. There are twelve of them.

The room is four metres square, a little larger than most in the camp. It is hot, though the shutters are half-closed against the midday sun. In the gloom, sitting upright and dignified on battered chairs, they wait with the patience of those who have been waiting for thirty years. They rise, courteous but wary. They have heard the world denounce their children and grandchildren as 'terrorists'. So they are the fathers of terrorism? They would like to know what purpose it could serve to ignore the insult and explain their truth to those who did not wish to know.

The question is resolved among themselves. They elect a spokesman.

'You are British and we find it hard not to perceive the British as our enemy, because it was you who permitted our country to be stolen from us. But we make you welcome. At least you wish to hear. We will speak with you.'

The formality is disconcerting but short-lived. These old men live for the past. When they speak of Palestine, they use the present tense. Their faces become animated as they compete to recall stories, remembering forgotten details, arguing about names and places and correcting dates. They talk without pause for over four hours about a world which they still inhabit.

They explain that most of the Palestinians living in the refugee camps of Lebanon come from Galilee. Most of them were peasants. They, the elders, come from families which were generally more prosperous than the other peasants. They owned land, and employed labour to work it. They raised cattle, and ran flocks of sheep. In their orchards, they grew oranges and lemons. They had vineyards and olive groves. On the better land they grew wheat and maize. They were not so much rich as less impoverished than the poor. The prosperous had slightly larger rooms in slightly bigger houses, a few more cattle, and they supported a larger entourage. But they still slept ten in a room and lived in simple style. Each offers a similar account of his history.

'I come from a place which is mentioned in the Bible, near Nazareth in Galilee. There I had an orchard where I grew vegetables, and apples and lemons. The orchard was almost square; I had seven acres altogether, which was a good size. It was half an hour from the house so I used to walk there each day. There was a shed in the orchard where I kept my tools and stored the fruit. During harvest-time I had a guard who stayed there to protect the fruit.'

'I had four oxen for ploughing, and a horse, and four donkeys to take my produce to market. There was a shepherd in the village who looked after everyone's sheep. Every family helped to support him and in return he cared for the animals. Each day he would walk the sheep, and each night he would return them to their owners. And it was the same with the cows.'

'Altogether there were twelve people in my family, including my parents and my children. When I got married I had to add two rooms and a kitchen to the house. We were all villagers so we were used to sharing. I had another room in which I stored the wheat and the seed; and another in which I kept the cattle.'

There is a pause, and the oldest man in the room walks slowly over to ensure that his words are recorded accurately. 'You should note this fact,' he says. 'I am eighty-five years old. I left Palestine in 1948 when I was fifty-five. But I am no older now than I was then. My life ceased at that moment.' The other men nod in agreement, fiercely silent.

The villages of Palestine were isolated, small communities. Virtually all the inhabitants worked on the land. The routine of their life was ordered according to strict custom. The hierarchies were well established. The elders of the village, the most powerful families, selected the muktar, who thus became their spokesman, the village leader. It was his responsibility to organize the labour for the communal harvest, to entertain visiting dignitaries and to provide hospitality for passing travellers. Each village had at least one guest-room where there was always coffee brewing on the charcoal brazier, and mattresses on which any visitors were entitled to take their rest.

Although one village looked much like another from the outside, inviting the indifferent stranger to see only their shared lowliness, each was in reality sharply individual. Not only were they run by different and often competing families, but their inhabitants spoke in differing accents and used their own idioms. One village was famous for its fighters; another for its olives; another for its singers; yet another for the beauty of its women. Sometimes they fought each other, jealously guarding traditional water-holes and grazing rights, and occasionally they would fight together against the new tax or the conscription of their young men into the Ottoman armies. They shared certain ruling principles: loyalty, hospitality and respect for age. And they lived by a common code of honour, which

'It is our revolution, the revolution of the old and young'

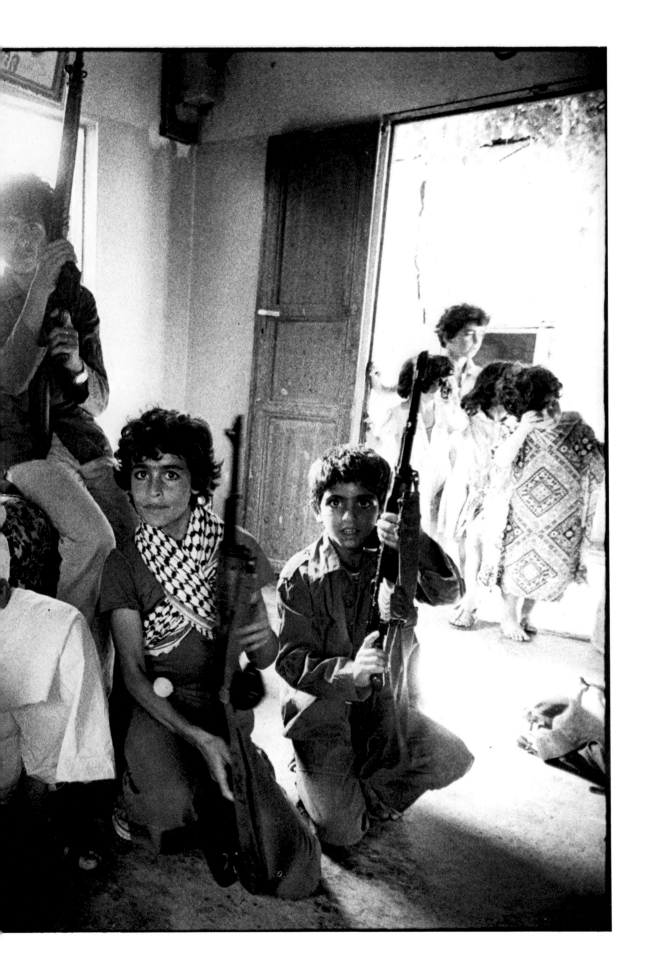

was upheld by the ritual of revenge.

The leading families sent representatives to sit on the village council, so that, according to the elders, their community was structured upon democratic lines.

'Within each family, we had respect for age. The old were given deference, but they listened to the young men. It was a good life. It was true that we had no cars, or electricity, or schools. Our roads were rough tracks, but we were happy and orderly.'

The muktar believes that it is time to move to the heart of the matter.

'Put this in your book. The British cheated us. They promised us freedom and instead we had the Mandate. And do you know what the policy of the Mandate was? It said that we, the people of Palestine, were not mature enough to govern ourselves. That is what it meant. That we were not mature enough. And worse than that even, they

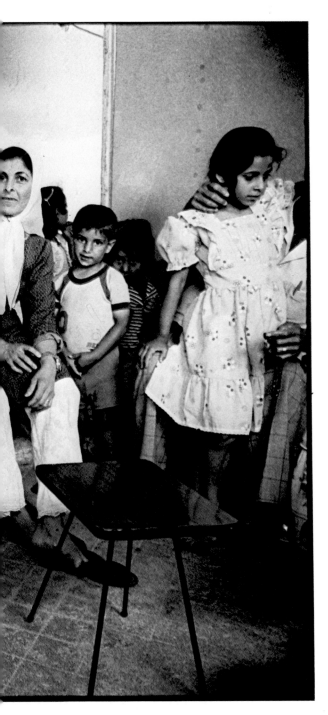

brought ruin to our land and made us homeless; you, the British, brought foreigners to Palestine and made us exiles.

'Now you, the British, and the rest of the Western world, say it is terror when our Palestinian fighters attack the Zionists. Our sons are not terrorists. They understand our tragedy. And we share their revolution. It is our revolution, the revolution of the old and young.'

The muktar has raised his voice, indignant, out-raged. Others join him. There is much talking at once. Then the old man comes over once more to ensure that what he says is noted. He speaks in a high frail voice.

'I have sacrificed so much. One of my sons was killed in Palestine. He was a commando. But I say this to you: the caravan of martyrs will continue to grow until the last drop of the blood in our bodies has been spilled. We can never forget and we will never give up.'

Outside in the evening sun the camp still seems normal, unnaturally so. An infant plays with a tin can in a gutter. Children in school uniform walk down an alley, shouting mild abuse at each other and anyone else in range. An old lady, catching the last of the sun, scolds them, muttering to herself. From a courtyard where supper is being prepared on an open fire, the smell of beans and oil drifts across the alley to compete with the heavy scent of blossom. A commando strolls past in khaki uniform, like any soldier on his way home, smiling at a young girl, who laughs back at him provocatively. Down a side-street, a donkey drawing a water-cart skilfully avoids the pot-holes in his path. In the café, the old men hardly glance up from their cards and their coffee, talking into the lengthening shadows.

But the last words of one of the elders lingers: 'A man without a country is a man without dignity. And our dignity is more important to us even than our life.'

'The smell of beans and oil drifts across the alley'

Two
The Roots of Zionism

It is unlikely that many of the inhabitants of Palestine took great notice of a conference which was held in Basle in 1897, under the direction of a prominent Jewish writer called Theodor Herzl, already renowned in Europe as the father of a new political movement called Zionism. At Basle, before a distinguished gathering of European Jewry, Herzl stated his purpose: 'We are here today to lay the foundation stone of the house which is to shelter the Jewish nation.'

The programme adopted by the delegates at Basle called for Jewish settlement in Palestine under the protection of international law. As symbols of their purpose and their identity, they chose both a flag and an anthem.

Zionism was an inspirational movement, mobilizing a downtrodden people, offering them a glimmer of a future, an alternative to the oppression and humiliation of the European ghettos in which they were isolated and imprisoned. At its birth it was morally unblemished, and spiritually innocent. It was not, however, either a uniform creed or a monolithic movement. There were those who perceived in Zionism an opportunity for the rebirth of the Jewish people as a cultural force in the world. Others dreamt that Zionism would lead the Children of Israel back to the 'promised land', and secure their ancient claim to Palestine. But for the great majority of those Jews who were attracted by its missionary zeal, who were to provide its limitless energy, and therefore its almost unstoppable historical momentum, Zionism was a political solution to their grave social predicament, an invitation to escape.

Theodor Herzl had been willing to contemplate either Argentina or Uganda (though the latter was rejected because of the fear that the white colonialists already there might rise up against the new immigrants) for settlement, in the belief that the solution to the 'Jewish question' lay in the 'establishment of a Jewish state for those whose position has grown intolerable' in the countries which persecuted them.

From the beginning, the new political creed was surrounded by controversy. There were those Jews who believed that Zionism was a blasphemy, a violation of the Word of God, who would – in His own time – lead the Jews back to the 'promised land'. Others, more pragmatically, believed that Zionism would feed anti-Semitism; that it would both confirm Gentile prejudice against the 'exclusive' character of the Jewish people, and offer an excuse for the forcible expulsion of Jews from their homes in Europe to the 'Zionist home' elsewhere. Such dissenters (and among Jews they were in the majority at the time) asserted that, since Jews were not in any sense a 'nation' – their self-definition being exclusively in terms of their religion – their escape from oppression should be by the route of assimilation into Gentile society.

Moreover, they asked a simple but fundamental question: 'By what right could Zionists expect to create a state in Palestine?' That country was not a wasteland in search of an identity. It existed upon the world map, it had borders, and – most crucially – it was inhabited. It was hardly conceivable that a Zionist state could be established in Palestine without the displacement and dispossession of the people who already lived there – unless, of course, these people could be persuaded to surrender their own aspirations to those of Zionism. Otherwise the project would have to be abandoned or pursued by force. This dilemma was the womb in which was to be nourished the tragedy of the Middle East.

The leaders of Zionism were unmoved by such dissent. They shared a set of unshakeable assumptions, pillars of certainty without which the edifice of their belief would have collapsed. They were convinced that all Jews in the world did belong to one nation; that their state was to be created by Jews for *all* Jews; that all Jews would eventually be driven to the Jewish state by the pathological anti-Semitism of the Gentile world; and that the fundamental purpose of the state was to secure 'the in-gathering' of the exiles. None the less they were careful to avoid using the term 'state' in public, choosing instead the carefully less provocative expression 'national homeland'. In their zeal they fostered the myth that Palestine was 'a land without a people, waiting for a people without a land' while assiduously denying that they sought to create a state in that territory. However, only two years after the congress, Herzl recorded in his diary: 'At Basle I founded the Jewish state . . . if I said this out loud today, I would be answered by universal laughter. Perhaps in five years, and certainly in fifty everyone will know it.'

Half a century later, the state of Israel was founded in Palestine.

The peasants of Palestine had little apparent cause for alarm. By the turn of the century there were rather more than half a million people living there, a mere five per cent of whom were Jews, who owned rather less than one per cent of the land. Many of these belonged to small religious groups which had been settled in and around Jerusalem, the focal point of the Jewish faith, for generations. It is true that others had recently arrived to establish a number of agricultural colonies which they had bought from absentee Arab landlords; and the alien customs and exclusive attitudes of these settlers aroused the suspicion, and sometimes the hostility, of those agricultural workers who had

been expelled from their jobs to make way for the immigrants. Indeed, the attitudes and behaviour of these early settlers had dismayed some early Zionists: 'They treat the Arabs with hostility and cruelty, unscrupulously deprive them of their rights, insult them without cause, and even boast of such deeds: and none opposes this despicable and dangerous inclination.' Those words were written in 1891 by Ahad Aham, who was fearful that the Jews in Palestine would fail to resist 'that inclination to despotism that always occurs when the servant becomes the master'.

This aside, the Palestinians had more pressing matters with which to deal, the rise of Zionism coinciding with an upsurge of Arab nationalism. Although the peasants of Palestine were ill-acquainted with the concept, they were displaying all the signs of a people which was determined to emerge from the long dark night of colonial – in this case Ottoman – rule.

For thousands of years their forefathers had obstinately and tenaciously clung to the soil upon which their lives depended, while a succession of foreign armies had churned their land into the battleground upon which they fought each other to secure the destiny of great empires. But by the early 1900s, the Ottoman Empire was in decay. As its foundations began to collapse, so the Arabs emerged to hasten the process. The Turkish response to this subversion was simple if ruthless. In the summer of 1915, for example, they hanged thirty-two leading dissident Arab lawyers, writers and army officers, who by challenging the Ottomans were committing treason against the Empire. The British, more cunning in the colonial arts, had sensed this new atmosphere and believed they could turn it to advantage. Two months after the hangings, the British High Commissioner of Egypt and Sudan concluded negotiations with Sherif Hussein of Mecca, who in the absence of any other leader was held to represent the Arabs, with the solemn declaration: 'Great Britain is prepared to recognize and support the independence of the Arabs in all regions within the limits demanded by the Sherif of Mecca.'

Various areas were excluded from this commitment, including 'portions of Syria lying to the west of the districts of Damascus'. Since Palestine lay to the *south* of Damascus, the people of that area not unnaturally concluded that their independence would follow an Allied victory in the First World War – their support for which against the Ottoman Empire was the unspoken condition of the British promise.

British diplomacy was, however, not as guileless as it appeared. A year later, their agreement with the Arabs notwithstanding, the British made a secret agreement with the French and the Russians, in which they divided up the Arab world into spheres of influence between them; deciding specifically that Palestine should be placed under international administration.

The British were careful to keep this act of duplicity hidden. Indeed, it became public only when the Russian Revolution allowed the Bolshevik leaders to open the diplomatic files of their Tsarist predecessors, where they duly discovered the Anglo-French plan which was so embarrassing to the British that the new Russian régime found the temptation to make it public irresistible.

Until 1917, the question of Arab independence was of far greater moment to the inhabitants of Palestine than the Zionist aspirations formulated in Europe, and pursued in secret diplomacy. But in that summer the issue of Zionism suddenly emerged as a most dangerous threat to the aspirations of the Palestinian people.

The Balfour Declaration was phrased in carefully ambiguous terms, but its implications were brutally clear. In a letter to Lord Rothschild (the novel form selected for this declaration of government policy), Lord Balfour wrote that the British 'viewed with favour the establishment of a national home for the Jewish people' in Palestine. And what of the Palestinians? So far from supporting 'the independence of the Arabs', the British now promised to protect 'the civil and religious rights of the existing non-Jewish communities in Palestine'. By a stroke of the British colonial pen, the people of Palestine – 92 per cent of the population – had been reclassified for the convenience of grand strategy as 'non-Jewish communities'.

The impact upon the Arab mind was devastating: it was now obvious that the British intended not merely to renege upon their promise of independence, but to hand over Palestine to the Jews. It was an act which the Palestinians found both inexplicable and treacherous.

Any doubts about the import of the Balfour Declaration were soon clarified by the Zionists themselves. A modestly triumphant Chaim Weizmann, whose passionate intellect had moulded the British declaration, was in no doubt that embedded in its ambiguities was the foundation-stone of the Jewish state. Nor, in his account of it to the American Secretary of State, did he disguise the matter:

I define the Jewish national home to mean the creation of an administration which would arise out of the natural conditions of the country – always safeguarding the interests of the non-Jews of the country – with the hope that by Jewish immigration, Palestine would ultimately become as Jewish as England is English.[3]

Elsewhere he was even more explicit, informing a British audience:

I trust to God that a Jewish state will come about; but it will come about not through political declarations, but by the sweat and blood of the Jewish people.[4]

A variety of reasons has been advanced to explain the tragic tangle of self-contradictions which passed as British policy. Was Balfour erasing his guilt for his own unseemly part in the 1906 Aliens Act which expressly sought to exclude Jews from Britain? Was Lloyd George honouring Weizmann as the distinguished scientist he undoubtedly was? Did the British hope that American Jews would push the government into the war on the side of the British? Or were they attracted by the thought that their strategic interests concentrated in that corner of the Imperial map – the Suez Canal, the route to India, the buffer between British and French spheres of influence – could best be protected by implanting in Palestine the advanced Western attitudes and sympathies represented by Zionism? Or was it an amalgam of all these reasons and more besides? Whatever the case, the British decision displayed a breathtaking disregard for moral principles side by side with an absence of intellectual conviction. Balfour revealed his own cynicism in a memorandum to the Cabinet in 1919:

In Palestine we do not propose even to go through the form of consulting the wishes of the present inhabitants of the country . . . the four Great Powers are committed to Zionism. And Zionism, be it right or wrong, good or bad, is rooted in age-long traditions, in present needs, in future hopes, of far profounder import than the desires and prejudices of the seven hundred thousand Arabs who now inhabit that ancient land . . . So far as Palestine is concerned, the Powers have made no statement of fact which is not admittedly wrong, and no declaration of policy which at least in the letter, they have not always intended to violate.

The Middle East tragedy was born.

Historical illustrations and photographs

1875-1948

1875–80

In the Holy Land
Radio Times Hulton Picture Library

Harvest
Popperfoto

The author of the Balfour Declaration
Syndication International

The founder of Zionism, Theodor Herzl with his mother
Snark International

A demonstration in Jerusalem by Palestinians
against Jewish immigration (1930)
Popperfoto

The father of Israel, Chaim Weizmann (right)
Central Press

David Ben Gurion
Central Press

The Arab rebellion, 1938. The first 'terrorists'
Popperfoto

Reinforcements arrive in Palestine. 20,000
British troops were needed to fight the rebels
Fox Photos

Barnabys Picture Library

Fox Photos

Action and reaction. To fight terrorism, the
British used terror

The war was fought in the hills
Fox Photos

The British confront the Palestinians at the
walls of Jerusalem (1938)
Fox Photos

By 1939 more than 3,000 Palestinians had died
Fox Photos

WANTED!

REWARDS WILL BE PAID BY THE PALESTINE GOVERNMENT TO ANY PERSON PROVIDING INFORMATION WHICH LEADS TO THE ARREST OF ANY OF THE PERSONS WHOSE NAMES AND PHOTOGRAPHS ARE SHOWN HEREUNDER

Wanted by the
British
Popperfoto

President Roosevelt (right) and his successor, Harry Truman (left): a transformation of American policy
Fox Photos

The Arab Higher Committee; banned and deported after the general strike
Popperfoto

The slaughter at the King David Hotel
Fox Photos

The Arab liberation armies were 'ill equipped, disorganized and in intense rivalry, one with another'
Popperfoto

The Palestinians were out-gunned
Popperfoto

Members of the Stern gang demonstrate against
the UN mediator, Count Folke–Bernadotte, 1948
Popperfoto

'A broken people, scattered, dispossessed and
powerless'
Popperfoto

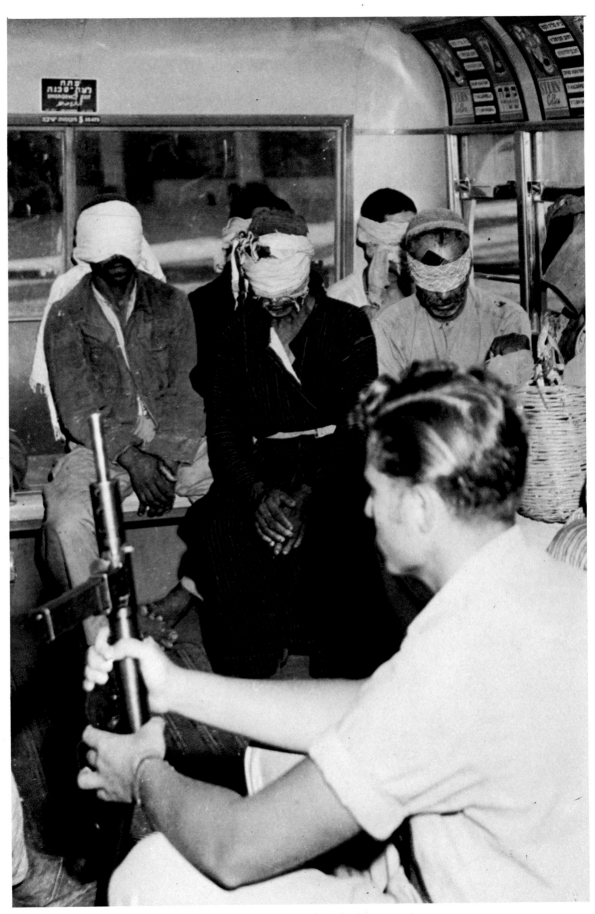

Captured Palestinians are taken from Ramleh to Jerusalem for interrogation
Popperfoto

Prince L. Faisal (left), second son of Ibn Saud,
arriving at Heathrow Airport to lead the Saudi
Arabian delegation to the London Conference on
Palestine, September 1946
Central Press

Exile
UNRWA Photo: Munir Nasr

over
The defeat left Israel in occupation of one of
the holy centres of Islam, the Dome of the
Rock from where the Prophet is believed to
have ascended into Heaven. The future of
Jerusalem thus became a crucial if intractable
issue uniting the Arab world against Israel

Three
The British Responsibility

Ahram Zuayter is an unlikely rebel. He is courteous, old-worldly, ushering his guests to elegant chairs and offering them, with Arab hospitality, whatsoever may be their wish. He has been an ambassador for most of his adult life, a writer and historian of the Palestinian cause. In print, he is calm and measured; scholarly in the presentation of his case that the Palestinians are the victims of a great and terrible injustice which must, and will, be rectified.

When he speaks, it is with intensity and excitement, words bubbling from him, ideas desperate to escape. He piles argument upon argument, with meticulous addition of detail, rehearsing an endless flow of private outrage, desperate to convince those who will listen that the tragedy of the Palestinian people is a crime that must be answered:

'I will never despair; I believe we will get our country back. You know the history of Carthage? If we are defeated in one battle, there is the second, the third, the fourth. We will never surrender. Those that are now fighting were not born in Palestine but still they fight. For generations the struggle will continue. We'll make mistakes, we will be defeated, we will make sacrifices, we will be broken, but the Resistance will not die. I will never accept the loss of my country – never.'

The passion seems unlikely in an otherwise gentle person. His words are those which the Western media have portrayed as extreme, fanatical. Yet he is evidently a sane man. He riffles through his file in search of evidence, alighting upon a document signed by the assistant district commissioner for Samaria, ordering that Ahram Zuayter be detained in the village of Anja El Hafir for three months:

I hereby direct that Ahram Zuayter of Nablos shall be detained for a period of three months in detention camp No. 1 Sarafand . . .

Given under my hand this fourth day of July 1936.

In the same file there is a letter signed in the same hand, written more than thirty years later, by the former assistant district commissioner for Samaria, Mr Hugh Foot, who had now become Lord Caradon, Britain's representative at the United Nations, and one of the architects of UN Resolution 242, upon which any hope for lasting peace in the Middle East is held to rest.

The letter is couched in affectionate terms, and with it there is a brief verse:

From a Tyrant to a Rebel

He was resolved while still at school
Bravely to challenge British rule
The rebel Ahram did not fear
Exile to Anja El Hafir.

'One day they'll see the Promised Land'

But from all malice he was free;
With Arab magnanimity
Forgiveness brought a happy end
He let the tyrant be his friend.

One day they'll see the Promised Land
Return to Nablos hand in hand
Acknowledging as just and true
The principles of two-four-two.

Zuayter's route to the concentration camp was simple. He had been born in Nablos where his father was mayor under Ottoman rule; his brother was a noted professor of law in Jerusalem. He remembers with pleasure that his home town was noted for the quality of its young scholars, commonly sending two hundred or so students a year to Istanbul and another two hundred to Beirut to study at the universities. Ahram had been one of those at the American University in Beirut, though he had to cut short his studies when his father died.

'I became a teacher in a government school in Nablos. My father had always been a political man, and naturally I followed him and joined the Nationalist movement. You see we all knew what was being prepared for us, for our country, and we knew that we had to resist it.'

Ahram Zuayter was twenty-seven when the Palestinians finally rose up in revolt against the British Mandate, which they had come to see as the Trojan Horse within which the Jewish state was to be secreted into Palestine. It was the National Committee in Nablos which began in a modest way what was to become the first organized mass action by the Palestinians. The committee's secretary-general was Ahram Zuayter.

'We felt we had to do something to force the British to change their policy, otherwise we would lose Palestine to the Zionists. So we decided on the General Strike. It was a great step for us and daunting to take on the British Empire, can you imagine? But we believed that the strike would bring about a peaceful revolution. That with every single person on strike in Palestine it must lead to that. So we called for an indefinite strike until the British changed their policy.'

The Palestinians had been remarkably patient. For eighteen years, since 1917, their leaders had protested against the policy of the British Mandate. They had sent deputations to London, furnished evidence before Royal Commissions, made representations to British Ministers, had offered full explanation and careful argument in support of a case which those who had heard it found most compelling. Already a host of British dignitaries had descended upon Palestine in search of the truth and had returned to London to confirm, in the words of Winston Churchill, after the first such foray, that : 'The cause of unrest in Palestine, and the only cause, arises from the Zionist movement and our promises and pledges to it.' The observation, astute as it surely was, had no discernible effect either upon Mr Churchill or the government of which he was a leading member and which was unshakeably committed to the Zionist cause.

Indeed, successive British governments evidently felt obliged to act as if the irreconcilable conflict which their eminent servants had detected between Zionist aspiration and Palestinian nationalism could in some way, one day, resolve itself by itself. The British presided over the approaching disaster with all the moral authority, intellectual honesty and political dexterity of those who choose to see no evil, speak no evil and hear no evil. To the Palestinians, the choice had become clear. Fobbed off with empty expressions of goodwill from the British, they could either watch as the Zionists took over Palestine or they could resist.

The Palestinian peasants had already been drawn irresistibly to the same conclusion as their leaders, not by theoretical analysis of Zionism, nor by incoherent instinct, but by that most overwhelming of arguments – their own harsh experience. While their leaders followed a diplomatic route which led them round in circles, the peasants had come face to face with Zionism on their land, in their villages, at their work. They found Zionism alien and threatening. They had no doubt that the new settlers who poured into the country each year intended to rule in Palestine, and there was no one who seemed prepared to stop them. The statistics merely confirmed their deep anxiety.

In 1917, the year of the Balfour Declaration, there were about 57,000 Jews in Palestine, and they comprised 9.7 per cent of the population. Nineteen years later, in 1936, their numbers had risen to 384,000, or almost 30 per cent of the population – an unprecedented increase in the history of settlement. To the Palestinians, it seemed evident that, while the politicians offered them bland words of reassurance, the immigrants would continue to arrive in ever greater numbers until Palestine was in their hands.

Although the ambiguity which had characterized the public utterances of Zionist spokesmen before the Balfour Declaration persisted, it became steadily easier to read between the lines and detect the purpose : if the Zionists were to be believed, then the Palestinians were right to be fearful. Indeed, as early as 1921 men like Dr Eder, the acting chair-man of the Zionist Commission, had been quite blunt, stating before a British Commission of Enquiry with a candour which deeply impressed the British that :

There can only be one National Home in Palestine, and that a Jewish one, and no equality in the partnership between Jews and Arabs, but a Jewish predominance as soon as the numbers of that race are sufficiently increased.

The Committee of Enquiry had been sent to Palestine following riots in Jaffa, the principal port of Jewish immigration. As elsewhere in Palestine, the Arab frustration had erupted with hideous ferocity against the immigrants. In a week of murder and pillage, the Palestinians killed some 200 Jews and suffered in consequence 120 casualties among their own people. Arab atrocity begat Jewish revenge. Innocents – women and children among them – were clubbed, stabbed and beaten to death in a frenzy of atavistic bloodletting in which neither side was innocent and which was incomprehensible only to those who were ignorant of how brutal man can become when driven by fear. The British Enquiry understood, and offered its conclusion that indeed it was fear and hatred of Zionist immigration which was the root cause of the Jaffa pogrom.

As the rate of immigration increased, so did the fear. It was not simply a matter of numbers, but of purpose. In 1935, the British High Commissioner for Palestine, recognizing what was happening, wrote to the Colonial Secretary at Westminster of : '. . . a genuine feeling of fear that the Jews will succeed in establishing themselves in such large numbers that in the not too distant future they will gain economic and political control of the country'.

Nor could the peasants have been expected to appreciate that the immigrants were themselves victims, escaping from the virulent anti-Semitism which had now taken a fierce hold on Europe, and from which no Jew was safe. Whatever form it took – public insults, silent contempt, open brutality, sudden pogroms – it seemed to receive official sanction, and it provoked the prescient fear that there was worse to come. While the compassion of the Western world was being demonstrated by the failure of every major government to increase its quota of immigrants to meet this crisis, Zionism offered both self-respect and refuge in Palestine.

To inculcate a sense of national purpose among Jews of different countries and class, Zionist propaganda had for long depicted the Jew in terms which, from any other source, would have been deeply offensive : the Jews in Europe were parasites,

middle men, shopkeepers and moneylenders, despised by their fellow men. Only through Zionism in Palestine – so the propaganda ran – could the Jews liberate themselves, working together with their hands and brains, participating in a great national movement in which all men were equal. In isolation, out of context, it might have been a heroic vision. As it was, it served to clothe a cool political strategy with fervent moral purpose.

In this purpose there was no place for the Palestinians; the Jews did not need the Arabs. Not only did the Zionists speak their own language, follow their own separate faith and enjoy a different culture, but they also insulated themselves from the Arab world in every way possible. They formed their own industries, trade unions, banks, schools, hospitals – and from all of these Palestinians were carefully excluded. When the Jewish Agency bought Arab land, the new settlers to whom it was bequeathed expelled the Arab families who had

The old men do not forget the British

farmed it for generations, thus depriving them of their means of subsistence. The Histradruth (the Zionist trade union) forbade Arabs to join, and picketed any Jewish employer who took on Arab labour. Those employers who persisted were branded as traitors.

The leader of the aggressively exclusive Histradruth was David Ben Gurion, whose equivocal public pronouncements were belied by his deeds, which made it plain that there was in his national home no place for the Arab as an equal citizen enjoying equal rights with the Jews. The zeal of men like Ben Gurion clearly embarrassed some of the Jewish immigrants who were new to Zionism and who were obliged to defend its principles when they travelled abroad.

To defend the fact that I could not accept Arabs in my trade union, the Histradruth; to defend preaching to housewives that they not

69

buy at Arab stores; to defend the fact that we stood guard at orchards to prevent Arab workers from getting jobs there . . . to pour kerosene on Arab tomatoes; to attack Jewish housewives in the markets and smash the Arab eggs they had bought . . .[5]

This policy was hardly calculated to inspire goodwill in its victims, who remained stubbornly unmoved by the heroic achievements of those who now worked on their land and took their jobs. They saw invaders not idealists; arrogant settlers not selfless pioneers.

Soon after he succeeded Lord Balfour as Foreign Secretary, Lord Curzon had asked rhetorically of the Palestinians:

What is to become of the people of this country . . . they and their forefathers have occupied the country for the best part of fifteen hundred years. They own the soil . . . they will not be content either to be expropriated for Jewish immigrants, or to act merely as hewers of wood and drawers of water for the latter.

Ever since the Balfour Declaration, the British had been pinioned by the incompatible objectives they had set themselves in Palestine. As the years of the Mandate wore on, the consequences of this became even more clear. By 1936, senior British civil servants felt obliged to inform the High Commissioner for Palestine that 'the Arabs have been driven into a state verging on despair; and the present unrest is no more than an expression of that despair'. It was evident by now that the only way in which Lord Curzon's question would be answered was with the gun.

It was in this atmosphere that the Arab leaders in Nablos called for the general strike in what was, in effect, a last desperate effort to head off a violent confrontation with the British. Ahram Zuayter was uncertain about the response, anxious lest the people should be too frightened to heed the summons.

'It was my job to make an appeal to the other towns in Palestine and to make the announcement of the strike to the newspapers. At first we were worried. But it wasn't necessary. Within twenty-four hours Palestine was on strike. The people were with us. Everything stopped.

'The Zionists have sometimes tried to suggest that this was a revolution of the upper classes. This was not true. We had national committees in every village, not just in the cities. It was the fellaheen, the peasants, who played the most important role in our movement. We held meetings in scores of villages, preaching the cause. The people would gather in the main square. Then day after day

people from different areas would march on the cities, and the cities would offer them a feast on their arrival. We had huge demonstrations. And the people would provide all the food – cheese, meat, eggs, butter, every household offering what would have been their own meal for that day.

'Our message was simple. During the period of the Mandate the British should gradually have enabled us to move towards independence. That was supposed to be the goal of the Mandate. But it was clear that the real goal was different. It was to establish a Jewish state on our ruins, to uproot the Arabs from their country. That was how we felt, that they were going to replace us with a Jewish state.

'For this reason the British were the cause of our catastrophe, and the catastrophe was Zionism. So we asked the people, "Who is your first enemy?" "Britain." "The second enemy?" "Zionism." "Why?" "Because Britain is responsible. Britain protects them and persecutes us."'

The strike lasted six months: offices and factories kept their doors locked. Market stalls and shops were shuttered. There were no lorries or buses or taxis for hire. Civil servants, public employees, industrial workers, students and schoolchildren remained at home. Only the hospitals remained open, and even the ambulance drivers needed the authority of the local strike committee to pass. For an impoverished community which had never before tested its strength in this way, the general strike was an impressive demonstration of a national unity which offered conclusive testimony to the depth and scale of Palestinian dismay at British policies.

Ibrahim Ghannan, the painter, was a child of six when the strike began.

'Our neighbours were Jewish and we were friendly with them. They never caused us any problem. And many of us worked for the British. At first they were welcome because the army gave the Arabs work at their camps. Of course I was much too young to understand their politics or their presence at the time, but I do remember the day when I discovered that the British were foreigners. I can't remember exactly when it was, but there was a demonstration in the streets outside our house. And the people were shouting, "Down with Balfour, down with Balfour." It was during the general strike. I was astonished, you see. My brother had a monkey and his name was Balfour. And I couldn't understand what my brother's monkey had done wrong to make all these people so angry. So I went out into the backyard, and Balfour was still there, doing no harm, quietly in his cage. I was very upset. I went to my brother

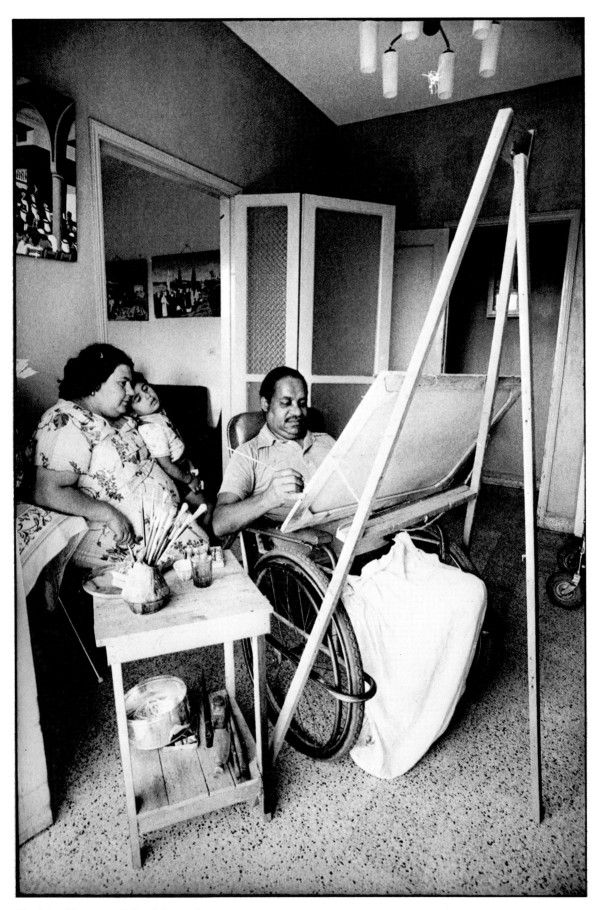

Ibrahim Ghannan, Palestinian painter

and asked him why the people were so cross with his monkey. But he just laughed at me. So I went and asked my father, but my father was agitated and much too busy to answer me. And outside in the street, the people went on shouting, "Down with Balfour, down with Balfour." And then I went out and overheard two people talking, and I realized that there was another Balfour, and that they were angry with him, not with my brother's monkey. After that I wanted to call our Balfour by another name, because he wasn't our enemy. And from then on I knew that the British weren't our friends.'

Although Ibrahim Ghannan was not aware of it at the time, one of his uncles, Sheikh Arattieh, had already advanced beyond the strike, taking up arms against the British presence, convinced that only a war could defeat the British alliance with Zionism. In 1935 he had joined a small band of guerrillas led by Sheikh Qassan, who had sworn to give their lives for Palestine. Sheikh Qassan is known to Palestinians as the 'first martyr'. His campaign began in November 1935, but almost before they had an opportunity even to use their rifles, bought with the proceeds from the sale of their wives' jewellery, the rebels were ambushed by a British force. There was a brief battle. Sheikh Qassan and three of his followers were killed, and most of the rest captured.

In Nablos, Ahram Zuayter read the British communiqué which announced the news.

'They talked about "a band of vagabonds or gangsters which had clashed with the British police force". These were the Qassanists, and they were fighting for Palestine. Always – even then – they used this language. They called him a terrorist, and he was fighting to preserve our people, ready to sacrifice himself for Palestine.

'I dictated a statement at once proclaiming that Sheikh Qassan and his martyrs were our national heroes and appealing to the people to attend their funeral. And they came. Thousands upon thousands of them. It took us two hours to walk from the mosque to the cemetery. We carried their coffins above our heads.

'They were – and are – our national heroes. Heroes for us, gangsters according to the High Commission.'

The contempt with which the British treated Sheikh Qassan doubtless reflected the ease with which their trained soldiers had crushed his ragged uprising. If so, it was a foolish conceit. Sheikh Qassan was not an aberration, an absurd excrescence or a futile gesture. He died calling for a holy war to save Palestine. In that moment he expressed the yearning of the people for liberation. As a martyr, he offered them a mission and the will to

attempt it. If *he* could die for Palestine, it was argued, so could they. The Arab rebellion had begun.

Two months after the start of the general strike, in the spirit of Sheikh Qassan, Ahram Zuayter found himself using the language of war, not peace.

'I remember it well, my last demonstration. It was huge. And peaceful. But we had been ignored by the British. They ignored our demands. Nothing had changed. They were obviously hoping simply to wear us down.

'I remember that one of the marchers carried a gun. And he shot in the air. And in my speech I said, "You have no right any more to shoot in the sky. From now on, if you use the gun, you must shoot at the British. So goodbye; no more speeches, no more processions. Now we must explain our demands by using our rifles."

'That night about eleven o'clock my house was surrounded. Two Arab police officers came and knocked on the door. My brother opened it, and they told him, "We have come to arrest Ahram." He came and told me. My first thought was to escape, to run away and lead a movement in the hills. But there were fifty soldiers surrounding the house. I had no means of getting out.

'So I dressed and I walked downstairs and I walked out of my front door. It was the happiest moment of my life. I felt so proud. I was twenty-seven years old, and fifty British soldiers with rifles were needed to take me away. I walked through the streets of Nablos at their head, under arrest. And on that day I became the first person to enter a British concentration camp in Palestine.'

Such members of the intelligentsia as Ahram Zuayter played a key part in the early days of the rebellion. But it was not their movement. In the concentration camp at Sarafand to which Zuayter was sent, the overwhelming majority of the inmates were peasants. It was, above all, their rebellion. Men like Zuayter were in fact greatly distrusted by the big political families, who had wished to lead the nationalist movement according to the diplomatic principles which had preserved their influence with the British since the First World War. Although the leading families of Palestine wrangled fiercely with each other, competing for control of the nationalist movement, they were united in finding the militancy of Nablos embarrassing. It had been with reluctance that they supported the general strike, and they did so in the knowledge that, if they did not, the Arab masses would desert them entirely. It was therefore with relief that, in September 1936, the Arab Higher Committee, under pressure from neighbouring régimes, which were themselves pressed by the British, urged their people to end the strike, six months after it had started. It had achieved nothing except the promise of another – yet another – Royal Commission.

But the spirit of Sheikh Qassan now ruled among the peasantry. Unmindful of Royal Commissions, suspicious of the diplomacy by which they believed their old leaders had been seduced and ensnared, even more fearful of the inexorable invasion of their land by Zionism, the young men of Palestine took to the hills with their guns.

It was a spontaneous uprising. Local leaders formed small bands of fighters almost overnight. They knew little about guerrilla tactics and had virtually no training; their weapons were an ill-assorted collection of antique hunting guns, pistols and old British rifles bought from army corporals by middle men in return for the family heirlooms and jewels. By the end of 1936, however, there were perhaps 5,000 men in an unknown number of groups, each of which owed no allegiance to any other, had no central direction, but all of whose members were pledged to die for the cause of Palestine.

Acquiring almost by instinct the habits of the guerrilla fighter, these men fought by night and hid by day. One or two of the old men in the refugee camps remember leaving their rifles hidden in the branches of the olive trees where the military patrols never looked, or hiding in caves in the mountains, which only they and their animals could find. At night they moved out of the hills. They ambushed military convoys, attacked British bases; they laid mines on busy roads and railway lines, blew up bridges with dynamite and cut telephone wires; they burnt the crops belonging to Jewish settlers, uprooted their plantations, and sometimes murdered individual Jews with a terrorist bomb or a sniper's gun.

By day they would return to their homes, slipping back unnoticed into the protective routine of the village where, since they came from the bosom of the peasantry, they never lacked for food, shelter or support.

In the official British accounts of the period, this national uprising is referred to as 'the disturbances', alleged to have been caused by 'terrorist and gang activities'. This distortion of its nature may have helped to justify the ruthless and sometimes brutal methods used to combat the rebellion, but it could not disguise the scale on which the war was fought. Between 1936 and 1939, Palestine was in a state of insurrection. In the first year alone, nearly 1,000 Palestinians were killed or wounded in action against the British army, although it was not until 1938 that the rebellion reached its peak.

By this time the traditional leaders of Palestine were at a loss. Their diplomacy had patently failed. For nearly twenty years they had patiently argued variations of a familiar case: the British should stop Jewish immigration and commit themselves to the establishment in Palestine of a democratic government in which all inhabitants should participate in proportion to their numbers. Again and again they had been rebuffed. Moreover, their leadership was under direct challenge from the fighters who had taken to the hills and who held their diplomacy in contempt. There was little doubt that the Royal Commission, promised in return for ending the general strike, offered them at best a last chance to find a peaceful escape from their dilemma. There was, in early 1937, a pause in the guerrilla war as all Palestine waited for the report of the Peel Commission which was to be published in July 1937. The report's appraisal when it came was blunt:

> The situation in Palestine has reached deadlock. We cannot – in Palestine as it is now – both concede the Arab claim to self-government and secure the establishment of the Jewish national home.

Twenty years on – and twenty years too late – the self-contradiction contained in the Balfour Declaration was at last openly acknowledged. But if the Mandate was unworkable, what was the alternative? To the astonished horror of the Palestinians, the commission made the fateful suggestion that their country be divided. Although the Jewish sector owned only 5 per cent of the land, the Peel Commission proposed that almost half Palestine should be handed over to a Jewish state, from which – if necessary – the Arab population, which would number more than 200,000 people, was to be forcibly transferred into the Arab Palestinian state to be established in the other half of Palestine.

The proposed Jewish state was too small to meet the aspirations of Zionism, with the consequence that its leaders were ambivalent about the Peel Commission. The Palestinians, on the other hand, facing the dismemberment of their country, reloaded their rifles and came down from the hills to fight to the end.

One of their first victims was the district officer in Galilee, Lewis Andrews, who was assassinated outside the Anglican church in Nazareth by four gunmen. The British authorities were understandably outraged at the crime, but as ever refused to reflect upon the fact that Upper Galilee, populated and owned almost exclusively by Arabs, was under the partition plan to become part of the Jewish state. To the Palestinians Lewis Andrews was therefore the agent of their national destruction.

The authorities responded with alacrity. Most of the leaders of the Arab Higher Committee which had striven in vain for a diplomatic solution, were summarily arrested and deported to the Seychelles. Without any political leadership to protest through diplomatic channels to the world beyond, the Palestinian peasants were now to experience bitterly the full severity of a colonial power bent on the suppression of rebellion. The elders do not forget.

'Some of us were fighters, some of us were not. I was a revolutionary like all the peasants. We were protecting our country, fighting for our independence. But what did we have to fight with? I had my gun and five bullets against British planes and artillery. And you British were unjust. Your soldiers arrested us, guilty or innocent. They tortured us. And sometimes they hanged people.'

In fact 110 Arabs were hanged during the rebellion. Among the first to be executed was a prominent nationalist, Sheikh Farhan Sa'adi, who had admitted owning an elderly rifle and who was suspected of organizing a terrorist outrage. He was summarily tried and sentenced to death. Ahram Zuayter heard of it from his concentration camp, and remembers Hugh Foot appealing to the High Commissioner that sentence be postponed because it was Ramadan.

'You see it was against our law, our tradition and our character to hang a person who was fasting. It was shameful to execute a sheikh during Ramadan. But the High Commissioner refused to hear Mr Foot's plea and he was hanged.'

There were other officials who, like Hugh Foot, evidently had grave doubts about the policy they were obliged to defend and enact. Sir Alec Kirkbride has described how he was 'committed to playing a leading part in a triple killing' in his role as District Commissioner of Galilee. On his way into the prison at Acre, where he had to witness the hanging of three young Arabs, he remembers passing a Moslem priest,

... who had been to prepare the victims for death. The priest exchanged salutes with us and had a look of the blackest hatred. I, for one, felt guilty and mean ...[6]

In the execution chamber, the governor was obliged to read out the death sentence to the young Palestinians.

In this instance, the man protested at the delay and said, 'I know that you are going to hang me. For God's sake get it over quickly!' He soon had his wish fulfilled. He came in with his hands handcuffed behind his back, then the warders pinioned his elbows and slipped over his head a hood of black cloth which not only blindfolded him but mercifully hid his face from us ... The Governor slammed over a lever and the man fell forward through the trap to be brought up short, when the rope ran out, with a shock that shook the whole platform ... I was filled with an overwhelming feeling of pity, mixed with the hope that I might be able to meet my end, whatever it might be, with the same courage and fortitude which was being shown by these men ... the feeling that I was doing something shameful, which had bothered me the whole morning, grew more intense.[7]

If these acts of 'judicial homicide' – as the hangings were known – eliminated some 'gangsters', it had little discernible effect upon the course of the 'disturbances'. The war on the 'terrorists' inevitably became a conflict between the British army and the Palestinian people – a fact which was not understood in London by those politicians who, on behalf of the British people, sanctioned British policy in Palestine. Isolated in London, ignorant of the full dimension of the Palestine issue, susceptible to adroit diplomacy by the Zionist lobby and responsive – if occasionally with cynicism – to the persecution of the Jews in Europe, the political consensus had been unwavering in its support of the Jewish national home in Palestine. On the one hand, socialists in the Labour Party, indulging a romantic attachment to the ideals of the kibbutzim, erroneously assumed that these formed the principles upon which the national home would be founded. On the other, Conservatives, with whom Zionism's most formidable advocate, Chaim Weizmann, enjoyed the closest relationship, chose to insist that the Balfour Declaration was a solemn and binding commitment, enshrined in international law – which incidentally greatly served Britain's imperial position while offering a solution to the 'Jewish problem'. Both groups chose to ignore the voice of Palestinian nationalism, which urged with growing desperation that the land upon which the British wished Zionism to flourish was not at their disposal.

The 'disturbances' in Palestine quickly degenerated into all-out war. The elders of Galilee, sitting in their refugee camp, insist with vehemence today that their experiences at the hands of the British should be recorded. The former muktar of Souffari had been – of necessity – an intermediary between the people of his town and the British authorities.

'The British army had two regiments in the castle on the edge of our village. Now many of the people were revolutionaries and so I was in a very difficult position. One day I was summoned to the castle and was interrogated. How many rebels were there in Souffari, what were their names? I refused to tell. I knew nothing, I said. So they sent me away and told me to find out. But we all supported the revolutionaries, every single person in the town. And I'd have been a traitor to give the British any details. So when I went back I told the British that no rebels ever came into the town. When I said this, the official hit me with his stick and I was knocked to the ground. Two of my companions were also beaten. Then they took our shoes from us, put us in the back of a jeep and drove us out of the camp on the road to Tiberius. When they had driven us almost twenty kilometres, they ordered us out of the jeep and began to hit us, so that we started to run, barefoot, back up the road towards our home. And they began to shoot at us – not to hit us, you understand, but at the ground around us – to frighten us.'

The problem faced by the British was simple: it was impossible either to distinguish or detach 'the terrorists' from the people. To fight terrorism they therefore had to use terror, and since the enemy was the people, the terror was indiscriminate.

'Put this down, put this down – I swear by God that this is the truth. I saw all this with my own eyes. I protested personally to the castle about it, but the soldiers went out of their way to humiliate me, although they knew who I was.'

The muktar's agitation is not only at the memory of deep wounds, but at the fear that his testimony may be discarded.

'You know what they did whenever there was trouble? They would surround the village, and stop you from leaving. They paralysed the life. Anyone who tried to leave the village in secret would be shot down as a suspected patriot. Then the women were taken from their houses to the yard where the threshing was done. The men were taken up to the castle. The soldiers came into the village, searching the houses for weapons. They hanged people for having guns. Did you know that? When they'd searched a house, they'd put a cross on the door. They walked into our houses without permission, quite freely, violating our privacy. And if they found a house with weapons, they would destroy several other houses in the vicinity as a collective punishment.

'I remember on one occasion when they took us up to the castle. It was surrounded by barbed wire. And they drove us through the narrow entrance with such ferocity that our clothes were torn on the wire and we were cut and bleeding. One or two people tried to get out of the mêlée by climbing over the wire, and they got caught and were left suspended like clothes on a washing line.'

The British authorities imposed severe punishment upon villages suspected of harbouring rebels. If telephone lines were cut or roads blocked or mined, the near-by village could expect a visit from the army and a huge fine to be levied on every resident. Sometimes a village was ordered to pay £500 or even more – an impossible sum to raise without selling off livestock and food. On occasion villagers were forced to take their entire flock of sheep or goats to the market to raise the money. The muktar of Souffari remembers one fine of £1,000 imposed because no one in the village would yield information about an explosion which had damaged an army vehicle on the road to Nazareth.

'It was impossible to raise even £200 so they arrested many of our youths and put them in concentration camps on the Lebanese border, where some of them stayed for six months.'

To Palestinians, the significance of such stories is not that the British behaved cruelly, but that to endure such treatment and still fight is overwhelming evidence of their refusal to accept the dismemberment of their country.

'You may find it difficult to believe this, but I assure you it happened . . .' The speaker is Abu Rahman Youssef, who came from the village of Zeib, not far from the coastal town of Acre.

'In 1938, a Zionist colony was set up near the Lebanese frontier, in an area which the Peel Commission had designated to the Jewish state. But it was our land. So the settlement was at risk from our revolution. It was the responsibility of the British to guard it. So the revolutionaries planted a mine on the road and it blew up a tank on its way there. Now this happened ten kilometres from Zeib. In their normal fashion, the army went to the nearest village, which was called El Bassa, and invaded it. They took the young men from the houses and shot some of them; the rest they threw into the bushes which we call "sidir", the "needle bush", because its thorns are so long and sharp. And they trod the people down into the bushes. Then they went into the houses; they took food and clothes. They looted from the shops and set fire to some buildings.

'Now Zeib overlooks El Bassa and our people saw what was happening. And they saw the army when they finished there coming to our village. We were all forced to leave our villages, and we were lined up outside the houses. And then they went through our houses.'

He raises his voice in anger:

'They found nothing – as usual. So they collected the grain and mixed different seeds together – can you imagine: wheat, barley, sesame, millet, lentils, all our produce. They took our belongings, they set fire to our houses. They overturned our jars of olive oil, twenty-gallon drums they were. They took our jewellery. And our gold.'

Independent corroboration of the innumerable similar accounts of British military behaviour has been offered by an English nun called Frances Newton, who lived in Palestine for many years, becoming Dame of Justice of the Venerable Order of St John in Jerusalem in 1930. She had been horrified by the reports of British reprisals brought to her by Arab villagers who trusted her good faith. Nevertheless she was scrupulous in recording and evaluating the evidence, relying greatly on her personal experience.

On 22 February 1938, she visited the village of Igzim, which had been punished following the assassination of a British officer, Squadron Leader Alderton.

> I entered many of the houses and can only say that the havoc which had been wrought was indescribable, and, unless seen with one's own eyes, unbelievable.[8]

She made notes of what she saw: doors torn from their hinges, mirrors smashed, cupboards upturned, chairs broken into fragments, sewing machines battered to bits, clothing and bedding soaked in olive oil, cereals of all sorts mixed up and scattered on the floor with broken glass, china and crockery. At least sixty houses had been laid waste in this manner. In addition, all the sheep and goats from the village – 900 in all – had been rounded up by the soldiers and taken to Haifa as security against a collective fine. Those who could afford the price were permitted to buy their animals back. Those who did not have the requisite 8s. (40 p) a head, lost their goats and sheep, which were then sold or slaughtered by the army.

> I saw a pitiful sight on the way home just outside the village – an old man on a donkey which was laden with household articles, carrying two tiny infants on his lap; behind walked a woman carrying what she could, together with a big goose; two quite small children toddled after her – true refugees! – but from *British* barbarism.[9]

A month later Frances Newton returned to Igzim to discover the village empty of its former inhabitants, except for the muktar, who had been forbidden to leave, and the school-teacher, who had been warned that if he went the authorities would dismiss him. The villagers had evidently left *en masse* after the government billeted a detachment of forty policemen in Igzim as a collective punishment, requiring that the cost of their pres-

ence there be met by the people. As this was £90 a month, they could not raise the money. So rather than let the authorities seize their possessions in lieu of payment, they had fled. Some of them were still living in shelters made of old sacks under olive trees in the fields near by.

Sister Newton's dismay at such evidence of inhumanity did not blind her to the consequences of these tactics. So far from breaking the back of the rebellion, she judged that even more recruits were attracted to the cause:

> It is this kind of thing which drives the young men to join the 'bandits' in the hills . . . they have nothing more to lose than their lives.

By the end of 1939, the authorities had incarcerated more than 5,000 Palestinians in concentration camps. Among them was an elder, Abu Abdul Rahman, who now lives in the Lebanese refugee camp. He is crippled. His leg is badly broken just below the knee, an old wound. He points to his jaw, which is swollen and distorted, again an old disfigurement. He wishes to explain how it happened.

'I was arrested along with scores of others from my village. They took us in lorries to one of the concentration camps near Acre, in a place called Akrit. There we had to pass between two lines of soldiers who beat us as we entered the camp. They used their guns as sticks.'

With his arms he demonstrates a scything motion, as if the end of the barrel of the rifle was clenched in both hands.

'Then we had to crawl through barbed wire while they hit us all the time. We were herded into a compound. Day after day we sat in the open under the sun, and in the night we had to endure the extreme cold. We had no blankets. For several days we were without water. When we were allowed to drink it was from fouled water in large barrels in which we'd been forced to wash the wounds which the soldiers had inflicted on us when we first arrived. The water was fouled.'

The rebels used to launch their assaults by night, waiting in the olive groves or behind the rocks which bordered the rough winding roads, to ambush military patrols. Their skirmishes were usually brief. A burst of fire; a soldier killed or wounded; a vehicle set on fire with a hand-grenade; and then silence. The rebels disappeared into the dark.

In response, the British night patrols instituted the practice of taking hostages with them, selecting the men from the concentration camps, forcing them to travel in cars or buses in front of their military vehicles – a practice which dismayed

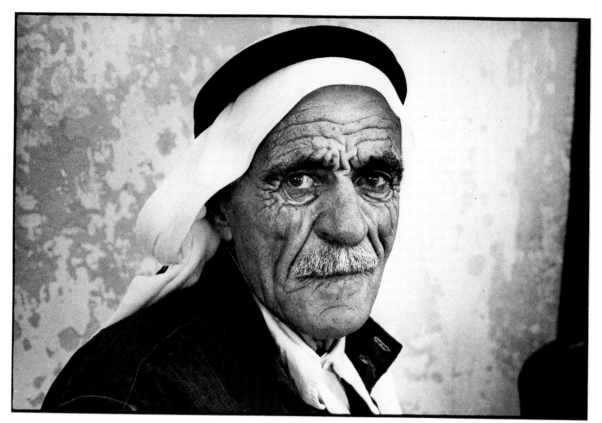

The British took hostages

certain British officials who were nevertheless powerless to intervene.

On the tenth day of his detention at Akrit, Abu Abdul Rahman was forced to join one such patrol. Earlier in the day, the army had unearthed four crates of explosives which had been hidden in a farm on the outskirts of Acre. The military was doubtless irritated – and in those days there were few inquisitive outsiders with an inconvenient concern for human rights. Retaliation and reprisal were unencumbered by any concern for public relations.

Abu Rahman was placed with a group of twenty other detainees who were ordered into two buses which were to travel at the front and rear of the convoy. According to Abu Rahman, the rebels were tied into their seats:

'As soon as the convoy got under way, and we had left the camp, we began to sing. We had a Palestinian song, but we changed the words, knowing that the British did not understand, singing, "We are in the front bus and the last bus, don't shoot at us."'

'We had to go slowly. If we went faster the jeeps behind us fired their machine-guns on the road to slow us down. We drove for most of the night. For ten hours. Eventually we came to the military camp at Nahkoura [now the headquarters of UNIFIL in South Lebanon]. I remember it very clearly. The soldiers called out to our driver, who was a very dark Palestinian, "Well done, Sambo," as we drove into the camp. Then they refuelled with petrol, and prepared to return to Akrit.'

On the way back the bus drove over a mine. It exploded:

'The people in front were thrown fifty metres in every direction. They were smashed to pieces. I can give you their names. There was Younis Tiha, Fadal, Youssef, Hassan Sambo, Youssef Hawani. I was lucky because I was at the back of the bus so I escaped simply with my jaw and my leg broken.'

'Afterwards the British had to collect the pieces of flesh of those who had been killed. They tried to piece together the bodies, but it was impossible. So they put their remains in sacks and took them back to the village to hand them to the women.'

The elders allege that the soldiers had laid the mine themselves, claiming that they used the same explosive which they'd discovered at the farm. To doubt that allegation is to be shouted down.

'You don't understand, you don't understand. They did anything and got away with it. They wanted to frighten us, to turn the people against the revolutionaries. We know they did it. If they

77

weren't guilty, why did they pay our families compensation? It was known that they paid this money. And by paying it, the British admitted their crime.'

It took three years of such tactics to break the Arab rebellion. The acts of sabotage against British installations, army camps, pipelines, did only minor and temporary damage to the colonial authority. More serious were the assassinations of British officials, policemen and soldiers, which kept the entire region in a state of alert and pinned down 20,000 trained soldiers. With the approach of war, the British could not afford to permit an insurrection in so sensitive and vulnerable an outpost of the Empire, which may have helped to explain the ruthlessness with which the uprising was crushed.

According to the official statistics, the British had killed more than 3,000 rebels by the end of 1939 – 2,000 by 'military and police action'; 961 in 'gang terrorist activities'; and 110 by 'judicial homicide', meaning hanging. However, by their own admission, these are conservative estimates. Palestinians argue that the true figure was in excess of 5,000 killed, and, on the basis of a one-to-three ratio, more than 14,000 wounded – which would raise the casualty figures to almost 20,000 for the whole campaign. Whatever the precise number, it is evident that 'the disturbances' exacted a terrible toll upon a Palestinian population of little more than one million souls. It is not surprising that, by the end of it, the rebellion had been crushed. Its leadership had collapsed or was in exile; its best men had fallen or were in jail; their villages had been punished and terrorized; and – perhaps most important – their fighters had almost run out of weapons and ammunition. The rebels had been defeated in a struggle which they could never have won. What did they gain? Desperation had sent them into war against the British; and from that struggle, they emerged with only their desperation intact.

Four
Terror and Retreat

On 10 April 1948, the head of the International Red Cross delegation in Palestine drove into a small Arab village outside Jerusalem. He was met by a detachment of a Jewish organization called the Irgun.

> All of them were young, some even adolescents, men and women armed to the teeth: revolvers, machine-guns, hand-grenades, and also cutlasses in their hands, most of them still blood-stained. A beautiful young girl with criminal eyes showed me hers still dripping with blood; she displayed it like a trophy.[10]

It is always dangerous to stumble upon an atrocity. Jacques de Reynier was fortunate to emerge alive with his official Red Cross report of what happened the previous night in the village of Deir Yassin.

The Irgun commanders coolly explained – in a familiar phrase – that they were engaged in a 'cleaning up' operation. The Red Cross delegate walked into one of the houses.

> I found some bodies cold. Here the 'cleaning up' had been done with machine-guns, then hand-grenades. It had been finished off with knives, anyone could see that. The same thing in the next room, but as I was about to leave, I heard something like a sigh. I looked everywhere, turned over all the bodies, and eventually found

a little foot, still warm. It was a little girl of ten, mutilated by a hand-grenade, but still alive . . . everywhere it was the same horrible sight.[11]

Altogether 250 men, women and children had been butchered to death. The survivors, at the point of hysterical collapse from shock and grief, recorded their hideous experience for the British authorities: families had been lined up and shot down in a barrage of machine-gun fire; young girls raped; a pregnant mother was first slaughtered and then had her stomach cut open by her murderer with a butcher's knife; a girl who tried to remove the unborn child from the woman's womb was shot down. Some of the Irgun fighters slashed their victims to pieces with cutlasses. All this was meticulously recorded by the British authorities, even to the detail observed by Assistant Inspector-General Richard Cutling, the British interrogating officer, that: 'women had bracelets torn from their arms and rings from their fingers, and parts of some of the women's ears were severed in order to remove ear-rings'.

There is evidence that the massacre at Deir Yassin was not, as some apologists have urged, an inexcusable but isolated act of bestiality, a horrific aberration, or a sudden and inexplicable upsurge of fanaticism, to be weighed in the balance against the wild excesses of the 'Arab hordes', and therefore to be relegated into the footnotes of history.

The facts appear to be otherwise. The capture of Deir Yassin was part of a carefully formulated strategy; the massacre of its innocents – embarrassing and excessive as it may have been – greatly facilitated the success of that strategy, and was instrumental in securing the Zionist dream formulated by Herzl fifty years before.

Although the outrage was condemned in public by the official Zionist leadership, no action was taken against its perpetrators, all of whom could easily have been apprehended. Moreover, and even more significantly, the assault on Deir Yassin by the Irgun had been approved by the Jerusalem commander of the Haganah, the 'official' Zionist military wing, who wrote:

> I wish to point out that the capture of Deir Yassin and holding it is one stage in our general plan. I have no objection to you carrying out the operation provided you are able to hold the village.[12]

In a survey of the charnel house that his men had made out of Deir Yassin, Menachim Begin was later to assess the consequences of their barbarism:

> Arabs throughout the country, induced to believe wild tales of 'Irgun butchery', were seized with limitless panic and started to flee for their lives. This mass flight soon developed into a maddened, uncontrollable stampede.[13]

A month later, the state of Israel was proclaimed in Palestine, on land 'purified' of its Arab population.

The ten years which had led up to this moment had not been wasted by the Zionists. The Arab rebellion had greatly clarified and simplified their strategic requirements. The policy of infiltration – of steadily buying more and more land on which to settle more and more immigrants – had been the basic cause of the 'disturbances'. The Arab rebellion had demonstrated beyond question that the inhabitants of Palestine would only surrender their land to the Jewish state by force. Zionists were not slow to draw the obvious inference. Joseph Weitz, the administrator in charge of Zionist colonization, confided to his diary:

> Between ourselves it must be clear that there is no room for both people together in this country . . . we shall not achieve our goal of being an independent people with the Arabs in this small country.[14]

From this assessment he drew the chilling but inevitable conclusion that the Jewish national home would have to be liberated from the Arabs who still inconveniently inhabited it.

> And there is no other way than to transfer the Arabs from here to the neighbouring countries, to transfer them all; not one village, not one tribe should be left.[15]

The vision is more startling when it is recalled that the Jewish immigrants in Palestine at this time formed only 30 per cent of the population; 95 per cent of the land was still owned by Arabs, who formed 70 per cent of the population.

The ends implied the means: a strategy for the acquisition of land, if needs be by the use of force. By 1939 the Jewish National Fund had evolved a most sophisticated policy for the purchase of Arab land. In the early days almost all land bought by the fund was used for the settlement of new immigrants. Even at this stage, however, according to Abraham Granott, the former chairman of the board of directors of the fund:

> The Fund strove to avoid the isolation of villages, as this was liable to impair the secure and smooth progress . . . endeavours were made to create blocks of settlements, a sort of skeleton of Jewish districts . . .[16]

By following the contours of this 'skeleton', it later became possible to define the outline of the Jewish state. As the opposition to their immigration intensified, so the Zionists began to erect settlements on land

> which bore a military value, either because they overlooked centres of Jewish activity, already operated or likely to be so in the future, or the occupation of which provided control over communications . . .[17]

By 1938, the strategy of the fund was governed above all by 'national policy': the determination to create a Jewish majority in as large an area of Palestine as could be secured for the immigrants.

> In the decade preceding the establishment of the state, the decisive stage in the struggle for the future state, a number of land operations were carried out which were of supreme consequence in the Jewish war of independence . . . When the great day arrived, and the United Nations decided to establish a Jewish state, those who were responsible for defining its boundaries were compelled to include the lands bought by the Jews, together with the settlements thereon. The frontiers of the new state which march in so curiously winding a fashion were largely determined by the success of the Jews in creating *faits accomplis*.[18]

It was a brilliant strategy, planned with meticulous foresight. It required one further element: the means to fight that 'war of independence' which would transform the skeleton into a state.

As early as 1933, one of Zionism's most moderate leaders found himself drawn by the ineluctable logic of his cause to the need for a violent assertion of Zionism in Palestine. According to Chaim Arlosoroff, who ran the political department of the Jewish Agency, the realization of Zionism might require a period of revolutionary rule by the Jewish minority,

> . . . during which the state apparatus, the administration, and the military establishment would be in the hands of the minority, in order to eliminate the danger of domination by the non-Jewish majority and suppress rebellion against us.[19]

This was, in effect, a call for a Zionist *coup d'état* in Palestine, which not unnaturally was made in a private letter to Chaim Weizmann, who continued however to assert the peaceful principles upon which the Jewish national home in Palestine was to be founded.

In accord with this policy, the official Zionists strenuously condemned those Jews who had begun to take it upon themselves to retaliate against the Arab guerrillas who, during the rebellion, had from time to time descended from the hills to ravage their crops and snipe at their settlements. These Jewish reprisals took a spectacular form: they placed bombs in urban centres where Arabs were sure to congregate. A single explosion in the Arab market of Haifa, for instance, killed fifty-four people, fifty-three of whom were Arabs. The scene was of a kind that was later to become familiar: mangled bodies grotesquely trapped in piles of upturned fruit, blood and juice intermingled, running down the gutters.

However distressing such independent action might have been to the Jews of Palestine, it beckoned them – however crudely – down the military route towards which Zionism, however reluctantly, was being remorselessly drawn. In its early days, Zionism had embraced the principles of non-violence, enshrined in the Jewish Havlaga. But militants in the movement were not slow to point out that it was precisely this passivity which had led to their oppression and humiliation for so many centuries. Moreover, it was now evident that there was an irreconcilable conflict between the Havlaga and the Zionist aspirations for a Jewish state. Although men like Jabotinsky, the leader of

the militant wing, was once alleged to have said: 'I can't see much heroism and public good in shooting from the rear an Arab peasant on a donkey . . .',[20] he subsequently endorsed such tactics. Nor was he unaware that in such retaliation 'it was not only difficult to punish the guilty ones, in most cases it was impossible'. Quite bluntly, he recognized that the choice was between 'retaliating against the hostile population or not retaliating at all'.[21] And he was for retaliation.

If the Jewish terrorists broke through a moral barrier, their assaults were not isolated incidents, out of step with the times. For, at the same moment, the underground Jewish army, the Haganah, was taking formidable shape as the future army of the Jewish nation.

By the time the British had crushed the Arab rebellion in Palestine, the Haganah – in collusion with the authorities – existed as a formidable force. The British had openly trained 14,500 Jewish fighters whom, although the authorities knew that they belonged secretly to the Haganah, they chose to designate as 'supernumerary policemen'. Their function was to help defeat the Arabs. In addition to the arms provided to these 'policemen' by the authorities, the Haganah had acquired no less than 6,000 rifles, a million rounds of ammunition, 600 machine-guns, 24,000 hand-grenades, 12,000 rifle grenades, either manufactured locally in Jewish underground workshops or imported illegally from Europe.

The training given by the British was invaluable. The leadership of Colonel Orde Wingate was, in particular, to leave a lasting impact upon the Zionist movement. Wingate was a military genius of idiosyncratic mien, who was given to scratching his naked body in public with a toothbrush – a habit evidently regarded with wonder by his devoted followers. He was a ruthless and unorthodox commander who led the Jewish night squads which, from 1938, took the offensive against the Arabs, not quite with and not quite without the permission of the British. David Ben Gurion, the first Prime Minister of Israel, was to record that:

> The Haganah's best officers were trained in the night squads, and Wingate's doctrines were taken over by the Israeli defence force which was established twelve days after the birth of the Jewish state.[22]

One of Wingate's most celebrated disciples was a young settler called Moshe Dayan, who records in admiration that Wingate's disdain 'could make you feel as tiny as a mouse'. Dayan went on the first mission led by Wingate. It was an illegal expedition of revenge against an Arab village allegedly

81

responsible for attacks upon a new Jewish settlement known as Hamita in Upper Galilee on the border with Lebanon. After a thirty-mile march through rough country, the eight-man squad arrived at the suspect village. Wingate disappeared into the darkness and his followers waited for his signal.

Soon they heard a shot and they moved into the positions Wingate had mapped out for them. From the outskirts of the village there was another shot; after which there was a fusillade of fire, obviously from the Arabs, a firefly spray of lights in the distance, shouts, screams and wails. And then straight into the trap which Wingate had laid for them, came the Arabs . . .[23]

As the Arabs ran from the village – whether with or without weapons is not recorded – Wingate's men, Dayan among them, surrounded them with ease. Then, in the words of the author of this account, the British journalist, Leonard Moseley, they 'began to pick off their victims. They killed five and captured four.' Wingate returned, full of praise for his men, and began to interrogate the prisoners:

He said in Arabic: 'You have arms in this village. Where have you hidden them?'
The Arabs shook their heads and protested ignorance. Wingate reached down and took some sand and grit from the ground; he thrust it into the mouth of the first Arab and pushed it down his throat until he choked and puked.
'Now,' he said, 'where have you hidden the arms?'
Still they shook their heads.
Wingate turned to one of the Jews and, pointing to the coughing and spluttering Arab, said: 'Shoot this man.'
The Jew looked at him questioningly and hesitated.
Wingate said in a tense voice, 'Did you hear? Shoot him.'
The Jew shot the Arab. The others stared for a moment, in stupefaction, at the dead body at their feet. The boys from Hamita were watching in silence.
'Now speak,' said Wingate. They spoke.[24]

At the time this action was officially regarded as an unforgivable offence by Wingate's superiors, who had not even been informed of his enterprise, which violated the policy of the Mandate. In the event, the offence was quickly forgotten, and Wingate was subsequently given a free hand to organize the Jewish night squads according to his own principles – explaining to the British: 'The Arabs have caused great damage and made the British army look fools. I can stop all that. I will wipe out the gangs for you . . .' And to the Jews: 'We are establishing here the foundation of the army of Zion.'

By one of those ironies which are the hallmark of an incoherent policy, no sooner had the British crushed the Arab rebellion than they decided to reverse the policy which had provoked it – at precisely the moment when the Zionists were more powerful and militant than they had ever been. In a White Paper of 1939, the Colonial Secretary, Malcolm MacDonald, summarily revoked his own government's Partition Plan and declared that the Jewish national home had now been established; that to develop it further would violate British undertakings to the Arabs and could be pursued only by force. He urged, therefore, that after five years, during which Jewish immigration and land purchase would be phased out, 'self-governing institutions' should be set up to prepare the way for independence at a later date.

This pious and belated assertion of principle, a last lunge towards common sense, did not even gather dust before it was trampled underfoot by the irresistible force of Zionism which had been unleashed by the British themselves. Enraged by such a *volte face*, and obedient to the logic of their cause, the Zionists now turned upon the British: the Trojan Horse which had done its work was now in the way.

At many rallies in Palestine, Jews were invited to offer their allegiance on oath to a declaration of Zionist intent:

The Jewish population proclaims before the world that this treachery will not be tolerated. The Jewish population will fight it to the uttermost, and will spare no sacrifice to frustrate and defeat it.

As it was, the intervention of the Second World War held the military struggle for Palestine in suspension. But the political war was fought with unflagging vigour. And, for the first time, the battleground became the United States. Confronted on the one hand by the reluctance of the British to impose the Jewish state upon Palestine, and on the other by growing evidence that the future of the 'free world' was to be determined in Washington, Zionists decided with great foresight to switch their efforts from Whitehall to the White House.

Until this moment American Jewry had demonstrated no great urge to heed the cries of anguish which reached across the Atlantic from the ghettos of Eastern Europe. Even when Nazism had seized the soul of Germany, the White House came under no pressure to offer sanctuary to those millions who were to fall victim to that barbarism.

The Americans had therefore remained free to pursue the policy which they had adopted soon after the Mandate. In essence, this involved a tacit understanding between the Western Powers and the Zionists by which, in return for Western support of Jewish settlement in Palestine, the Zionists would refrain from criticizing the meagre quota of immigrants which the Western Powers were prepared to admit into their own states. Thus, between 1932 and 1935, only 14,000 Jews were permitted to enter the United States, while 144,000 descended upon Palestine. Such hypocrisy served both sides well: a burden of 'the Jewish problem' was siphoned off to Palestine where the Zionists, within the limits permitted under the Mandate, were free to choose only the most suitable 'pioneers' for settlement in the national home.

The decision to shift the focus of their attack from London to Washington was taken in the confident belief that, if American Jewry could be aroused from indifference, it was powerful enough to exert a decisive pressure upon the White House – not to lift restrictions upon Jewish immigration into America, but to secure a commitment not merely to Zionism but to the Jewish state. The Zionists judged well.

By 1945, American Jewry had raised more than $46 million for the cause. Moreover, a powerful lobby of American Zionists had been mobilized to adopt a programme which specifically called for the transformation of Palestine into a 'Jewish Commonwealth'. However, since this programme threatened to dispossess the 70 per cent of the population of Palestine who still owned 95 per cent of the land, President Roosevelt's response to it was cool. Indeed his immediate concern was not Zionism but the half a million or more refugees who were expected to emerge from the Holocaust, in need of the world's protection. He proposed that the Western nations – led by the United States and Britain – should alleviate this tragedy by absorbing between them all those victims who would wish to find sanctuary away from the scene of the Nazi atrocities. To this end he sent Morris Ernst as an envoy to sound out international opinion. Ernst was astonished and insulted when active Jewish leaders 'decried, sneered and then attacked me as if I were a traitor . . .'[25] Under this assault the Roosevelt programme collapsed, and it became an unquestioned assumption that the refugees from Europe could and would only go to Palestine. They were never to be asked, as Roosevelt had intended, 'Do you want to go to Ecuador, or Newfoundland, or Kansas, or Nottingham? The doors of the world are open. State your choice.' It was a significant victory for the Zionist lobby,

which now intensified its assault, not only in Washington by propaganda, but with guns in Palestine.

The end of the war had left the British exhausted, without either the will or – more especially – the need to preserve the Mandate in Palestine. It was left to the new Prime Minister, Clement Attlee, to undertake the monumental task of disentangling an enfeebled Britain from a disastrous policy. For a while he clung uncertainly to the ghost of the 1939 White Paper. But it was beyond his power to resist the battering which this provoked, not only from the Zionist guns, but – more especially – from a White House which, with Roosevelt's death, now had a new occupant, Harry Truman.

The new President soon demonstrated his grasp of the issues at stake by blithely adopting the Zionist programme as his own – confronting doubters with the memorable apology:

> I am sorry, gentlemen, but I have to answer to hundreds of thousands of those who are anxious for the success of Zionism; I do not have hundreds of thousands of Arabs among my constituents.[26]

This cynicism encouraged perhaps the most shameful but decisive hypocrisy of a shoddy and shameful historical record. In July 1945, Truman wrote to Attlee, endorsing the Zionist stand against the 1939 White Paper:

> The dramatic restrictions imposed on Jewish immigration by the British White Paper of 1939 continue to provoke passionate protest from Americans most interested in Palestine and the Jewish problem. They fervently urge the lifting of these restrictions which deny to Jews who have been so cruelly uprooted by ruthless Nazi persecutors entrance into the land which represents for so many of these their only hope of survival.

In that last sentence the White House gave its full authority to the grotesque proposition, which Roosevelt had already repudiated, that the 'only possible hope of survival' for the survivors of the Holocaust lay in their admission to Palestine. It is a proposition that Western public opinion has rarely been invited to question, and yet it has been of overwhelming significance. If the foundation stone of the Jewish state was concealed in the ambiguities of the Balfour Declaration, then the edifice of Israel was constructed upon the rock of a world public opinion which appeared genuinely to believe the deception propagated by Zionism and upheld by the White House: that salvation for the Jewish people lay in Palestine alone.

The momentum generated by the Zionists towards the Jewish state had now become irresistible. What had happened? The alliance of Zionism and the White House had led the world to believe that the political solution now to be imposed on Palestine was in fact an obligation owed by civilization to humanity.

Why in Palestine? Only agonized Palestinians murmured the question, and they were ignored then as they are today. Moved by the discovery of the horror which the victims of the Holocaust had endured, world public opinion was in no mood for reasoned debate. In the transit camps of Europe there were the pitiful survivors, the 300,000 who had escaped extermination in the gas chambers, but· who had witnessed the most dreadful and sophisticated atrocity ever perpetrated. Opinion was united: if these poor souls wished to go to Palestine, then in the name of humanity they should go. Yet the survivors were never asked. The choice was never offered. While the White House urged Britain to open the gates of Palestine to the refugees, Capitol Hill took three years – until 1948 – before grudgingly passing the legislation to permit a meagre 20,000 of them into the sanctuary of the United States. Instead of castigating Congress for its reluctance to demonstrate the humanity to which the American President had given such powerful expression, the Zionists remained silent, knowing that the alternative destination for the victims was Palestine. The refugees had become pawns in a brilliant propaganda campaign which skilfully exploited the horror, shame and guilt of the Western world at the atrocities committed in the bosom of Christian civilization.

The Zionists had succeeded in driving American Jewry to drive the President to drive the British to surrender Palestine to the Jewish state, and world public opinion, unmindful of the realities of Palestine, applauded them all along the way.

Buffeted by the White House, Britain was blitzed in Palestine in a coolly prepared and vicious campaign of terror, designed to drive them out of the country, the Zionists reinforcing their assault not by threats but in action. They turned their guns on those who had taught them how they should be used.

The explosion which destroyed a wing of the King David Hotel in Jerusalem and killed no less than eighty-eight people was the most notorious – and the most effective – single act of terror in the campaign which had begun spasmodically two years earlier in 1944, with explosions in government car parks and offices; and policemen gunned down in the street – eight of them killed in the single worst outrage. But by 1946 the campaign was in earnest. In competitive alliance, the Stern gang and the Irgun blew up radio stations, power stations and bridges. They mined roads and sank patrol boats. They dynamited aeroplanes and robbed banks. They raided military camps and killed soldiers in their beds. They kidnapped officers. Once they caught two army sergeants and hanged them from a tree for the public to gaze upon. They had learned all that Wingate had to teach them, and more.

Although the official Zionists in Palestine put on a public show of condemning the violence, their allies in America could not suppress their jubilation at each new outrage. An extreme Zionist like Ben Hecht, the Hollywood scriptwriter, was given space in the *New York Herald-Tribune*, in 15 May 1947, to urge the terrorists on to further exploits:

> The Jews of America are with you. You are their champion. You are the grin they wear. You are the feather in their hats . . . Every time you blow up a British arsenal, or wreck a British jail, or send a British railroad sky-high, or rob a British bank, or let go with your guns and bombs at the British betrayers and invaders of your homeland, the Jews of America make a little holiday in their hearts.

British protests were eloquently ignored. And the White House openly undermined – against the fierce advice of the State Department – British attempts to secure order in Palestine. In late 1946, Truman endorsed a Zionist proposal which would have handed over no less than three quarters of Palestine to the Jewish population, which by then owned a mere 7 per cent of the territory to be ceded to them. It was the most significant act of 'statesmanship' since the Balfour Declaration, and the most important Zionist victory to date.

Under these circumstances, the British position in Palestine became untenable. Although 100,000 British troops were available on the spot to confront the military assault of the terrorists, they were – to their intense frustration – virtually immobilized by the political considerations that dictated the policy of the British government. In April 1947, enfeebled and humiliated, the British government announced its intention of surrendering the Mandate to the United Nations, thus resolving – albeit in ignominious fashion – the contradiction it had imposed upon itself thirty years earlier.

Five
The Cleansing of Palestine

The peasants watched this struggle for their land with impotent horror. It took place over their heads, against their will, but they had no means to intervene, let alone prevent the fate being prepared for them. And their fields still needed ploughing and sowing. There were still olive oil and oranges to take to market; marriages to celebrate; deaths to mourn. The routine and ritual of peasant life continued with a resolution borne of the conviction that somehow the wisdom of nations would intervene to defend their rights and aspirations, to protect their homes, their land and their livelihood.

The children of the Arab rebellion had become young men. Ibrahim Ghannan, the painter, whose brother's monkey had initiated him into politics, had, like many other impoverished peasants, gone to work for the British army.

'I began when I was 11 years old, because I was intelligent and knew how to speak both Hebrew and English as well as Arabic. I started as a storekeeper, looking after the books. Then more and more British came into the country during the war, so my position improved. I used to spend a lot of the time with the English officers, translating for them, because most of them spoke no Hebrew or Arabic.

'I remember on one occasion, when there was a different officer on duty and I went for my salary. He went to kick me out, thinking I was a child. I insisted that I ought to be paid. And in the end the captain relented. He told me that I should go to school. "But there is no school in my village," I said.

' "No government school?" he said.

' "There is no government and there is no school," I replied. "And I wouldn't be here in any case except that my parents need the money." '

To Ibrahim's relief, the officer evidently liked his show of spirit and he was permitted to stay at work.

The innocence of the young was not a privilege enjoyed by their parents. They did not easily recover from the ravages of their rebellion, nor did they quickly forget the manner of its suppression. But the psychological thunderbolt delivered by the United States – the threat of upheaval, of a Jewish state on their land to fit a grand design which they could not comprehend – had led them, by 1945, to reconsider their feelings towards the colonial authority. The ambiguity of their attitude towards the British persists even today.

'You know,' one of the elders in the camp explains, 'we still regard the British as the architects of our misery. When the Second World War was waged in the Middle East some British soldiers came and asked me for water. I said, "No; you tortured and disfigured me, you destroyed my people, you may have no water." But they said, "We control

Palestine." So I said, "Only by force, and only by force will you get what you want. I'll give you no water." And they got no water.'

But this story does not provoke the general assent which accompanied earlier tales of confrontation with the British. Instead, to some approval, an old man who had not spoken hitherto recalled that he had worked for the British as a policeman.

'I still have a pension, you know. My pension number is 2293. There are many like us. I liked working for the British. They were just and good to me. I must say that. I worked for the CID. On political and civil crimes. But they didn't expect me to inform on the Arabs; they were very clever in not involving us in embarrassing circumstances. So for me there was no contradiction in working for them.

'You know that we depended on the British after the war. They had exhausted our strength in the rebellion, but I don't think they wanted our destruction. Some of the officers and officials in the British army were very sorry to leave Palestine, I'm sure of it. And they sympathized with us. But they had no power. Britain had come out of the war bankrupt. So her government was forced to obey the United States.'

Impoverished and ill-prepared to resist, the peasants were aware of how devastatingly the scales were now tipped against them. Ten years earlier, in desperation, they had fought the Mandate, believing that the British could be driven to resist the Zionist invasion. They had been broken in the struggle, and now the British, who stood between them and the openly declared intention of Zionism to establish the Jewish state on their land, were themselves being broken by a form of militant Zionism that had been bluntly expressed by terrorism's philosopher, Menachim Begin, in the memorable phrase : 'We fight, therefore we are.'

The peasants now had little choice but to wait for Zionism to turn its attention from the British to them. By 1948, the Haganah numbered no less than 35,000 armed men, with the additional support of what had been described in a British White Paper as 'a static force of 40,000 settlers and townsfolk'. And the Jewish military industries in Palestine had greatly expanded. Between 1942 and 1944, for instance, they had been able to supply $33 million of equipment to the British army. They manufactured machine-guns, mortars, bombs, anti-tank mines, tank engines, small naval craft, parachutes and a host of small arms.

Against this, the peasants – who had been systematically disarmed by the same British army which bought its military supplies from the Zionist arsenal – possessed an ill-matched assortment of weapons,

many of them relics from the First World War; they had perhaps 2,500 effective fighters; a leadership which had been dispersed or sent into exile; an organization in disarray with no central direction. Their strength lay only in the fact that they still formed the majority, that their villages were clustered in strategic positions, and that they had not lost the desperation which led them into battle against impossible odds ten years before. It was in this parlous condition that the people of Palestine waited to hear the outcome of the deliberations of the General Assembly of the United Nations in November 1947.

The result was never in doubt. The White House had threatened, cajoled, bullied and blackmailed those wavering UN member states which relied upon presidential goodwill into voting for partition. President Truman had demonstrated his skill in the martial art of diplomacy to such effect that it was described by the US Secretary of Defense, John Forrestal, in the privacy of his diary, as 'an almost scandalous use of coercion and duress upon other nations'. But it worked. Under the UN plan, the Jewish state was to be given 54 per cent of Palestine. Included within its borders were five sub-districts which had Arab majorities of 70, 67, 87, 53 and 99 per cent respectively. It incorporated almost all the most fertile land, including the main citrus groves upon which the Arabs depended for their main export earnings. It also incorporated the vast area of the Negev, which was populated by 100,000 Bedouin who produced from the desert, most of the barley and wheat grown in Palestine.

The land under cultivation in the Negev alone was three times that under cultivation by the Jewish settlers in the whole of the rest of Palestine. Despite the fact that there had been but 475 Jewish settlers in the Negev before President Truman made his declaration in favour of the Jewish state, the United Nations duly handed over this huge area to the Zionists, doubtless believing the myth that it was they, not the Arabs, who 'made the desert bloom'.

The outrage of a people at the dismemberment of their country at the behest of the international brotherhood of nations – albeit under duress – has been passionately expressed by the Palestinian scholar, Walid al-Khalidi. In a scathing assessment of the UN decision, he has noted that the 'ostensibly disinterested verdict of an impartial international body' endowed the concept of partition 'with the attributes of objectivity and evenhandedness – in short a compromise solution'. But there was no compromise to be made, since, by definition, a compromise is an arrangement, acceptable, even if grudgingly, to both protagonists. In the case of the partition of Palestine this was impossible.

It was Zionist in inspiration, Zionist in principle, Zionist in substance and Zionist in most details. The very idea of partition was abhorrent to the Arabs of Palestine and it was against it that they had fought their bitter, desperate and costly fight in the years 1937 to 1939.

Moreover, compromise implies a readiness by the protagonists to make mutual concessions.

What were the Zionists conceding? You can only really concede what you possess. What possessions in Palestine were the Zionists conceding? None at all.

On the other hand, the Arabs were expected to concede more than half their land.

Concessions of such a kind and scale are demonstrably alien to the very idea of compromise. It is surely utterly alien to this idea that one party should so revolutionize its position *vis-à-vis* the other, and at the latter's expense, that the relative positions between the two would be actually reversed. It surely goes against the grain of human nature to expect the party that would suffer this reversal to enter into the transaction just because some third party, itself affiliated to the potential aggrandizer, chose to befog the issue by calling this transaction a 'compromise'.[27]

The incredulous Arabs had no alternative but to resist partition as best they could against overwhelming odds. The British had little doubt about the outcome of a war which they knew was inevitable. General J. C. D'Arcy, the commander of the British forces in Palestine, had already informed a group of journalists that if the British withdrew 'the Haganah would take over all Palestine tomorrow'. But could the Haganah hold Palestine under such circumstances? 'Certainly, they could hold it against the entire Arab world.'

So when, soon after the UN vote had been taken, the British announced that they would surrender the Mandate on 15 May 1948, they knew what they were doing. Disaster was inevitable. Not only were the Arabs to see their country dismembered, they were also to face the destruction of their own identity, surrendering it, along with their majority rights, to the alien and exclusive culture of their new rulers in the Jewish state. No longer were the Zionists to be mere settlers, buying up land and dispossessing its inhabitants to make way for their settlements. It had taken seventy years of resolute planning for the Zionists to purchase 7 per cent of Palestine; now the United Nations was to hand over to them another 47 per cent of the country –

an overnight territorial increase of 800 per cent, over which they were to have sovereign rights before which, if the UN 'recommendation' had any force in international law, the inhabitants of that territory were supposed to offer obeisance. It was inconceivable, and everyone knew it.

Moreover, the Zionists themselves, who had been anxious to establish territorial rights throughout Palestine, regarded the UN partition as a formal declaration of principle rather than a final division of territory – as an 'irreducible minimum' of land upon which to establish their state. They did not for a moment doubt that the Arabs would resist; and the prospect perturbed them not at all. Indeed, it offered them – and later they were to be quite open about it – the chance to 'cleanse' the new state of the bulk of its Arab inhabitants, while extending its borders to undefined limits.

They were confident, too, that they would in the process escape the condemnation of a world community which, under the tutelage of the White House, had been rendered purblind to such irregularities.

The war began almost as soon as the UN vote had been counted. It was a chaotic communal struggle over which Great Britain presided with a dignity befitting the occasion, making little pretence that the Mandate any longer enjoyed the authority with which it was formerly invested. Those who cared to observe the humiliation were privy to the degrading shambles of a colonial power retreating on every front in as orderly a manner as possible under the circumstances, and over the fallen bodies of the combatants which the Mandate had been supposed to reconcile and protect.

As the British moved out, so the Zionist forces moved in to occupy their new territory, to protect their settlements and to confront the recalcitrance of an Arab population which stubbornly resisted its own national downfall. Although the Zionists had by now 100,000 potential soldiers out of a population of just over half a million, they were not all yet mobilized. Moreover, the Arab villages resisted with the defiance of desperation. Despite snipings, bombings and hit-and-run raids, the peasants stayed put. Thus, with only a few weeks to go before the end of the Mandate, the Zionists were presented with an apparently alarming prospect: no less than half the population of their new state would be Arabs who would rather die than submit to its diktat, who would never accept an arbitrary frontier dividing them (under occupation in the United Nation's artifice) from their compatriots in the dismembered 'Arab' state in Palestine who were equally committed to the preservation of their heritage throughout Palestine.

Abu Jihad, the co-founder of Fatah, in his Beirut office with his daughter

The Zionist solution to this 'Arab problem' was not arbitrary or sudden or taken in panic. It was carefully considered, superbly planned and – inevitably – utterly ruthless. To the Arabs of Palestine, it is known to this day as the Catastrophe.

In the summer of 1948 there was a grocery shop in the Arab town of Ramleh, which stood inland about sixteen kilometres from the new Jewish city of Tel Aviv and the old Arab port of Jaffa.

The grocer's son, Khalil Wazir, who was twelve years old, used to play with the Jewish children who lived near by. The two communities had lived beside each other in relative harmony. The conflict over Palestine had not yet touched his young life. The tranquillity was destroyed suddenly.

'I will never forget that day. The men had gathered together. And they were saying that the Jews were going to do to us what they had done in Deir Yassin. That they had surrounded the town and were about to enter it. I was frightened, terribly frightened. And then my mother and my sisters and I went to the church. The whole village went to the church. It was packed. And I remember the archbishop standing in front of the church. He was holding a white flag, and the Zionist troops came into the town. And the archbishop said to them, "We are civilians, not soldiers, not fighters.

Leave us in peace." They talked for a long time. And then some of the soldiers came into the church. And they picked out some of our youths. And they took them away and no one knew where they had gone.

'Afterwards we came out and the picture will never be erased from my mind. There were bodies scattered on the road and between the houses and down the side-streets. I can't forget it even now. No one, not even women or children, had been spared if they were out in the street. This was the first stage. After that, you might say, they dismissed us – they drove us out of the homes, and out of the town.'

On that July day the grocer's son – who is now better known to Palestinians as Abu Jihad, the founder with Yasser Arafat of Fatah, the Palestinian 'terror' organization – joined the remnants of 700,000 Arabs who fled from their homes in terror, out of Palestine into exile in the diaspora – so bringing to its desired conclusion the strategy initiated so spectacularly with the massacre at Deir Yassin.

The Israeli historian, Arie Yitzhaqi, has recorded the methods used by the Zionist forces to drive the Palestinians out:

If we assemble the facts, we realize that to a great extent the battle followed the familiar pattern of the occupation of an Arab village in 1948. In the first months of the 'war of independence' Haganah and Palmach troops carried out dozens of operations of this kind, the method adopted being to raid an enemy village and blow up as many houses as possible in it. In the course of these operations many old people, women and children, were killed wherever there was resistance.[28]

The cold fury of the Zionist assault was conditioned by the need to defeat and drive out the Palestinians before 15 May, when, it was feared, the Arab armies might pluck up courage to intervene to impede the Zionist advance. Village after village was overrun. The British journalist David Hirst, in a meticulously researched account of this period, has unearthed an article written by an Israeli army officer for the US Marine Corps magazine, about one of the more successful devices used by his men. It was called the 'barrel bomb'. As Hirst describes the 'weapon':

It consisted of a barrel, cask or metal drum, filled with a mixture of explosives and petrol, and fitted with two old rubber tyres containing the detonating fuse. It was rolled down the sharply sloping alleys and stepped lanes of Arab urban quarters where it crashed into walls and doorways making 'an inferno of raging flames and endless explosions'. Against such an assault the Arab civilians were powerless. As for their fighters – against machine-guns, mortars and, in the later weeks of the assault, aircraft, they could offer only ancient weapons, limited ammunition and almost no training.[29]

In addition to their physical onslaught, the Haganah forces waged a skilful psychological war. From secret radio stations, they broadcast in Arabic news that dangerous diseases like cholera and typhus had reached epidemic proportions; they warned of reprisals; and they gave details of escape routes from the advancing Zionist army. Loudspeakers mounted on armoured cars would reiterate the warnings, and – in full knowledge of how deeply Deir Yassin was seared into the Arab soul – instructed the villagers to flee to 'get out of the bloodbath . . . if you stay you invite disaster'.

In Jerusalem, the combination of barrel bombs and loudspeakers was particularly effective. As the same Israeli officer recalled,

. . . uncontrolled panic swept through all Arab quarters, the Israelis brought up jeeps with loudspeakers which broadcast recorded 'horror sounds'. These included shrieks, wails and anguished moans of Arab women, the wail of sirens and the clang of fire alarm bells, interrupted by a sepulchural voice calling out in Arabic: 'Save your souls, all ye faithful: the Jews are using poisoned gas and atomic weapons. Run for your lives in the name of Allah.'[30]

As the Arabs moved out, the Zionists moved in, sometimes killing, almost always looting and burning.

By now several hundred thousand Palestinians were on the move, criss-crossing Palestine or fleeing towards neighbouring countries, dodging the Zionist army, sleeping in olive groves and in mountain huts, or swamping villages not yet under attack. In the flight crops were abandoned, animals left to starve; families were separated, women and children going in one direction away from the war, and their men in another, skirting the Zionist forces but refusing to leave. In the chaos, men lost their women, mothers their children. Families were scattered, never to be reunited.

In April 1948, Ibrahim Ghannan still lived in the small village on the outskirts of Haifa where he had been born. It had been free of conflict, its 500 inhabitants being careful to avoid confrontation with the well-armed Jewish settlements that surrounded it.

'I never liked the settlements. I knew that it was those people who would cause the trouble. The Arab Jews, who wore Arab clothes and had Arabic customs, were quite different. They were part of us. This is an important truth for the world to remember. We were never like the Europeans. We were never against the Jews. Only against those who took our land.

'Even so I could not believe the news when it reached us, that the Zionists were killing people in Haifa. As children we had visited the local kibbutz. We didn't believe that they were now fighting us. So I went to Haifa, down the hill where I had spent so much time as a child drawing, to see if it was true that they had taken the city. And the city was filled with Jewish soldiers, thousands of them.'

The British began to move out of Haifa on 21 April, leaving the Jewish and Arab quarters to face one another in battle. There is evidence, corroborated by the journalist Jon Kimshe, who subsequently became editor of the *Jewish Observer*, that the British informed the Jews in advance of their intention to withdraw, but not the Arabs. As the British pulled back, a fierce struggle began as Arab fighters from neighbouring villages came to support their comrades. But the odds were impossibly loaded. The Arab inhabitants tried to flee, but the roads were blocked by the retreating British army, which looked on as the terrified refugees tried to find any escape route. As if determined to impress the ignominy of their role indelibly upon the Arabs, it was not until the population of Haifa surrendered and was rushing for the boats in the harbour that the British elected to send in ambulances to rescue the wounded. As the refugees left, driven from their homes for ever, they allegedly raised the cry: 'Deir Yassin' – to the apparent satisfaction of Menachim Begin, who paused to make a note of the event for posterity.

Two days after the fall of Haifa, the semi-official Zionist newspaper, the *Palestine Post*, announced that:

> Haganah forces in a thirty-hour battle . . . crushed all resistance, occupied many major buildings, forcing thousands of Arabs to flee by the only escape route – the sea.

Seeing the devastation, Ibrahim Ghannan returned to his village. But it was surrounded by Zionists.

'We had no choice but to surrender. The muktar telephoned to the British to ask for help to save our people. Eventually the British organized a convoy of all the villages which were under assault. But we weren't allowed to take anything with us. Even the toys of the young children had to remain behind. And we had no water.

'After that the British washed their hands of us – that is how it seemed to me anyway. At first they accompanied our buses, but when we were on the road they left us, and they went away smiling and laughing. Then the Jews began to shoot all around us at the buses, over our heads, on the ground, to humiliate us. And the British soldiers did nothing.

'We stopped in a Jewish village called Kofitra. In that village there were two kinds of Jews. Some of the women were kind and gave us food. Others spat at us.

'Finally we came to an Arab village called Shifal Amer and we stayed there three days. But the Zionists were forcing their way into Galilee and the village was attacked. So we went to Saffouri which is on the edge of Lake Tiberius. I remember the place vividly because it was my last day in Palestine. We stayed in a simple stone house, belonging to two ladies; they were very kind to us and I remember them with great respect. They fed a group of us, perhaps one hundred people, grinding the corn up for us. There was a water well in the yard from which we drank. They also prepared yoghurt for us.

'It was their last day too. For that night Saffouri came under attack and the ladies had to flee with us. You see my painting of the scene. I feel great joy when I see it, joy and sadness. Joy because I feel that I am still living in Palestine. I dream of it, it is always present. Sadness, because it is a dream. I feel that my life stopped at the age of seventeen, because that is how old I was when I left, and I only live when I dream of those days.'

The 'hero' of the 'war of independence' and the architect of Ibrahim Ghannan's flight was Yigal Allon, later to become distinguished as an Israeli Defence Minister. In the most unequivocal language, he explained why the Zionist forces adopted tactics which produced such a violent upheaval during the last few days of the Mandate.

> We saw a need to clean the inner Galilee and to create a Jewish territorial succession to the entire area of the Upper Galilee. The long battles had weakened our forces, and before us stood great duties of blocking the routes of the Arab invasion. We therefore looked for means which did not force us into employing force, in order to cause the tens of thousands of sulky Arabs who remained in Galilee to flee . . .[31]

In addition to the traditional military assault, Allon's tactic was therefore to gather together the Jewish muktars of the region and ask them to noise it abroad that a great Jewish reinforcement was on its way,

> that is going to burn all the villages of the Hulel . . . The flight numbered myriads. The tactic reached its goal completely.[32]

On 14 May 1948, a few days after the British had scrambled out of Haifa, the voice of the chief secretary of the British administration raised itself above the chaos formally to announce that the Mandate was at an end. He was asked by a journalist: 'And to whom do you intend to give the keys of your office?' Hiding his shame behind a stiff upper lip he replied: 'I shall put them under the mat.'

There was, by now, no doubt as to who would pick them up. On the same day, before an assembled crowd of 200 journalists, photographers and Zionist notables, David Ben Gurion declared the establishment of the state of Israel – a proclamation which was recognized within sixty minutes by the United States of America.

The following day, belatedly and reluctantly, the combined forces of three Arab countries entered Palestine to confront Israel's secured position. Some irregular forces had entered the country before the end of the Mandate, but they had not impressed themselves upon the situation. The official forces were designed, it appeared, to fare no better. They were ill-equipped, disorganized and in intense rivalry one with another. Although they were to be portrayed by Israeli propaganda as 'the invading Arab armies' bent upon driving the Jews into the sea, it should be recalled that they were incapable of such a feat against 100,000 Zionist troops; and that the only people thrown into the sea were the Arabs from the ports of Haifa, Jaffa and Acre, many of whom drowned in the scramble to reach the small flotilla of boats evacuating them from their homes.

In proclaiming the new state, Ben Gurion was careful not to define its borders. Indeed, Zionists were to argue that, since the Arabs had rejected the UN Partition Plan, the Israelis were under no obligation to accept it either. This was an obfuscation: Ben Gurion had a great territorial ambition, as he revealed a few days after his proclamation, when he sketched out a dream in his diary:

The Achilles' heel of the Arab coalition is the Lebanon. Muslim supremacy in this country is artificial and can easily be overthrown. A Christian state might be set up there, with its southern frontier on the Litani. We would sign a treaty with this state. Then when we have broken the strength of the Arab Legion and bombed Amman, we would wipe out Trans-Jordan; after that Syria would fall. And if Egypt still dared to make war on us, we would bomb Port Said, Alexandria and Cairo. We should thus end the war and would have put paid to Egypt, Assyria and Chaldea on behalf of our ancestors.[33]

As it was, the intervention of the Arab armies was to postpone the satisfaction of Ben Gurion's ancestors, much to the frustration of Yigal Allon, who later recorded:

If it wasn't for the Arab invasion there would have been no stop to the expansion of the forces of Haganah, who would have, with the same drive, reached the natural borders of western Israel . . .[34]

According to this interpretation, then, the Arab 'invasion' posed a threat, not to the survival of the Jewish state, but to its indefinite expansion.

It has long been asserted by Zionists that the Arabs left Palestine of their own accord, or under orders from the neighbouring Arab states. This revision of the facts by Zionism was to prove of immense consequence: for years it encouraged the pragmatic conscience of the West to believe that the solution of the 'Palestinian problem' lay not with the Jews, but with the Arabs who had 'caused' it. The inhabitants of Jaffa, Jerusalem, Haifa, Acre, Safad, and hundreds of other small towns and villages – the 650,000 men, women and children who became refugees – knew who had caused it,

and why. To them it was no accident that Ben Gurion refused to define the limits of the Jewish state; nor that immediately after its establishment he refused to permit the right of return to the refugees, citing before the United Nations that this would present 'an insuperable problem'. Neither was it an accident that four fifths of the new state was to comprise land abandoned by the refugees, including half the citrus-fruit holdings, a quarter of all the standing buildings, and no less than 10,000 shops and stores; nor was it by accident that, within a few years, one third of the Jewish population of Israel would be living on what was to become euphemistically known as 'absentee property'. At least, to the Palestinians, it was no accident. As the victims of one Catastrophe, they would have found themselves in agreement with the judgement of one of the original Jewish settlers in Palestine, Nathan Chofshi, when he wrote:

We came and turned the native Arabs into tragic refugees. And still we have to slander and malign them, to besmirch their name. Instead of being deeply ashamed of what we did and trying to undo some of the evil we committed . . . we justify our terrible acts and even attempt to glorify them.[35]

And, being in agreement with Nathan Chofshi, the Palestinians would wonder why, until this day, Western opinion has remained so indifferent to their plight, so reluctant to find out why they reject the state in Palestine that was acquired from them only by force of arms, so eager to accept the Zionist version that the 'right of return' which the Palestinian people claim is but a devilish concoction, brewed by the 'Arab hordes' who would drive the last outpost of Western civilization into the sea.

The grocer's son may not have known it at the time, but the assault on his home town was approved in person by David Ben Gurion; it was led by Yigal Allon, and one of the officers at the head of the attack was Moshe Dayan. On the previous day, 11 July, Dayan had led his troops into Lidda, which with Ramleh formed an important strategic salient that the Zionists wished to take so as to secure the route from Tel Aviv to Jerusalem. The author, Jon Kimshe, has described how Dayan

. . . drove at full speed into Lidda shooting up the town and creating confusion and a degree of terror among the population . . . Its Arab population of 30,000 either fled or were herded on the road to Ramallah. The next day Ramleh also surrendered and its Arab population suffered the same fate. Both towns were sacked by the victorious Israelis.[36]

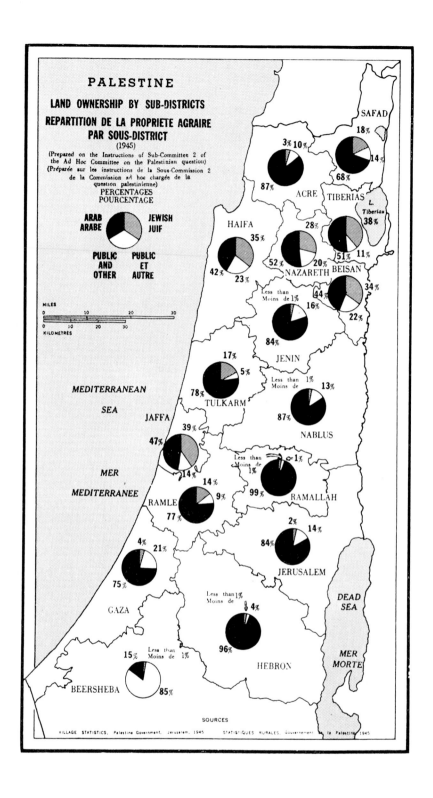

Land ownership in Palestine as prepared for the
United Nations Sub-Committee on the
Palestinian Question in 1947. Data obtained
from the Rural Statistics prepared for the
British Administration in Palestine, 1945

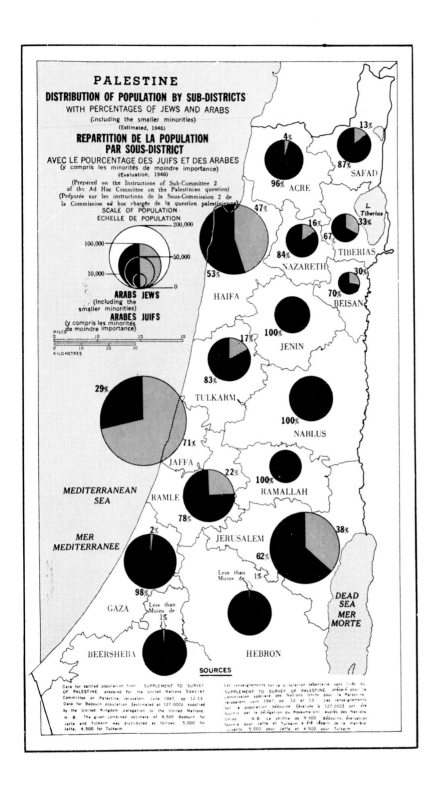

Distribution of population in Palestine, as
prepared for the United Nations Sub-Committee
on the Palestinian Question in 1947. Data
obtained from the Supplement to the Survey of
Palestine, United Nations Special Committee on
Palestine, June 1947

Abu Jihad now sits behind a desk in an air-conditioned PLO office in Beirut, coolly planning guerrilla war against Israel. He is anxious that others should know why he does this, though it is the first time that he has ever discussed the matter with an outsider. His voice is hoarse with contained emotion as he remembers the details.

'After the cathedral, and the bodies, we were, as I said, very frightened. We all knew about the massacre at Deir Yassin, where children had been killed too. We knew about it from the Israelis in the broadcasts. They had done it before, and therefore every child expected it again. This fear put pressure on us. And you should know that they did do it again, here and there where there were other massacres. And Begin, the man who is now Prime Minister, he was the head of the groups who did this.

'We hurried back to my house, we had been ordered to leave and I wanted to collect my best suit – I was a child, you see, and I was proud of my suit. But my father would not let me, saying we couldn't take too much luggage. We can only take a little. Then we left our house. We were gathered, thousands of us, in the road. We put our few things beside us and waited. And I will never forget. The Israelis wouldn't let us take anything. We had just brought some warm clothes, some bread, some food, that was all. I walked back to have a last look at my house and there, before me, the Zionists were taking everything out of my house, everything. I wanted to go in and take something. But they stopped me, and pointed their guns at me, telling me to get out. I went back to the place where the bus was to pick us up. We were to go towards Latrun, which is on the road to Ramallah. But first they separated the men, including my father and my grandfather, and they forced them to walk. My father was ill but they forced them out of the town by shooting over their heads you see, like this, over their heads. And I was standing there.

'We told the driver that we wanted to take some food with us. And although the soldiers had said no, he saw that I was a child, and he relented. I went to pick up our parcels. An Israeli soldier saw me, and fired towards me, not less than ten bullets, I swear it. My mother drew me to her chest to protect me, and those bullets hit a neighbour of ours in the leg, and he is still alive, and he could tell you about it. All I wanted was the bread – can you understand?

'Then they put us in the bus and took us out of the town where they stopped the bus. We were supposed to walk through to where the Arab armies were up in the hills at Ramallah. We could have walked along the road, but they didn't let us. Instead they forced us to go through the valleys and mountains. And do you know, we spent four days walking. There was a huge multitude of us, all gathering and walking. We had nothing. We were thirsty and hungry. Children died. How many things happened.

'On the third night some of us reached an Arab village. But when we arrived there was an attack on it. I can't forget it. The sky was lit up. There was a terrible noise. Everywhere there were mortars and artillery around us. Many were killed. Many fled, losing their children, their sons. Some fled towards Lebanon, taking nothing. We reached Ramallah. And for two weeks we stayed there, living under the trees, and then from there we went to the Gaza Strip. All that I've told you I remember exactly. I was twelve years old. I was a witness to great suffering.'

After briefly stemming the tide of the Israeli advance, the Arab armies were soon on the retreat, to the dismay of the Palestinians who had been led to believe that their Arab brothers would easily conquer the Zionist 'occupation'.

Six
After the Catastrophe

The forlorn column of refugees which stumbled out of Palestine were a broken people, scattered, dispossessed and powerless. They clutched a few belongings, some clothes, a little food, perhaps some silver and jewellery which they had managed to conceal from the looters who sacked their towns and villages. Their exodus was hardly recorded at the time. In the eyes of the world the matter was simple: the Arabs had fled and then they became refugees, dispossessed people, stateless. Their humiliation has to be pieced together from the scraps of personal agony which individuals remember: the Lebanese peasant who refused his Palestinian brother a jug of water until he had paid for it; the filthy dust-caked clothes which they had to wear for days at a time, without any means to clean them; the need to beg for bread for half-starved children; and the children who died of hunger, thirst and disease. There were the goats and sheep which collapsed; the hostility and contempt; the isolated acts of violence; the insults of the citizen directed at the exile, the silent but perpetual assertion, as he watches you pass, that you are nobody, that you do not belong, and that you are not wanted.

On both banks of the Jordan, in Lebanon and in the Gaza Strip, the authorities constructed makeshift camps to house hundreds, then thousands, then tens of thousands, then hundreds of thousands of refugees. With characteristic and impetuous generosity, the world community sent donations: tents, blankets and medicine. But it was never enough. The United Nations, having sliced Palestine into arbitrary partition, now had observers on the ground to survey their surgical handiwork. They found a gaping wound, festering. Count Bernadotte, the Swedish UN mediator, who had been charged 'to promote a peaceful adjustment of the future situation in Palestine', and who later was to be murdered by the Stern gang for his reward, was horrified by the reality to which the United Nations had given its blessing. In Ramallah he was besieged by emaciated and terrified refugees, who stood around his car, demanding food and the right to return to their homes. 'Never have I seen a more ghastly sight than that which met my eyes here,' he said. He travelled from one makeshift camp to another, concluding early in his pilgrimage that 'the refugee problem was vaster and more baffling than we had imagined'.

His attempts to reconcile the Arab and Zionist establishments were fruitless. Although he had started out in the naïve belief that the Zionists would demonstrate a Western propensity for compromise, he found an unyielding Ben Gurion, who insisted that the refugees were an Arab not a Jewish problem. Count Bernadotte was soon drawn to the reluctant conclusion that the state of Israel 'had shown nothing but hardness and obduracy towards the refugees'.

The conditions in the camps were atrocious. Families, still traumatized by their loss, huddled bleakly in overcrowded tents. They were without adequate food or sanitation. When it rained, the narrow paths along each neat row were churned into a quagmire. The mud oozed into the tents. They lived in sodden clothes and slept in wet blankets. Influenza and pneumonia reached epidemic proportions. The young and the old perished. Malnourished children were too weak to resist, and the old, left with no purpose, lacked the will.

Even after rudimentary order had been imposed upon the camps, the conditions remained barbaric and degrading. Over the months, and into the years, the tents began to rot. They were discarded in favour of huts whose barrack rooms were often occupied by six or more families, sixty men, women and children, crowded together with only hanging blankets to offer privacy. They cooked, ate, washed and slept in public. Parents with many children could find no space in which to rest their own exhausted bodies.

The immediate sympathy of the world soon evaporated or turned elsewhere to offer its charity. The Palestinian camps were starved of funds. UNRWA, the relief organization set up by the United Nations to cope with the crisis which its most prominent member state had helped to create, began to complain – in language which would thirty years later be part of an annual ritual – that it could barely meet the basic needs of those it was charged to support, let alone begin to care for their future.

Apathy among the exiled Palestinians spread with the same virulence as disease. Anger, frustration and terror yielded to the sense of loss, the knowledge of impotence. The promise of the Arab nations – that they would rise up to destroy the enemy – had been revealed as an absurd and hollow boast. The bitterness of this discovery was sharpened by the evident indifference which the various Arab régimes now displayed towards their unwelcome guests.

To survive above the level of subsistence, the Palestinians had to find work. It was not easy. Although Abba Eban was to tell the United Nations almost ten years later that, since it was the Arab governments who had created the refugee problem, the obligation was upon them to solve it – a revision of history which by then had received President Kennedy's blessing – it was evident to anyone with any knowledge of the parlous social and economic conditions in the Arab world that no Arab government could absorb the refugees. No host country had either the jobs or homes to offer. Decrepit régimes in backward countries with rapidly rising populations were, as ever, too busy trying to contain the aspirations of their own impoverished people to open their economy to an invading army of unskilled peasants.

So the Palestinians were forced into such menial jobs as they could find, at the lowest rates. They were without protection or security, taking seasonal work on the land or casual jobs as labourers in factories or on construction sites. For this work – which only the youngest and strongest could find – they earned a few shillings a day. By 1952, four years after the Catastrophe, the average income of all Palestinians had fallen to one fifth of what it had been ten years before. Despite pensions and indemnities paid to former officials by the British government, and the earnings of successful entrepreneurs, the Palestinians received no more *per capita* than 8.9 Palestinian pounds a year, or $(US)21.7. The poverty was extreme but not isolated, and it was inescapable.

Nor did the impact of the Catastrophe recede. The memories of a particular life, a particular home, in a particular village, with particular neighbours – the memories of those images which provide a man with his identity – became, though remoter in time, sharper in perspective. The desolation of the camps accentuated the sense of the fragmented self. Although each Palestinian community grimly stayed together, forming 'villages' within the camps, attempting to re-create the old social structure, they existed in a nowhere world: behind them was the history through which they defined themselves, from whose womb they had been brutally torn; before them lay an uncharted map, an opaque, unnavigated emptiness.

Inevitably they turned in upon themselves, upon their memories. They shunned contact with outsiders and were themselves shunned in return. Isolated in the camps, they regarded themselves, and were regarded, as 'other', to be despised and even mocked for their 'cowardly betrayal' of Palestine, their surrender to the Jews. Without a passport, without a country, without a home, dependent on UN rations and UN schools, the Palestinian refugee became an object of scorn, an inferior being who had nothing and who belonged nowhere. The humiliation of this disrespect blended with a sense of loss to produce a deep longing to return. 'The Return' became the driving passion of the Palestinians, protecting them from disintegration, summoning them out of oblivion into the hope of a future.

The desperation of the fathers communicated itself to the sons. Yahya Rabah was five years old when his family was uprooted from their village in southern Palestine and driven to the Gaza Strip.

'I have a vivid memory of our flight. First the mortar bomb which fell on our house. The Israelis were attacking. It was dawn. The village was in panic, absolute panic. We just left our houses and fled, taking nothing. That afternoon I was hungry, and I started crying. My mother told me that she had no food, and I should stop asking. "We can't help you," she said. "It causes us pain, so please don't ask." This was my first lesson : I never asked my parents for anything after that, because I did not wish to let them feel that they would deny me anything.

'In Gaza we have nothing. The pain of a child is never forgotten. We used to sing a song: "Rain and rain as much as you like, our home is made of iron." But we lived in a tent and the rain poured in. We came to realize that we were nothing without a homeland. We inhabited a void and we filled it by talking about our country. A homeland is not only land and security. It is songs and happiness. When we ate bread or drank water, our first thought was that the bread in our country was better, and the water tasted more sweet. Palestine became a living legend to us, the children. I used to learn the stories of our home and retell them to other children.

'Our sensitivity was no less than that of our fathers, though they carried the country with them into exile. I could articulate my feelings and this has been my outlet. The very concept of a "camp" is for me an equation with death. For this reason you have to fight all the time in the camp to preserve yourself from demoralization, from a moral and spiritual death.'

Yahya Rabah soon revealed himself to be a child of unusual talent. He is now well known, not only as a senior member of Fatah, but as a poet, writer and broadcaster.

'The school in our camp was in a large tent, and we sat on sacks. When I went to secondary school I walked fourteen kilometres each day, seven kilometres there and seven kilometres back. We already knew that learning was very important to us. Our parents had the feeling that it was ignorance which had contributed to our being thrown out of Palestine. We were not equipped to deal with the political ploys and manoeuvres to which we fell victim. We did not understand the plans and alliances made over our heads, and we had failed therefore to fight Zionism in the early stages. The crucial part is this: the world map was altered between the wars for the convenience of the great powers, and we couldn't recognize what was happening.'

At secondary school Yahya Rabah was quickly recognized to be a promising writer. He wrote short stories and contributed to the school newspaper. The imagination of the child was captured by the sea :

'I came to consider that the sea was my only friend, only the sea was great enough to contain our sorrow.'

In 1951, Gaza was struck by violent storms which almost demolished two of the camps, uprooting tents and tearing worn canvas to shreds. In Demelbalach, where Yahya lived, the tents were close to the sea, and on one terrifying night the storm was so great that the waves swept up over the tents, demolishing two rows and sweeping them with their occupants and their belongings into the sea.

'I remember how this symbolized and intensified our fight for life. I remember so clearly the frightened children and the screaming women, trying to escape, and rescue their possessions from the attacking waves. Why, why, I asked, why were we driven to this? Only gradually through incidents like this, did we begin to realize that no one could help us unless we began to help ourselves.'

Yahya Rabah used the image of the sea to express the Palestinian yearning for the homeland in a short story called 'The Sea Became Blue'. It is one in a book of short stories which has an introduction by the PLO Foreign Information Department, phrased in language which the West is seldom invited to hear, although it is pervasive in the Arab world.

A lover usually talks frequently about his loved one, because she dominates all other thoughts in his mind. In the same way we Palestinians like to talk about our loved one, Palestine . . . We resist persecution and oppression, we resist until we win, we resist so that we may see our beloved country, Palestine. Whoever among us falls along the way is like the thousands of heroes. The lovers who fall are transformed into candles to light the way for the heroes who come after them. Our lovers never die. They rise to the heavens to be transformed into stars in the sky of Palestine . . .

How it angers us lovers to see our beloved one the object of the enemy's attentions, and grasped between the enemy's arms, as we sing her love songs which she does not hear. How it angers us that people speak and write of her, falsify the facts, and find willing listeners among those who do not know the truth, or do not wish to know it.

They seized our land and our country from us, they seized our loved one Palestine, and have been singing, writing and talking about her so much that the world forgot that this land is the loved one of someone else, who lives in torment and forgotten in the refugee camps of oblivion, dying from the pain of suffering and deprivation.

The raw extravagance of expression, disconcerting to the modern Western ear, none the less offers a moving insight into the passions which lurk behind the diplomatic and military masks that the Palestinian usually chooses to wear before the rest of the world. A similar yearning speaks through 'The Sea Became Blue' itself. The story begins with the image of a storm.

Foamy, O sea, foamy . . . your strong winds blow, the tall cliff collapses on to the beach, the ropes of the tents are snapped, the tents fly away and drown, the palm trees are smashed down . . . and Al Habash, your ardent lover who rides the violent waves, spreads out his sail for the journey and goes westwards, far, far away, not returning, his voice no longer heard . . . We hear nothing but your roaring, sea, and your white foam the colour of a funeral shroud, your foaming face the colour of death.

In the story, Abu Al Habash is a fisherman who becomes a myth, a romantic expression of the need to struggle for the Return. The other refugees cannot understand him. He is a remote, isolated and steadfast figure, striding the beach, collecting driftwood. The refugees are used to this hermit in their midst, but they ignore him.

One winter day they are astonished by the sight of Abu Al Habash when he arrives among them, gesticulating towards the sea and shouting, 'I saw him. I swear by Almighty God I saw him.' It transpires that the fisherman was walking along the sea shore when he noticed a black shape in the water which looked like part of a barrel. When he got closer to it he recognized a large black dolphin, the same dolphin that used to swim around his boat in Palestine.

I knew him from his head, his eyes, from the way he swam and played in the water. I knew him, and he knew me. He came to me, he came calling me. I swear to God that's what happened.

The refugees think that Abu Al Habash has gone mad. He is indifferent to their looks, filled with a restless, fierce determination. He builds a small boat. The muktar tells him that fishing is forbidden by the authorities. He ignores him, and when his boat is finished, jumps into it and heads out to sea, disappearing over the horizon. He is a brave man and desperate. And he has decided to return.

The men waited,
And the women waited,
And the small children waited
Even in their sleep.
They all waited through the night.
The wind howled as if in mourning,
And the colour of the sea was changed . . .

But Abu Al Habash had gone away and did not return, and the people in our refugee camp are still waiting for him to return.

In Gaza, in Lebanon and in Jordan, the wound festered. The new state of Israel perceived this but remained unmoved, adamant that the exiles should never return. The propaganda was insistent: the 'refugees' were an Arab problem to be solved by the Arab world. It was no concern of the Jewish state.

Israel began to flourish within the boundaries defined at the 1949 Armistice. It was this territory which now had to be defended against an Arab world committed – at least by rhetoric – to the recovery of their land. Inflated Arab sentiments, and the illusion which the Israelis fostered that the might of the Moslem world was ever about to wage relentless war against their small and fragile young state, were brilliantly exploited by their official propaganda.

The leaders of Israel were free to undertake almost any military exercise that the defence – or the advance – of Zionism appeared to require, in the knowledge that the West would not question whether the adventure had really been forced upon the fledgling state to pre-empt its strangulation. Moreover, those who now challenged Israel were to be identified before the world as Arab 'hordes' or 'terrorists'. The fact that no combination of Arab armies either could or wished to offer serious challenge to the Israeli military régime was conveniently ignored by all parties to the deception perpetrated with such zeal by Israeli propaganda.

For a few years after the exodus, some Palestinians did make pathetic attempts to return to their homes and villages. Often they came across the borders by night, to seek out relatives or unearth hidden possessions. One old man returned on his donkey from Lebanon, determined to live in his home village. Fear of detection made him hide in the fields by day and return to his house at night. Others would cross over to pick oranges and olives from their orchards. Those who lived in villages along the border with Israel suffered a double indignity. The Armistice had separated them from their land, but because they were not 'homeless' according to the criteria adopted by the United

Nations, they were not officially refugees and therefore received no benefits from UNRWA. It was from these villages that the most persistent 'infiltrators' came, desperate both to rescue what they could from their land and to demonstrate a daring and futile resistance.

When these 'terrorists' were captured, as many were, they were driven back over the border with the warning, reinforced on occasion by a volley of shots, that they should never return. Those who were unwise enough to come armed with a gun for protection were almost certain to perish in an unequal duel with waiting Israeli patrols.

The grocer's son, Abu Jihad, had been in one of the last cars to leave from Hebron for the Gaza Strip, crossing the war-lines between the Zionist and Arab forces. In Gaza he had been fortunate. His father had been able to rent a room, ten metres square, and here the family – eleven people in all – made its home.

Like Yahya Rabah, Abu Jihad excelled at school.

'It was difficult. We had missed two years during the upheavals and when the secondary school finally opened, it had no books, and seventy pupils in each class. Our teacher used to read from his book and we would copy out what he said word for word, thus making our own textbooks.'

Abu Jihad came top of the form, and second in the Gaza Strip Elementary Certificate for his year. In the final certificate exam he came seventh in all Egypt – an achievement in which he takes particular pride. In 1955, he was elected secretary of the first Students' Union in the Gaza Strip. It was out of the bitterness and frustration which General Dayan had so clearly perceived that students like Abu Jihad began at this time to formulate the plan of escape now known as 'The Resistance'.

'We had already begun to organize ourselves, selecting young Palestinians, patriots, to begin the struggle. We had to do this in strict secrecy because it was forbidden by the Egyptian authorities.

'It is worth recalling our circumstances at this time. In 1948 the Arab armies had entered Palestine, and they told us: "Okay, we are here, you are militia, civilians, we are with you, but we are organized, so hand your arms over to us, let us win the fight." And we handed over our guns. And even now, you know, we have receipts from various Arab governments for the arms which we handed over.

'What happened was simple. The Zionists had been in Palestine for seventy years and we had not surrendered. And yet, when the Arab armies withdrew, they handed over 20,000 square kilometres and we were left with a mere 6,000. It was – and it is a tragedy to have to say it – a mock war.

'Thereafter we were forbidden to carry arms. The Arab régimes were under great pressure from the Western countries to keep us disarmed, and at that time they found it difficult to resist. We were not permitted by them to form any organizations. So we had to organize and plan in secret.'

Though they were to be more of a nuisance than a threat, the Gaza 'patriots' organized several raids against the enemy: they blew up a military jeep on the coast road near Jaffa, and reported back that its occupants had been killed; they scattered mines near the Gaza border, which they claimed had destroyed a number of Israeli tanks; they attacked the military settlement at Side Bohar in the belief that Ben Gurion was resting there; and they mined roads in the Negev. Most spectacularly, they managed to blow up a reservoir used to irrigate Zionist settlements in the valleys bordering the Gaza Strip. Abu Jihad is still exhilarated at that memory.

'The next day I went to the border and saw that the water had flooded through many settlements. It had swamped valleys. The people were up to their knees in water. And their corn was drowned.'

These incursions neither alarmed nor surprised the Israelis. When a young pioneer was killed by Palestinian 'terrorists' as he harvested grain near the Gaza Strip, it was Moshe Dayan (the Haganah officer who had driven Abu Jihad out of Ramleh) who delivered the funeral oration. Dayan was not so insensitive that he did not understand what it meant to the Palestinians to watch their land being tilled by the enemy.

> Let us not today fling accusations at the murderers. Who are we that we should argue against their hatred? For eight years now they sit in the refugee camps in Gaza, and before their very eyes, we turn into our homestead the land and the villages in which they and their forefathers have lived.[37]

And then came the sting. Zionism would not yield.

> We are a generation of settlers, and without the steel helmet and the cannon we cannot plant a tree and build a home. Let us not shrink back when we see the hatred fomenting and filling the lives of hundreds and thousands of Arabs, who sit all around us. Let us not avert our gaze, so that our hands shall not slip. This is the fate of our generation, the choice of our life – to be prepared and armed, strong and tough – or otherwise the sword will slip from our fist and our life will be snuffed out.[38]

General Dayan had already demonstrated his conviction that Israel would live by the sword. The dashing cavalier of 1948 was by now a distinguished, even a revered figure in Israel, greatly admired for his flamboyant leadership in the new nation. It was Dayan who had been the moving spirit behind the creation of a special force, known as Unit 101. Its most spectacular operation was the assault on the village of Qibya on 14 October 1953 as a 'reprisal' for the death of a mother and her two children, blown up by a terrorist grenade.

The magazine of the Israeli airborne corps, the *Paratroopers Book*, described the operation as 'an ambitious undertaking surpassing anything in the past'. The UN military observers who arrived on the scene soon after the Israeli troops had left witnessed the results of this 'ambitious undertaking'.

> Bullet-riddled bodies near the doorways and multiple bullet hits on the doors of the demolished houses indicated that the inhabitants had been forced to remain inside until their homes were blown up over them . . . witnesses were uniform in describing their experience as a night of horror, during which Israeli soldiers moved about in their village, blowing up buildings, firing into doorways and windows with automatic weapons and throwing hand-grenades.

That night, in its first major operation, Unit 101 slaughtered sixty-six men, women and children. If 1948 had determined the nature of the struggle between the Palestinians and the Israelis, the scale of the latter's 'retaliation' – about which Western statesmen were to become conspicuously tolerant – had now been established by Unit 101.

Despite such provocation, the Arab world resolutely turned its face from confrontation. Egypt was particularly disposed to avoid conflict. In the early spring of his revolution, President Nasser went out of his way to assure the West that his expulsion of the British in no sense signalled an intent to embark upon military adventures against Zionism. And the West, led by the United States, believed him. To secure his revolution, Nasser needed to spend his nation's slender reserves, not on arms, but on the rescue of his impoverished people from the misery which had burdened their lives for centuries. And if the most powerful state in the Arab world did not propose to confront the Jewish state, then war against Israel was out of the question.

This prospect frustrated the Palestinians greatly. Under the tutelage of the Jordanians, the Lebanese and even the Syrians, they had already discovered that the Arab rhetoric which called for the liberation of their homeland was perhaps an expression of popular will, but certainly not of political intent. Now it appeared that even Nasser, the apostle of the Arab nation, was to disown them. It was a bitter discovery to make: that the Arabs feared Israel more than they loved Palestine.

The young students of Gaza realized quickly that their hope lay with the leaders of Israel, whose bellicose statements in 1954 and 1955 had so irritated the White House that President Eisenhower had even threatened to suspend aid to the American offspring. In this atmosphere the raids from Gaza against 'occupied territory', so far from being inarticulate acts of revenge, had a clear purpose. The tactic was not so much to harass Israel as to draw a reluctant Egypt into confrontation with the Jewish state by provoking Israeli 'retaliations' against Egyptian troops stationed in Gaza.

Their wish was fulfilled – though whether it was their provocation or Ben Gurion's stated urge to create 'a dynamic state bent upon expansion' which caused the 'Gaza raid' remains uncertain. Whatever the cause, the effect of the Israeli assault on

28 February was a crucial moment in the history of the Middle East.

President Nasser had just been to visit his troops in Gaza. He told them that their positions were not to become a battle front. He returned to Cairo only to discover a few hours later that Israeli forces had raided Gaza, killing twenty-eight Egyptian soldiers, some of them while they still slept in their beds. The seeds of war had been sown. No longer could Nasser resist the demands from his army for modern weapons. When the Americans turned him down, he sought arms from Eastern Europe, acquiring them from Czechoslovakia, and thereby permitting the Soviet Union to enter upon the Middle East stage for the first time.

In Gaza, Abu Jihad was quick to seize the moment.

'It was a real chance for us. The day after the raid we demonstrated in the streets in honour of the martyrs, and to mobilize all the people in the Gaza Strip, in the villages and in the camps. Our demonstration was an angry response. It was against the Egyptian authorities, against Abdul Nasser. And the tactic worked. Thereafter – you must have heard him – he would always say, "This was a turning point in my life" – he repeated it again and again.'

Free for a moment to vent their feelings, the young went on the rampage. They attacked UN positions and Egyptian installations, burned their vehicles and stamped their flags into the ground. Under this pressure, and driven by popular opinion in the Arab world, the Palestinian cry for weapons – 'so that we can defend ourselves' – could no longer be ignored. Six months later, armed reluctantly by President Nasser, the first Palestinian fedayeen went on a mission into occupied territory. The 'Resistance', so it seemed, was now cradled in the arms of the father of the Arab nation.

Seven

The Road to Karameh

In the hills above Tyre there is an old villa with peeling yellow walls and a battered roof, whose broken tiles have slipped so far that they promise to cascade to the ground at a mere vibration. Doubtless a Lebanese merchant once sat here in the shade of his veranda, contemplating his good fortune, looking down into the valleys where the citrus trees stand in neat distant rows, cradled by the white rock of the mountains which rise up to meet a far-off blue skyline. Now there is no tranquillity.

This villa is the headquarters of the local Fatah command, and it is due to receive a visit today from Yasser Arafat. The preparations are intense. Under the cyprus trees in what was once an elegant garden, some women are stirring three vast blackened cauldrons from which a smell of chicken stew wafts across to the audience waiting under the trees for the arrival of its leader. There is much jostling and laughing. Old friends embrace warmly as they encounter each other; mothers proudly produce self-conscious small children to be admired by relatives who are astonished at how much they have grown since last they saw them. A boy wearing jeans with a US flag sewn on the back pocket stands proudly beside a father dressed in military uniform, a pistol at his waist, talking to an elegant elderly man who wears a flashily cut summer suit

and who fiddles with his worry beads as they wait. It is a gathering of the committed élite: a military picnic for the middle class – Lebanese and Palestinian – who are members of Fatah, and who belong to the University Brigade. The villa is surrounded by Fatah commandos, sitting in Japanese jeeps and British Land-Rovers, which block the roads, their 106-mm recoilless rifles pointing menacingly at the sky. While the guests drink tea and coffee or beer, the young men in the jeeps are on the alert. Not only is their commander-in-chief about to arrive, but there is always the possibility that Israeli Intelligence will have heard about this occasion, and that their defence forces will honour it with a lightning bomber raid which could, in a single attack, obliterate a score of Fatah's most influential leaders.

At noon, and precisely on time, Arafat's convoy sweeps up to the villa, throwing into the air a dust-cloud through which it is just possible to detect the outlines of military men in a hurry, shouting orders and slamming the doors of the Mercedes, Range-Rover and BMW cars which have brought them from Beirut. Families from the adjoining refugee camps smile and wave excitedly as the entourage hurries into the villa. There the diminutive figure of Yasser Arafat is lost in the embracing arms of his supporters, who crowd around him to

Palestinians await their commander-in-chief

shake his hands and kiss his face according to Arab custom. He wears a wide smile and is delighted by the welcome.

The informality of the greeting is not permitted to delay the schedule. Within a few moments Arafat is moving briskly to the garden to deliver a speech in memory of a student 'martyr' who has been killed in the Lebanese war. But first there is lunch. Trestle tables stand under the cedars. Music plays through loudspeakers. Plates arrive, filled with rice and stew. Suddenly the entire gathering is eating in silence, pausing only to offer one another choice morsels from their own dishes, side-stepping young children who play hide-and-seek under the adult legs. Arafat sits in the centre, jovial and diplomatic, ensuring that those around him have food and managing both to eat and smile encouragingly at the deferential conversation which surrounds him.

After twenty minutes the tables are whisked away. A detachment of commandos emerges from

the trees, marching in time to the music. They halt on what was once the patio and which now forms a natural stage above the audience. They present arms and stand at ease. Slowly the audience forms itself into a semi-circle around the dais. There are university lecturers and students, old men from the camp, young fighters, bodyguards, peasant women and the wives of Beirut executives, silent in anticipation. After an opening barrage of speeches, a singer plays mournfully on his guitar,

telling of wars and struggle, death and victory. The song pleases Arafat, who calls out that he should record it for the revolution in a cassette.

The commander of the student battalion is a tall thin young man, who has a reputation for military cunning and fearlessness. He stands nervously clutching his notes, smiling uneasily, to welcome Arafat:

'In the name of the battalion, in the name of all Fatah battalions, we say to our chairman that we

will continue the revolution until final victory is ours. The man who can best speak for us at this moment is our leader, the chairman himself.'

Arafat walks up to the microphone, unprepossessingly paunchy, squashed uncomfortably into an ill-fitting uniform, almost comical, certainly unglamorous. It seems strange that this is the leader of the Palestinian revolution, who is a hero to millions of people in the Arab world. Where is the charisma?

The question is answered almost at once. His listeners are as discerning an audience as he ever has to face – educated, political, critical and informed. Arafat is utterly at ease. Without a text or notes, he launches into a powerful assault on 'imperialism', his voice rising with passion, his gestures timed perfectly for dramatic impact. His audience waits on his words, understanding and enjoying every ambiguity, responsive to the radical thrust of a speech which is directed not so much at

them as at the nations of the Arab world which have for thirty years competed for influence in the inner councils of the Palestinian people.

'History tells us that when the Crusaders entered Jerusalem, 70,000 martyrs died to protect the city. In 1967, when Israel occupied East Jerusalem, only seventy-one people were martyred defending the city. We must be ready to sacrifice one martyr for every mile of Palestine in order to liberate our land.'

He warms to the theme. His oratory has his audience entranced.

'We have no choice. Brezhinski says, "Bye-bye PLO." We know when he says that, that Begin and Carter are in league to destroy us. And yet, when they sent their army to fight us, we resisted for eight days and eight nights. And they failed to destroy us. That was indeed a battle but it was you' – he gestures slowly around the audience – 'you who carried the flame of victory. And it is you

'Peasant women and the wives of Beirut executives, silent in anticipation'

'It is thirty years since the Catastrophe'

who will bear it in the future.

'The United States has plotted with Hussein and Sadat and the Zionists to decide the future of the Gaza Strip and the West Bank. But they cannot do this. All this is finished. They can no longer decide our destiny. It is our people who must decide . . . We are a mountain which no wind can blow over.'

The audience murmurs in approval, and one or two soldiers spontaneously raise a clenched fist, crying out in support.

'Our future can no longer be decided in an embassy of another land. It is our decision, a Palestinian decision. Those who think they can buy us with oil – we say we don't need you, we can go elsewhere for what we need.' (The reference is to Iraq, with whose leaders at that time the PLO was fighting a brief but bitter feud. The breach was healed at the Baghdad Summit which saw the closing of Arab ranks against the Camp David accord between Israel and Egypt.)

The audience breaks into cheers and chants in unison, 'Revolution until victory.'

Arafat finishes suddenly and hurries towards his car, surrounded by bodyguards and a stampede of young children who are shouting and scuffling to get close enough to touch him. In a moment the powerful engines are roaring. The doors are slammed, the tyres squeal and the convoy disappears urgently into the dust-storm on the road back to Beirut. It is thirty years since the Catastrophe.

The tents of the refugees gave way gradually to concrete walls and corrugated roofs, squashed up against each other, rising in disorderly fashion, a storey added here and there to accommodate a son and his new wife, or grandparents arrived from another camp. The camps became villages, the villages grew into towns, their populations permanent but unsettled – yet remaining in the abject misery they had insisted was temporary.

From the start, the Lebanese authorities looked askance at the Palestinians, fearing that their volatile presence would disturb the uneasy balance between Christian and Moslem upon which the structure of their state was precariously perched. Although successive leaders of the Lebanese people went out of their way to pay sanctimonious tribute to their own 'hospitality', they were assiduous in their attempts to isolate the Palestinians, erecting around the camps a political, social and economic *cordon sanitaire* that only the most versatile and persistent could penetrate. Under Lebanese law, Palestinians were specifically excluded from government service; they were forbidden to send their children to Lebanese schools; they were denied the right to claim Lebanese social security, even though those who managed to obtain Lebanese work permits were obliged to contribute to the Lebanese national insurance scheme. They were not, however, for the most part permitted to become Lebanese citizens. Nor were they allowed to travel freely where they wished. Lebanese policemen stood guard outside their camps, controlling their movement. Neither 'nationals' nor 'aliens', they were rarely free from the knowledge that they were unwelcome in Lebanon. Moreover, so anxious were the authorities to avoid vexing the Israelis that they sought to block the only avenue left open to the refugees: the assertion of their national identity. It was forbidden – not in law but in practice – to say, 'I am a Palestinian.' The Lebanese secret police – the Deuxième Bureau – was ruthless in the suppression of those who dared to whisper such sedition. Arrests, detention and the usual abominable cruelties devised by sadists serving statesmen were routine. By their own account, the Palestinians in Lebanon were a spiritually cowed, politically impotent and psychologically broken people. And to a lesser degree, if not significantly so, the same was true in the Gaza Strip, in Syria and in Jordan. Until, that is, the revolution.

The decision by President Nasser to rally the Arab world to the Palestinian cause at first exhilarated the handful of young exiles who wished to rouse their people from the torpor of their demoralization.

Soon after the Israeli raid on Gaza, Abu Jihad received a delegation of Palestinian students from Cairo. It was led by one of the emerging spokesmen for the cause, an articulate twenty-six-year-old engineer called Yasser Arafat. This was the first meeting of the two men. They quickly became friends, beginning a close relationship from which can be traced the origins of the 'Palestinian Resistance'. Yasser Arafat returned to Cairo, from where he continued to forge links between those students whose families had escaped the camps to be dispersed throughout the Western world, and upon whose commitment it was evident that the mobilization of the Palestinian people would depend. Abu Jihad remained in Cairo to help organize fedayeen raids against Israel, although he acknowledges:

'We were not very effective. It was "armed struggle" but of a very limited kind.'

On one occasion they went to plant mines in 'occupied territory'. They were interrupted by UN troops as they went to cross the border, and had to retreat. They buried their mines in the earth, taking the detonators back with them to the camps.

'Unfortunately an Egyptian camel corps patrol

came that way and saw where the earth was disturbed. They discovered the mines. Mustafa Hafez (who was later blown up by an Israeli letter bomb) was the Egyptian Intelligence officer in charge of fedayeen activities. He immediately tried to find out who had put them there because the raid did not have his clearance.

'The bombs were home-made. I had bought wood and iron plate in Gaza. So his Intelligence officers were sent to all the carpenters and blacksmiths to find out who had bought the materials. At last they found the right shop, but the owner refused to say who had bought the materials. His young son was there, however, and he said, "It was Khalil Wazir." They came to arrest me. I was put in prison. After some weeks my lawyers arranged for me to be bailed out; arrangements were made with the authorities and I was allowed to go to Cairo.'

Before he left, however, the authorities interrogated Abu Jihad to find out who else had been involved and whether they had arms. 'I told them that I alone was responsible. They accepted my story and put all my details in a file.' A year later, when the Israelis occupied Gaza, they captured those files when they were left behind by the Egyptians. They included the one on Khalil Wazir, who is better known to their Intelligence Services today by his code name as the Fatah commander in overall charge of guerrilla operations inside Israel.

After the 1956 war, in which Israel occupied the Sinai, only being forced back to the 1948 Armistice lines under extreme pressure from the United States, President Nasser scrupulously avoided confrontation with the Jewish state. Instead he devoted his energies to the creation of a united Arab nation, which was, under his visionary guidance, to rescue the oppressed masses of the Middle East from the neo-colonial clutches of the imperial powers; an inevitable consequence of which was to be the Arab reclamation of Palestine from Zionism.

The vision intoxicated the Arab world, and at first captured the pragmatic imagination of those Palestinians who recognized that their return depended upon the will and the strength of the Arab states to challenge Israel.

But the vision was elusive, retreating mockingly before the advancing Arabs, drawing them to the reluctant conclusion that Arab unity was after all a romantic illusion, fragile and without substance, destined to be swept aside by the rival nation-states competing for power in the Middle East.

The rupture of the carefully nutured unity between Egypt and Syria in 1962 was brutal and chastening: the most dedicated advocates of the Arab ideal had, humiliatingly, destroyed their own cherished case. A decade of Nasserism had been wasted. Thus, at least, it seemed to the Palestinians.

Abu Jihad and Yasser Arafat were dismayed by the collapse of the ideal upon which they and thousands of other Palestinians had at first believed their liberation depended. The disintegration of Arab unity, the fragmentation of Arab power, revealed the appalling prospect that the 'Palestinian problem' would for the indefinite future be relegated to the bottom of the Arab file, while the refugees were left to rot in the camps in which they were incarcerated by the paralysed will of their 'host' régimes. To escape this predicament, men like Abu Jihad determined to turn the divisions within the Arab world to advantage. He still speaks with bitterness of the waste and decay that began in 1955.

'We had been driven from our homes. The Arabs paid lip service to our cause, but we were forbidden to organize. We were scattered. And we were told to wait. The great hero of the Arab world, President Nasser, would liberate our country for us – so we were told. So we waited. We waited for the Arab armies. And we waited. We believed that it was their duty because they were the cause of our exile. But we waited too long.

'We believed that the overthrow of the reactionary régimes would bring progress, that the Arab world would then be in a position to struggle in unity. So we watched the *coups d'état* – in Egypt, Iraq, Lebanon and Syria – waiting for the new spirit to emerge that would liberate the Arab world. Nothing. We tried to organize through the Arab parties throughout the Middle East. We were powerful in these parties, the most influential organizers. We were trying to build the base for our return. But nothing happened. Instead the Palestinians were humiliated and tortured: they investigated us, imprisoned us, hundreds of us, claiming that we were subversives or some such nonsense. It happened here in the Lebanon, in Jordan, in Gaza Strip, in Syria.

'So we began to realize that we should organize independently; that this was the only way to return. We were forbidden, of course, to do this openly. It was a crime to assert our Palestinian identity, even in those countries which indulged in much posturing on our behalf. We were unable to organize in any way. No unions – we couldn't even organize the shoemakers; no parties – political activities were forbidden us. To say in public, "We want to return home," or, "The Arabs are the cause of our misery," was to invite the severest reprisals. So we could draw only one conclusion: that we should work in secret to organize ourselves into a resistance movement.'

Other Palestinians, scattered across the Arab

world, were feeling their own way to the same conclusion. By the early 1960s there were numerous secret cells, organizing in isolation, recruiting members and exploring means of escape – both political and 'military' – from their predicament.

In 1957, Yasser Arafat and Abu Jihad moved from Cairo to Kuwait, where they joined another young militant, Salah Khalaf, who was to become well known as the third man in Fatah's triumvirate, Abu Iyad. Like so many Palestinians, Abu Jihad was a teacher. In the relatively liberal atmosphere of a kingdom which had come to rely upon the technological and managerial expertise of educated Palestinians, he and the other Fatah leaders were able to organize without undue hindrance. They raised funds, argued their cause and attracted recruits.

By now they had determined that only by taking up arms themselves would the Palestinians be able to force the Arab régimes into confrontation with Israel. It was at this time that they founded the Palestine National Liberation Movement, called, in Arabic, the Harakah al-Tahrir (al-Watani) al-Falastini, the initial letters of which read in reverse the word which was to reverberate throughout the world: Fatah.

'You can liken Fatah to a small river running in a certain direction. But everywhere where there were Palestinians there were streams which were flowing in the same direction and they joined up with the river, which was made mightier by these streams.'

The voice of Fatah was soon heard more widely, speaking in a wildly passionate language through the pages of a magazine, *Our Palestine*, which Abu Jihad and Yasser Arafat published in Beirut. Abu Jihad was its chief editor, and through its pages he gave public expression to the bitter yearning of a people, summoning them to join the struggle.

> Where are you, dispersed people . . . where? Are you just flotsam, just jetsam strewn around . . . How do you live? What's become of you? Are you living with your kith and kin, or are you scattered far and wide?
>
> Have you grown rich, children of the Catastrophe, or are you still dragging out the years in the shadow of hunger and sickness? Sons of the Catastrophe, you cannot forget that terrible Catastrophe . . . the loss of land and honour moulds you in the crucible of the Catastrophe . . .
>
> Our destiny is being shaped, but our voice is not heard . . . we tell you that our voice, the voice of the Palestinian people, will not be heard until the sons of Palestine stand together in one rank . . . then you will find the world attentive to your merest whisper . . . yes, just a whisper.

Had it reached them, the summons – callow and crude though it sounds to the Western ear – would have stirred the frustrated soul of the Palestinian people. But *Our Palestine* was low in circulation. It reached hundreds not thousands, and at first the message was distributed mainly to those who were already advocates of the same cause.

But even if the voice of Fatah did not yet reverberate through the refugee camps, *Our Palestine* expressed the national will. Of that Abu Jihad was never in doubt.

> There is one primordial, immutable reality: our fundamental desire is for the land, the land which is ours, whose loss we deem not merely material, but, above all else, a national dishonour, a badge of ignominy and shame. Our land is therefore our freedom, the land is our honour . . . If that is taken from us, then everything goes, everything is taken from us, our very being, our humanity, our name . . . So strong have these feelings become that we only desire life in so far as life enables us to begin the battle for our land, our earth, our freedom and our dignity.

Doubtless because its circulation was so limited, and its origins so obscure, the Arab régimes – like the Israeli Intelligence Services – ignored *Our Palestine*, even when it assaulted their honour in the most strident terms:

> The Arab governments have stopped the Palestinian mouths, turned their hands, deprived them of their freedom of action in what is left of their country, resisted the idea of their regroupment, turned them into a theatrical claque which applauds this and reviles that . . .

But if the régimes chose to dismiss *Our Palestine* as a shabby and shrill little rag, undeserving of their serious attention, its authors had no doubt that its message would be spirited to wherever there were Palestinians in search of an escape from the diaspora, giving them strength to resist the suffocating embrace of their Arab 'hosts'.

> You who went with many parties, and fought for many causes . . . what was the result? Did you restore your honour? Or one inch of your land? Did any of your slogans relieve your distress? You remain scattered, without honour, or personal or collective identity. Let us raise the banner of our own unity, of revolutionary Palestine, and put this aim above any other.

It took time. The mass of the Palestinian people were still apathetically isolated in their refugee camps, yearning for the Return, but impotent and leaderless, a people still apparently destined for extinction. The international community had by now made it abundantly clear that their future lay in a rejection of their past – which, it was now legitimate to suggest, was in any case a fiction of their wandering imaginations.

Israeli leaders began to give unrestrained expression to a new version of the *fait accompli*. Without noticeably impairing their international standing, politicians like Levi Eshkol felt free to ask witheringly: 'What are Palestinians?' – to be answered by Golda Meir in her chillingly memorable phrase: 'They did not exist.' These excesses of revision may have been facilitated by the evident inclination of the Western world to simplify the 'Palestinian problem' by detaching it from its roots, but it was surely inspired by the uneasy sense that the Palestinian identity would not so easily wither away.

If so, it was an accurate perception. The refugees may have lost their homes, their land and even their dignity, but they still clung fiercely to their identity. It was to this identity that *Our Palestine* spoke. Ironically, it was the attempts not by Israelis but Arabs to suppress that identity which guaranteed its survival; the more ruthlessly they chopped it down, the more fiercely it grew up again.

The message of *Our Palestine* was simple: the only escape from humiliation was through the Return. The only means of return was by armed struggle. As the message seeped home, it was answered by the exiles. Schoolchildren began to chant the ritual oath:

Palestine is our country,
Our aim is to return.
Death does not frighten us,
Palestine is ours,
We shall never forget her.
Another homeland we shall never accept!
Our Palestine, witness, O God and history,
We promise to shed our blood for you.

One of the schoolchildren who used to make this oath of allegiance was called Haj Talal. His parents had fled from Jaffa in 1948 to Beirut, where they settled in the refugee camp called Sabra. In Palestine, Haj's father had been a leading member of the illegal Communist Party. His mother was Jewish, an immigrant from the Ukraine. She had arrived in Palestine as a Zionist zealot. By chance she met Haj's father and fell for the young communist, who shared so many of her ideological ideas. Under his tutelage she began to look more closely at the nature of Zionism and, being fiercely nationalist herself, soon found herself in sympathy with the Palestinian cause becoming an ardent anti-Zionist. Her family was outraged, and did all that it could – to no avail – to break the relationship.

When they fled to Lebanon, Haj's father, who was trained as an accountant, managed to find work in an ice-cream factory in the centre of Beirut. Both he and his wife were political activists, and from the beginning Haj was brought up to understand that Palestine was his home. In the UNRWA school and in the streets, such seditious talk was forbidden, but his mother spoke to him of her own experience and of his father's struggle against Zionism which led to his imprisonment under the Mandate.

Haj speaks with reticence, shyly. He finds it difficult to discuss his life – even with other Palestinians – explaining that he believes as a revolutionary that personal experiences are a private matter. He is tall and thin, with delicate features, mild-mannered, smiling frequently but with diffidence. The appearance is deceptive. Haj Talal is a leading member of Fatah. He sits on the PLO executive, and he works closely with Abu Jihad and Yasser Arafat. He is known to have one of the best minds in the movement, being responsible for organizing and coordinating all PLO activities in seventeen Palestinian camps throughout Lebanon. It is a responsibility which he bears lightly, though his authority and influence are considerable. His involvement began in the early 1960s when his family rallied to the summons of *Our Palestine*.

'My father died in 1961, but my sister helped me to continue my education so that I was able to study commerce at the Arab University of Beirut. I'd always known about Palestine. It was in our house that the first secret cells met; and although she was a Jew, my mother helped organize and distribute our secret pamphlets. And the authorities never discovered her. I will never forget that when she died in 1970 her fellow fighters remembered what she had done. They came to her funeral, the founders of Fatah, to honour this Jewish lady who had served the Palestine revolution.

'In 1965, the Intelligence Services were very strong in Lebanon. The secret police were very brutal; the notorious Deuxième Bureau was able to torture at will. And we were imprisoned in the camps, not allowed in or out, not even allowed to take a Lebanese newspaper home with us.

'We were forbidden to hold meetings, so we began to organize by using the social organizations that we were permitted – like sporting clubs – as our base. In this way, because we were able to travel from one camp to another for sport, we were able to establish a network of contacts. In each camp we chose a few people to work in selected areas. Very few in number but very serious. We chose a student to work with students; a teacher with teachers; a worker with workers; a woman with women; an elder with elders – and so on.

'What are Palestinians?'

'They were selected as people who were respected in the community, who were popular, and who would uphold the honour and the image of Fatah. They began the work of creating cells within the camps. It was done in absolute secrecy and it was very dangerous. At this stage we wanted the highest-calibre people. We needed quality not quantity.'

Until at least 1964, Yasser Arafat and Abu Jihad controlled Fatah almost alone. Although they had established a small central committee, the most important decisions rested with them, as Abu Jihad recalls.

'We were running everything. For instance, while Yasser Arafat was travelling, I was in charge of military affairs, the finances of the revolution, the details of the secret cells all over the world, as well as being chief editor of *Our Palestine*.'

Yasser Arafat criss-crossed the Arab world to raise funds and secure alliances. In Algeria, he attracted the support of the young leaders of the revolution which had expelled French colonialism. Ben Bella offered Fatah training facilities for the young men who were to form the military corps of the Palestinian revolution. Fatah opened an office in Algiers, and it was from here that Abu Jihad distributed *Our Palestine* and other pamphlets and publications throughout the Arab world. From

here, too, they made contact with the revolutionary movements elsewhere, travelling to China, Korea and Vietnam. In 1964, Abu Jihad met Che Guevara. These contacts helped to establish Fatah's claim to the leadership of the Palestinian people and secured for its leaders a reputation in the West as a gang of dangerous revolutionaries. Yet Fatah was neither communist nor socialist in inspiration. Radicals were to describe both Arafat and Abu Jihad as *petits bourgeois*. Nasserites were particularly hostile, condemning Fatah for surrendering Arab unity to the cause of Palestinian nationalism. Saudi Arabia, on the other hand, the most conservative of all Arab states, was attracted by Arafat's political independence – and from the early days gave Fatah its blessing, and thereafter supplied 'the revolution' with the bulk of the funds upon which its survival and growth were to depend.

With military and financial support coming from Algeria and Saudi Arabia, Fatah and Yasser Arafat in particular established 'the revolution' as a movement devoid of ideology, committed exclusively to the armed struggle for the Return. It was an astute assessment, both of the diplomatic realities of the Middle East and of the instincts and aspirations of the exiles in the camps and elsewhere in the diaspora. The mass of the Palestinians were not by tradition, education or inclination equipped to become the shock troops of a Marxist upheaval in the Middle East; they were, however, ready to die in a struggle against the enemy for their land – whether the enemy be 'Zionism', 'imperialism' or 'reactionary Arab régimes'.

Arafat excelled in the skills required to navigate Fatah through the diplomatic minefields of Middle Eastern politics, though he was not yet treated by the Arab régimes with the deference he is now accorded as the leader of a mass movement. But Fatah was a threat. The establishment of the Palestine Liberation Organization (PLO) at the behest of the Arab Summit Conference under the auspices of the Arab League in 1964 was designed to siphon off support from Fatah and the other smaller but equally militant movements which had sprung up, and thus to refrigerate the excessive aspirations of the Resistance, which had sent a frisson of anxiety through the Arab régimes.

By using the PLO to reassert their control over the guerrillas, they hoped to redirect the bitter energies of the Palestinians away from the dangers of independent armed confrontation with Israel, as promised by Fatah, towards the rhetorical war favoured by most of the Arab governments.

The PLO deferred to the Nasserite sentiment, which proclaimed that 'Arab unity is the route to the liberation of Palestine'. Fatah had already reversed the principle, urging in *Our Palestine* 'that the liberation of Palestine is the route to Arab unity'. Thus while both Fatah and the PLO affected a show of common purpose, they were in reality at odds with each other. The leaders of Fatah were determined to destroy or take over a PLO which they judged to be President Nasser's creature, whose leader, Ahmed Shuqairy, would make windy speeches, raising false hopes, while carefully suppressing the irridentism of his followers. President Nasser had stated his position quite bluntly:

> If we are today not ready for defence, how can we talk about an offensive? . . . We must prepare the Arab defences and then prepare to carry out our ultimate goal.

It was precisely this procrastination which Fatah had already rejected. Despite the pressures put on its leaders by the Arab governments to restrain their independence initiatives, Fatah was irrepressible.

On 1 January 1965, a communiqué from Fatah under the pseudonym 'Asifah', which means 'tempest' or 'storm', announced that 'detachments of our strike force' went into action against the enemy 'performing all the tasks assigned to them'. The tone is measured, military; the confidence unbounded. Yet the language is carefully ambiguous. And not without reason. History questions whether 'the action' in fact ever took place, it being thought that the 'strike force' was in reality arrested by the Lebanese authorities some hours before it claimed to have left for the border with Israel. It is an irony upon which Palestinians reflect ruefully to this day (although their leaders rarely permit themselves the luxury of giving vent to their feelings on the issue in public), that the obstacles put in their way by their Arab 'brothers' have to a large extent been just as effective as the might of the Israeli army.

In the months following this setback, however, Fatah squads did penetrate Israel, though with somewhat less effect than their communiqués would suggest. If these were to be believed, then Israel should have been reeling under the guerrilla onslaught: communications were smashed, army patrols were under constant ambush, civilians were exhausted to the point of collapse. In truth, the guerrilla campaign had only a marginal effect upon Israel, though it was enough to cause Levi Eshkol, the Prime Minister – perhaps sensing future threats – to issue a severe warning to the Arab world that it would not escape unpunished if the guerrilla adventures continued.

Setting a familiar pattern, the Arab governments responded with alacrity. In Jordan, King Hussein ordered all guerrillas to be hunted down and captured (Fatah's first casualty was killed by a Jordanian bullet early in 1965). In Lebanon, Fatah suspects were arrested and imprisoned and – in the accustomed fashion – subjected to brutality and torture at the hands of the Deuxième Bureau. In Syria, whose Ba'athist leadership had provided Fatah with training facilities and bases from which to launch the revolutionary war against Zionism, Yasser Arafat, Abu Jihad and Abu Iyad were summarily arrested and detained in jail. Abu Jihad remained there for forty days. It is a painful memory for him, not so much because of the frustration or the discomfort, but because it was the occasion of a personal tragedy which stemmed directly from his incarceration.

His wife was accustomed to visit him regularly in jail. On one such occasion, she was unable to find anyone to care for their three-year-old child. They lived in a fourth-floor apartment and while she was out, her son climbed on to a sill, opened the window and fell to his death on the street below.

Abu Jihad now brushes aside the memory, recalling that when the Syrians released him to attend his child's funeral, he took the painful but proper path of duty as he saw it, and instead of joining his family in mourning, fled from Damascus to Lebanon 'to continue the struggle'.

Soon after that, Abu Iyad and Yasser Arafat were released, it being impossible for the Syrian 'revolutionary' government both to proclaim the cause of Fatah and to keep its leaders in jail. The guerrilla raids continued. The Israelis protested; threatened; and then 'retaliated'.

The events which led up to the Six-Day War in June 1967 – Nasser's Aqaba blockade, the clashes on the Golan Heights and the heightened rhetoric which accompanied both – can in major part be traced back to the emergence of Fatah as a force in Arab politics. Although the myth still prevails in the Western world that Israel was forced into a pre-emptive strike against the overwhelming might of an Arab nation committed to driving the Jews into the sea, the evidence is to the contrary. The Arabs were reluctant to go to war. They knew that the military power of the 'embattled' Jewish state exceeded by far their own resources. On the other hand, they were driven, not least by their own rhetoric, to make at least a show of commitment to the Palestinian cause. Hence the rumblings, the threats, the military manoeuvres. One of the architects of the Israeli victory, General Matty Peled, was later to avow that Israel had, in effect, manufactured the 'external threat' to the survival of the state which had been the pretext for the Israeli assault.

There is no reason to hide the fact that since 1949 no one dared or, more precisely, no one was able to threaten the very existence of Israel. But in spite of that, we have continued to foster a sense of our own inferiority, as if we were a weak and insignificant people, which, in the midst of an anguished struggle for its existence, could be exterminated at any moment.[39]

It took Israel six days to complete the occupation of that part of Palestine which remained in Arab hands after the exodus of 1948, as well as territory belonging to Syria on the Golan Heights, and to Egypt in the Sinai.

The Arab world was mortified. Its army had been swept contemptuously aside. It was a crushing blow to morale and prestige. In bitterness, the Arab forces reflected on how the absurd excesses of rhetoric which had led them to believe that they were invincible had ricocheted off the advancing Israeli army to taunt, mock and humiliate them.

Only the Palestinians escaped the moral trauma into which the Arab world had been plunged. Arafat sensed at once what might be rescued from the disaster. Fatah leaders debated briefly their simple choice: 'Do we give up or do we go on?' It took them two days only to plan their next steps, as Abu Jihad described it.

'We had no choice but to continue the armed struggle. Now all our people were under Israeli occupation or in exile. But in this we could see an opportunity. For the first time our own people were in contact with the enemy directly. We could work through them. It was our right and our duty to fight against this new occupation. So we sent cadres into Jordan and into the West Bank to invite people to come and train with us. In Damascus we opened new camps to train hundreds of recruits. We sent groups to the Golan, the West Bank and to the Sinai to collect arms left behind by the Arab armies. This was to be our main source of weapons for a long time. We picked up grenades, rifles, rockets, RPGs and many other supplies. By 1 September 1967, we began to fight once more, despite the reluctance of many Arabs to support us.'

Yasser Arafat and Abu Jihad went to the West Bank to organize Fatah cells. One of their leaflets, distributed in the West Bank during this period, offers a vivid example of the fervour with which they urged the Palestinians into resistance.

The Zionist occupation is nothing but the rise of a new crusade. We shall continue to rebel until final victory. We must boycott all economic, cultural and legal institutions of the Zionists . . . we must set up secret resistance cells in every street, village and neighbourhood. For even one fighting cell, operating in any region, has the power to inflict great losses upon the enemy.

Although the West Bankers did not exactly flock to this call, the guerrilla war intensified – to such an extent that, in January 1968, it was announced in the Israeli Knesset by the Minister of Defence, Moshe Dayan, that the 'terrorists' had been responsible for killing and injuring no less than ninety-seven Israeli soldiers in the six months since the end of the June War.

The Israelis retaliated with customary ruthlessness, blowing up houses with the same abandon of the British thirty years before. Yasser Arafat, the tactician, exclaimed:

Thank God for Dayan. He provides the daily proof of the expansionist nature of Zionism . . . after the 1967 defeat, Arab opinion, broken and dispirited, was ready to conclude peace at any price. If Israel after its lightning victory had

over
Israeli soldiers under fire

127

proclaimed that it had no expansionist aims, and had withdrawn its troops from the conquered territories, while continuing to occupy certain strategic points necessary to its security, the affair would have been easily settled with the countries that were the victims of the aggression.[40]

The Fatah offensive on the West Bank gave the Palestinians a standing in the Arab world which they had never before enjoyed. Almost overnight, the downtrodden and despised refugees became the brothers and sisters of heroes – the only Arabs who dared challenge the Zionist enemy. A wave of sympathy for Fatah spread through the Arab world, causing some anxiety to its rulers but forcing them to restrain their efforts to curtail the resistance. And for the first time a number of outsiders began to realize that the Palestinians had a history; that their actions against 'the Zionist oppressor' were not merely inexplicable outrages; that the ritual denunciations of 'Palestinian

Israeli paratrooper shot by Jordanian troops during the advance

terrorists' in the Western press were no less misleading than the attempts by the British government had been to characterize their fathers in similar terms thirty years before.

Salah Tamari lives on the ground floor of a large villa in Sidon. He is famous among Palestinians, though some of them know him by other names. When he walks into a PLO office he is at once surrounded by young fighters for whom he is already a legendary figure. His reputation among his devoted followers in the refugee camps is as a fearless leader and a man of unimpeachable honour. He is in charge of the militia in south Lebanon as well as of the overall political administration in the camps of the area. It is said by his friends that he would now fill an even higher post in the PLO if it were not for his inconvenient habit of saying precisely what he thinks in the fiercest terms whenever the mood takes him. Salah is greatly respected by men to whom deference does

Salah Tamari

not come easily but who will avoid crossing him at almost any cost. His anger is said to be as formidable as the warmth of his friendship.

'In 1967 in the West Bank, for the first time in my life I felt that I was a real human being. I had a gun in my hand. Between June 1967 and March 1968, I crossed into occupied territory thirty-five times. We always went across the Jordan, and because I couldn't swim, I was always fearful I would drown – and once I nearly did. I was saved just in time by my comrades. The fighters of that time were great men. They represented my ideal. I wanted to reach their standards. They were honourable men who loved their country and wanted it back. They belonged to a special age. We were isolated, lonely, but full of pride.

'It was a strange experience to be hiding in my own country. I felt both free and besieged. We were not just guerrillas. We were doing what others thought impossible. We were always being advised to withdraw and we said, "We will stand and fight." We always wanted to be in direct contact with the enemy, to stand up and face the Israelis in the open.'

Salah Tamari was born in Bethlehem to a Bedouin family of which he is immensely proud.

'The Bedouin society is unique. It has its own standards, its own discipline, its own way of life.

And when any of that falls, everything collapses. I remember my uncle. He was a tribal judge, a grand old man who used to ride on a horse, carrying a sword at his side. Everyone was in awe of him. You know what happened to his three sons? They ended up in Kuwait as refugees, as labourers.

'I miss Bethlehem, especially at Christmas. We used to live near the Church of the Nativity, and if you were to blindfold me now, I could find my way about the town with no difficulty, even today.'

He draws a map of the steep streets and the church, showing the way to his home. His parents had hoped that he would become a priest. Each Sunday, with his nine brothers and sisters, he was dressed in white and blue to attend the famous church.

The parental dreams collapsed in 1948. His father had been working in Jaffa. He fled back to Bethlehem. There was no work. He went to Kuwait, walking with four friends from Iraq across the desert, in search of a job. In Bethlehem, responsible for his family even as a child, Salah went to work – at first in a café, and then in a cinema, where he sold Coca-Cola in the interval from a tray hung about his neck. The job did not last; the Bedouin boy took unkindly to a customer who summoned his refreshment by a snap of the fingers. Salah banged his tray upon the unfortunate's head, and found himself out of work.

'In that period between 1948 and 1967, the injustice was unimaginable. The Jordanians, we felt, wanted us out of the area. When we met other Palestinians who had been scattered to Syria, Lebanon or the Gaza, we would talk about our situation and each of us would always think that the conditions that *we* endured were the worst. But they always envied us, saying that at least we had been able to keep our identity in the West Bank. Now of course it was very bad in Lebanon where really the people were in concentration camps. But we still believed that our experience was the most bitter. Although we were still called Palestinians, and although we were allowed to train militarily in the Jordanian army, we could get six months in jail for saying ourselves, "We are Palestinians."

'I could not bear this. I felt it so undignified, so offensive to human nature, to live under such a régime. It was a humiliation that was quite unbearable. And we felt too that they wanted us to get out of the West Bank. They permitted no development in the area and no work. All the heads of families in my street, like my father, went abroad to find work. The young men were driven to follow them.

'The West Bank became a land of the very old and the very young. Freedom of movement had been a trap – because we moved out. The villages near the front were without electricity or water supplies, and whenever we asked why, they said that it was a military zone.'

Salah found his way to Cairo, where he studied English literature – still borrowing from Shakespeare in stark and dramatic fashion to illustrate his argument:

'What choice is there for the Palestinians? To be or not to be, that is the question.'

In 1964 he joined Fatah, his intention to 'liberate' Jaffa and Haifa.

'It was like a Londoner wanting to defend Birmingham. We had leapt from infancy to maturity in one go when we realized that our only hope was to fight.'

In 1966, he gave up his studies and returned to the West Bank, only to be arrested and jailed by the Jordanians for belonging to Fatah. His mother and father were greatly disturbed, quarrelling with him and each other about whether he was right or wrong to land himself in such trouble. In the end they were persuaded that there was, for him, no other choice. By 1967, Salah was a commando.

The young men who joined Fatah had little ideological commitment. They were nationalists, for whom the concept of 'revolution' meant no more than the expulsion of the Israelis from Palestine. Fatah's strategy was based on unsophisticated certainties: the enemy occupation could only be challenged with the gun. The challenge would invite retaliation. The retaliation would provoke a wider conflict in which Israel would eventually be defeated, not least because the heroism of the commandos would so inspire the Arab masses that they would rise up to confront Zionism, sweeping aside the defeatists, the reactionaries, who sought to suppress the 'revolution'.

Crude as this proposition may appear, it seemed to those who were still dispossessed twenty years after the exodus to offer the only way back to Palestine. Indeed, for a brief moment in 1968 it seemed that Fatah had judged well.

On 21 March, 1,500 Israeli troops under air support advanced across the River Jordan towards the Palestinian refugee town of Karameh. Their purpose was to surround the town and destroy the Palestinian guerrillas – among them Salah Tamari – who had used it as a base from which to launch guerrilla raids into the West Bank. Three days earlier, an Israeli school bus had run over a mine which exploded, wounding some of the children and killing a doctor who was with them. According to the Israelis, this was but the latest of thirty-seven acts of 'sabotage and murder' in which altogether six people had died.

As they awaited the Israeli onslaught, the Palestinians debated their tactics: should they empty the town and retreat to the hills, according to the classic principles of guerrilla war? Or should they stand and fight, offering a convincing demonstration to the world that they were not simply 'terrorists' but men who were ready to die on behalf of their country? The debate was perfunctory – political strategy triumphed over military tactics.

As the Israelis advanced, King Hussein, who had hitherto been ruthless in the suppression of the fedayeen, radioed Cairo to alert the Arab states of the possibility that they were once more on the brink of war. President Nasser responded with alacrity, offering Egyptian aircraft to cover the Jordanian front. Embarrassed, and fearful of annihilation, Hussein demurred. By now, however, he had no choice but to commit at least some of his troops to the defence of his country. For Salah Tamari, who was in command of a commando group inside Karameh, it was a sweet moment. In 1955 he had seen four young friends, the oldest of whom was fourteen, gunned down in Bethlehem by Jordanian soldiers while demonstrating against the Baghdad Pact (the short-lived Arab alliance put together by the Americans to challenge Nasser's dream of Arab unity). A few weeks after that, he had been to witness the aftermath of an Israeli assault on the village of Abri Housa on the outskirts of Bethlehem:

'I saw the Palestinian soldiers who belonged to the Jordanian army lying on the ground, their bodies in grotesque shapes. They had been hacked to pieces, and before that they must have been beaten because I could see the wounds on their heads and their ankles. Scores of Palestinians had been killed.'

But the perpetrators of that attack had not been confronted by the Jordanians, who instead turned upon the fedayeen, outlawing their adventures. Only two months before, the Jordanian army had even besieged Karameh. Now it was standing side by side with the Palestinians, confronting the real enemy.

'We were so united. We were doing the impossible. We were waiting to fight the Israelis in open battle. Even if we were crushed under the wheels of the Israeli tanks, we believed that we were defending justice in fighting for our nation. We felt that we were avenging all the years of oppression. We never thought that we would survive.'

The battle of Karameh is now a legend in the history of the Palestinians. The Israelis advanced with their customary confidence. It was to be a massive but uncomplicated reprisal. In the past, when they had invaded refugee villages, attacking guerrilla bases, killing and wounding 'terrorists' and any other Palestinians who found themselves in the way, there had been no serious resistance. But this time it was different. As the columns of Israeli tanks rumbled over the Allenby Bridge, they were fired upon by Jordanian artillery.

The Israelis had to fight their way through to Karameh, only to find that the guerrillas were waiting for them. They were forced to take the stronghold street by street, fighting from house to house in hand-to-hand combat until they reached the centre of the town, which had already been evacuated of its 25,000 civilians.

By the end of the battle, the Israelis acknowledged twenty-one soldiers killed, though the Palestinians were to claim that the real figure was over 200. Palestinian casualties were heavy. Out of some 350 fighters, they lost almost half. Yet, for Salah Tamari, the battle of Karameh was the most heroic day in the Palestinian struggle.

'Those who died in that battle are still close to me. I remember their last words, their last gestures. I feel that I can see them still, as if it were yesterday.'

The news of the heroic stand at Karameh spread through the Arab world. The camps were ecstatic. And the Arab capitals rejoiced too, arranging huge funeral services to celebrate the death of the 'martyrs'. The Palestinians had fired the popular imagination of the Arab world. Thousands of young men began to arrive at Fatah recruiting centres and had to be turned away. And, in an uncharacteristically emotional statement, King Hussein declared, 'Maybe we will all become fedayeen.' For a moment it appeared as if the Fatah strategy was going to work.

After the 1967 war recruits flocked to join the fedayeen. The battle of Karameh in 1968 made the Palestinian fighters heroes in the Arab world. By 1970 the PLO could call on perhaps 20,000 fighters. Despite the wars which were to follow it is estimated that by the end of the seventies there were upwards of 25,000 fedayeen.

Eight

The State within the State

There is a sudden rat-tat of automatic fire. Is it a wedding? A funeral? Or bored young fighters shooting at tin cans? No one seems to care very much, though when Abu Douad strolls to the balcony to take a look, he is called back by Abu Moussa and Salah Tamari with some urgency. It is evidently neither a funeral nor a wedding.

The three men are in an apartment in a nondescript block near the centre of Beirut. It is rented by the PLO, and Abu Moussa and Abu Douad are living here for a few weeks before moving on. Israeli Intelligence Services are efficient: no wise PLO leader remains in one place for long, lest one day he carelessly open a letter bomb, or his car is blown up as he gets into it one morning, or a gunman breaks into his bedroom while he is still asleep to 'eliminate' another 'terrorist'.

Abu Moussa is very obviously a military man. His trousers are impeccably pressed, his hair, crinkly black, is neatly in place, and he walks as upright as possible with the help of two sticks. He is fortunate still to be alive. A few months earlier he had been crossing the street near his lodgings in Sidon when two gunmen rose up in front of him, firing at him with automatic rifles. He ran for cover and collapsed in a doorway, his body spattered with bullets. His assailants were not Israelis but Syrians – exacting revenge for an episode which took place two years before when Abu Moussa

had been in command of the Palestinian forces in south Lebanon, fighting against the Syrians who had then seemed bent on destroying the PLO's independent political and military power. A small group of Fatah guerrillas had ambushed a convoy of Syrian tanks as they trundled into Sidon, destroying four of them and incinerating half a dozen soldiers in the process. Revenge was inevitable, and Abu Moussa is without bitterness. He has long been resigned to the fact that, in thirty-one years as a soldier, he has seen more military action against Arabs than against Israelis.

Abu Moussa's first experience of war was in 1948, when he bought an old rifle and joined the Arab irregulars trying to resist the creation of a Jewish state in their land. After the rout of the Arab armies, he joined the Arab Legion, being interviewed by its commander, Glubb Pasha, who told him that they could make a soldier and officer out of him if he wished. He soon became a lieutenant. For as long as he can remember, Abu Moussa has wanted to be a soldier.

'As a small boy when we were fighting the British, I remember seeing the commandos in the village and saying to myself, "When I am big I will join them and do what I can for my country."

'During the rebellion I had a clear picture of the British army. I remember them getting us in a big circle in the centre of the village. And then they

Abu Douad

were firing in the air about us. There was panic. My father was hit by a bullet and he died. He was sixty years old. I soon knew that I had to fight for my country. Everyone supported the commandos. When one of them died, an entire town would turn out for the funeral.'

Silwan, the village on the outskirts of Jerusalem where Abu Moussa was brought up, used to provide the city with vegetables and fruit. The village was without electricity or cars. It was quiet. Abu Moussa's father had a small plot of land, enough for a simple living and to keep a family of seven in a small two-roomed house. Abu Moussa remembers the parties in the village square, the bonfires and the dancing. He played football. He and Abu Douad laugh as they compete to describe how they would fill an old sock with rags as a ball and then hobble back home at the end of the day with swollen, bloody toes to an anxious scolding from their mothers.

Abu Douad came from the same background. He has an early memory of his mother telling him about a family uncle who bought a gun for the revolutionaries.

'One day she showed me one of the guns he had bought. I'd never seen a gun before. He had got it from an Australian who was serving with the police, paying him £100 Palestinian for it. I remem-ber very clearly the day when some Zionists came to a village to ask the Jews to leave with them. These Jews were our neighbours and I was very close to them. As I was an only child my parents used to leave me with them while they went out to work. They came from the Yemen. I ate with them and drank their milk. I could never hate Jews, only Zionists. When they left I was only five years old. It was in 1942 when there was no fighting but the Zionists were already preparing for the war against us. I remember that the family, the man, the women and the girls, were weeping to leave us, and kissing and hugging me. But they had to go, leaving the "weak" villages to go to the "strong" ghettos, so that when the Zionist terror began, they would be safe.'

Abu Douad is now one of the PLO's most elusive and controversial leaders. He has been sentenced to death in Amman (being reprieved only after the intervention of the leaders of Saudi Arabia and the Soviet Union); he has been wanted in France; he was once thought – wrongly – to have master-minded the Munich massacre; and he has been banished from the Inner Council of Fatah, narrowly avoiding a PLO court martial for disobeying the order *not* to provoke the Israelis in south Lebanon. None of this impairs his reputation among young Palestinians as a man of fearlessness and daring.

Not one of the three men in the Beirut flat had much reason to suppose that the battle of Karameh, in which they were all engaged, would transform the future of the Palestinians. Both Abu Moussa and Abu Douad had learnt early to distrust the word of those placed in authority over them. At school they had been forbidden to discuss the Mandate or Zionism; Palestinian history was ignored. But the teacher told them in secret that the Mandate was not a British but a Zionist plan. They remember how scared their teachers had been, but how determined that their pupils should realize that the Mandate and their national rights were in direct and irreconcilable conflict. After the Catastrophe had conclusively demonstrated the truth of these 'subversive' ideas, they both discovered another contradiction between appearance and reality: the Jordanians were supposed to be in confrontation with the Zionist state, and yet, as Salah Tamari had also discovered, it was obvious that the truth was otherwise.

Silwan was on the border created by the new state of Israel. Abu Douad used to go to the fence which divided the city in half.

'I used to dream that one day I might share in unifying my lovely city, this beautiful and holy place. I remember on one occasion that a friend of mine who was from the other side of Jerusalem, who had been to school with me, tried to jump over the fence. He was coming to see us. Unfortunately the guards saw him. Both lots. He was shot at the same time in the front and in the back by the Jordanians and the Israelis.

'From the beginning the Jordanians had tried to crush our will. When we demonstrated against what was happening to our people in the Arab world, they would stop us in the most vicious fashion. It made us bitter. We believed that the Jordanian authorities did not want us to save Palestine.'

Abu Moussa, who was by now a Jordanian officer, was trapped between his duty as a soldier and his allegiance to Palestine.

'I saw that the Arab Legion did nothing to make Palestine face Israel. Our people had no guns (indeed they had been taken away from us); we weren't taught to become commandos. The army stopped us organizing. There was no resistance, no one to stop the Israelis.

'In 1967 I was stationed near Nablos. I was in command of a battalion. We were ordered to retreat to Amman. I remember it with great anger. I had never been so angry. I was weeping with rage. We surrendered without a struggle. I felt that Jordan wanted the city to become part of Israel. After that I joined Fatah in secret.'

Abu Douad, who had already joined Fatah in 1964, was in Damascus when the Six-Day War broke out. He drove at once by way of Amman to the West Bank. At Jericho, his car was stopped and he was told it was impossible to reach Jerusalem. So he went there on foot.

'I reached the city on the day it fell. I saw the Israeli tanks entering the city. We knew that historically Jerusalem is not easy to take if there is fierce resistance, with many thousands of people determined to die to defend it. What happened? It fell with hardly any resistance. I walked back from the city to Amman with the refugees.'

Three years later – despite the intervention of Karameh – Abu Moussa, Abu Douad and Salah Tamari were together in Jordan, fighting the bloodiest and most costly war of the Palestinian resistance – not against the Israelis, but against the Jordanian army, under the direction of King Hussein.

Between 1967 and 1970, the numbers of fedayeen had risen from a few hundred to perhaps 30,000. The prestige of Fatah had risen to unprecedented heights. Fatah had ousted the deferential leadership of the PLO, and was now in control of an organization with an honoured place in the councils of the Arab world. Foreigners who had hardly heard about the exodus of 1948 now made the pilgrimage to Beirut or Damascus or Amman to meet the Palestinian leaders and record their words for the world's newspapers and magazines. In the Third World, the fedayeen were now recognized as liberation fighters; Yasser Arafat had emerged as the spokesman for the PLO, his unshaven face and the black-and-white kaffir becoming familiar throughout the world. And fedayeen raids in the Jordan Valley and from Lebanon rose – according to the figures published by its own foreign information department – so rapidly that, by 1970, they were averaging thirty-four a month, almost three times as many as in 1967. They rocketed Israeli settlements, they blew up pipelines and railway tracks; they attacked Israeli army patrols; and for the first time since the Zionists had unleashed the same tactic twenty years before, they set off bombs in market-places, in Tel Aviv and Jerusalem – reasserting their presence in Palestine with 'terror' – and once more innocent victims died in the onslaught. The casualty figures announced by Israel in 1970 were a testimony to the efficiency of the guerrillas: in three years they had killed 543 soldiers and 116 civilians, wounding 1,763 soldiers and 629 civilians.

King Hussein viewed their achievements with growing concern. Despite his dramatic outburst after the battle of Karameh, the Hashemite

Israelis occupy east Jerusalem

monarch did not relish the resurgence of the Palestinians. In Jordan, they were beginning to establish themselves as 'a state within a state', the more dangerous to a king who relied heavily upon the unswerving loyalty of his Bedouin troops to preserve his authority against the uncertain support of a civilian population which was largely Palestinian in origin. For Hussein, the fedayeen were a disconcertingly militant presence, a destabilizing influence, a threat to the future of the Hashemite kingdom. Nor did the fedayeen behave with great tact. While Arafat sought to reassure Hussein, his followers openly flaunted their authority in the streets of Amman. They drove ostentatiously through the centre of the city in Land-Rovers bristling with weapons; they went out of their way to summon the populace, through loudspeakers, to join the revolution and fight the people's war; they set up roadblocks to check the credentials of Jordanian citizens, and – occasionally – they extracted 'contributions' for the resistance from civilians at gun-point.

Despite the PLO's attempts to stop these excesses and to effect a reconciliation, the tension between Hussein and the fedayeen grew sharper. Nor was it only Arafat's men in Fatah who were to blame. The Popular Front for the Liberation of Palestine (PFLP), the most prominent of the small radical groups which had sprung up after 1967 to offer an ideological alternative to the main guerrilla movement, ignored Arafat's calls for moderation. The leader of the PFLP, Dr George Habash, was a revolutionary socialist, believing that the liberation of Palestine was contingent upon radical upheaval in the Arab world. To this end, his followers had already caught the hostile headlines of the world with a series of spectacular hijacks in which many civilians died, and in one of which three airliners were downed at Dawson's Field in the remote south of Jordan and, after fruitless negotiations, blown up before the world's television cameras.

Arafat denounced these excesses, but to no avail. His inability to control the radicals was held in the Arab world to be evidence of the so-called

147

'inner sickness' by which the PLO had become infected. To Hussein, the hijackings were yet another symptom of the disease which threatened to eat into his kingdom and destroy his monarchy.

Salah Tamari was one of those Fatah leaders who was outraged by the radicals. He had been incensed when he heard that one group had broadcast Marxist propaganda from a minaret in Amman; he thought that the hijackings were scandals without purpose.

'The hijacker is not a hero. If we could liberate Palestine by hijacking, then yes, let us train 300 hijackers. We would be terrorists but at least we would have a purpose. But we cannot liberate Palestine that way. So why should our commandos up in the mountains for months at a time, in difficult conditions, waiting to inflict a real blow on the enemy have to endure the sight of one terrorist holding up a plane, and being proclaimed as a hero of the revolution by his friends? It damages our struggle.'

Salah had remained in southern Jordan after

The occupation of east Jerusalem is an outrage and humiliation for the Arab world

Karameh, working closely with Arafat, acting as his second-in-command, leading raids into Israel and trying to escape the heavy bombardments with which the Israelis retaliated against the Palestinian camps. He had long expected a show-down with Hussein.

'There is a law which governs Israeli behaviour towards us. They won't interfere so long as there is an Arab power to do it for them. The Jordanians had fought us only a short time before Karameh. They were bound to turn on us again, especially

as we were more powerful than ever. To under-stand this, you should see Jordan as a sponge, designed by the West, to absorb any Palestinian tendency towards the liberation of their land. Even if we behaved like angels towards his régime, Hussein would have been bound to try and annihi-late us.'

On 17 September 1970, King Hussein unleashed his frustrated army upon the Palestinians. His Bedouin troops went to war with a ferocious will, bombarding the refugee camps with merciless precision. The fedayeen fought back with desperation. When the struggle began, Salah Tamari was in the northern sector of Amman, where the fighting raged at its fiercest. Abu Moussa was elsewhere in the city, still in command of his Jordanian troops.

'I deserted at once, taking 300 soldiers with me. We went to try and stop the fighting. In one sector we intervened between the two sides, and I instructed the Jordanian troops to lay down their arms, saying that it would be dishonourable to shoot against the fedayeen. That is what I told them and they obeyed. Five hours later I was arrested and imprisoned. Another officer was put in my place to command my men. After a night in prison I managed to escape. I returned to my soldiers, and instructed my replacement to go, saying that I would command my own soldiers. A little later I heard an appeal on the radio: "Abu Moussa, please join us now." So I took my men, and we found our way through the lines and joined the fedayeen.'

Salah and his men fought heroically, but were unable to withstand the heavy fire directed at them from the planes and tanks which surrounded their positions. Salah moved from one fort to another between the pathetic remains of collapsing refugee huts, to urge his men to struggle on. He is reputed to have remained on the move for ten days, only taking time off one afternoon to hijack a passing priest and escort him to his headquarters where the poor man was obliged to solemnize Salah's marriage to a young Hashemite princess, Dina Abdul Hamid, who had been the first wife of Salah's protagonist of the moment, King Hussein.

By the end of ten days, after fearful bloodshed, the resistance was broken. Refugees and fedayeen fled before the Bedouin troops, who were determined to exact final vengeance. The PLO leaders, dismayed by the disaster of 'Black September', began to move out of Jordan to relocate their base of operations in Lebanon.

Some remained. Abu Douad, like Salah Tamari, did not willingly contemplate leaving the fedayeen positions on this front with Israel. Both men now sat on Fatah's Revolutionary Council, and they advised against an evacuation. Salah was insistent.

'There were very few of us left. We were moving in secret from house to house. I thought we should stay. Our people were still in the camps with nowhere to go, broken. And I thought that if we stayed there at least we would be seen to be sharing their misery. But it was impossible. We were pressed to the north. We tried to regroup. Again it was impossible. At Jarash, our last stand, the massacre was completed. I was required in Lebanon. I escaped to Beirut. I thought we'd be there for a few days. I have been in Lebanon ever since.'

Nine
Resolution in Lebanon

Those who were infants in 1948 now run the Resistance; young men whose memories fix arbitrarily on blurred images of the Catastrophe, for whom the Return is the sole purpose of life. The fedayeen are in control of the camps, organizing them in 'popular committees' which sit for long hours and have much the same responsibilities as any local council. They struggle against Zionism, but for most of their time their energies are more mundanely devoted to the administration of the volatile and complicated community for which they bear responsibility.

They make unlikely bureaucrats. The visitor to a large camp on the outskirts of Beirut finds them sitting in an office which is bare apart from numerous chairs and one desk, occupied by the chairman of the committee. Presiding over them with an avuncular smile from his portrait on the wall is Yasser Arafat. Their greeting is cold, the atmosphere uninviting. Their lives have been misunderstood and misinterpreted too often for it to be otherwise. They resent the zoological approach of those who arrive on the pretext of learning about the revolution, and depart with notes on 'international terror'.

The chairman is perhaps thirty years old, his young face hardened before its time, unshaven and stern. He is brief and to the point.

'How do we run the camp? We have a democratic vote. All decisions are made in democratic fashion. The committee is called the Popular Committee and it is made up of members from all the groups which form the PLO. It is the main authority in the camp. It operates with the military police who are responsible for discipline and security. It also deals with the relationship between the people in the camps and the Lebanese authorities. We deal with any problems that arise.'

'What kind of problems?'

'We are very crowded in the camps and there are many little problems.'

He gestures as if to indicate that to press further would be an indication of hostile intent.

'We also deal with health problems, and social problems, which are of course directly connected with the overall issue of the Palestine revolution.

'We are moving towards revolution. The nature of our existence in these conditions has a very great effect. We try to help our people understand the nature of our predicament, and the course which is required to solve it. It is not difficult, because we are still out of our land.

'Before we were just refugees, now we are a revolution. We are a revolutionary people, not refugees. Please understand that.'

'Before' and 'after' in the terminology of the

Lebanese exiles refers to the year 1969, which was the year in which Fatah emerged to challenge the Lebanese for control of the camps.

It had been generally intended that, in the years after the exodus, the Palestinians would disintegrate; that they would disperse in the Arab world, losing their identity in the slow struggle to rebuild their lives elsewhere. The intention – expressed in the crude demands made both by Israeli leaders and American presidents that the Arab world should 'absorb' the refugees – foundered on the rock of that stubborn passion which had fixed the refugee mind on the Return.

Fatmeh and Jihad live in Shattila Camp. She makes artificial flowers for sale, and he runs a news stand on the edge of the camp. They were babies when their parents fled from Saffad in 1948. Fatmeh's parents carried her into Lebanon in their arms. They stayed at Bint J'bail (the town near the border around and over which the war in south

Lebanon is now waged), but there was no work there. So they moved to Beirut and remained there. Fatmeh has seven children, and the family lives in three small rooms which are kept spotlessly clean. The sitting room is dark green, and the walls, because of damp, must be frequently repainted. The floor is bare concrete. There are three settees around the edge, covered in plastic. Three armchairs are similarly protected, and there is a low table in the middle of the room. Against one wall a tall cabinet displays an assortment of more than sixty cups and mugs which inform visitors that this is a home proud and able to be as hospitable as any. On another wall, there are hung a carpet and two prayer mats. Out of reach of the children, two garishly dressed dolls, made by hand but too treasured to be played with, hang limply from a nail.

Fatmeh is a resilient woman and a capable organizer, remorselessly optimistic and hard-

Jihad and Fatmeh : 'We are still an oppressed people . . . but now we are revolutionaries'

working. She answers questions about life in the camp with a shrug which says 'surely you must see what it is like for us, very difficult but we have no choice'. She then adds, 'If you are forbidden from entering your own country, you can imagine our feelings.' She is more interested in explaining the drainage project for which she, as a leader of one of the women's organizations, is helping raise funds. Every time the rains fall, there are streets in Shattila which are turned into rivers, houses which are flooded. They need $(US)2oo,ooo to pay for a new system. The money is being raised jointly by the PLO, international voluntary organizations and the people of Shattila themselves.

While Fatmeh explains this, her husband sits silently smoking in the corner. When she pauses, he speaks with unexpected agitation – saying that it is most important to understand how life has changed in the camp.

'We are still an oppressed people without our rights. But now we are revolutionaries. And the revolution is our passport. It is the only way of reaching our land. You, the British, are free – you live in a democratic state, you have human rights. When we return we too will have human rights. Here it is impossible, we have no rights. I've been in the revolution now for two years; it is the only way. Before the revolution, before Karameh, we had no hope. We were in a terrible way. We were nothing.'

He bangs his fist on the arm of the chair.

'We were nothing. Outside the camps they looked at us in disdain saying, "You are Palestinian. And this is not your country, you are refugees." '

His wife speaks about the future.

'My hopes? My hope is to build up my family with my children, as any other family in the world would wish. We are in a revolution so our family has to be strong. To be strong we have to work. Do you know something?' – she interrupts herself, now at ease – '. . . the Arabs tell us we are too much like the English. They say that we learnt too much from the English. "You think too much, you don't talk enough. And you talk quietly." What they mean by that is that we are too modern. And it is through this – being modern and in a revolution – that we will return.'

Outside in the street, standing by a stall selling fellafel, a young man with brick-wall shoulders is lounging against a shop front, an uncompromising expression on his face. A pistol is tucked casually into his belt. Then he begins to move off. The image falters; he is crippled, the shoulders and chest incongruously set on crooked, shrivelled legs. But he asserts the revolution with a swagger, laughing with friends and outstaring strangers with disdain. There is a brief, heated argument about the camera, should it be permitted? It is explained that the Popular Committee has given its permission. Smiles all round.

The presence of the PLO is everywhere: a poster, not of Arafat or of a martyr, but showing a mouse eating discarded food, carrying disease: it is a hygiene campaign. The vegetable market, under cover on a concrete floor, away from the road, was set up by the PLO to give traders space to sell their produce, and to keep their barrows from blocking the way. It is a Palestinian market, and you are informed that it is the busiest in Beirut. The police wear PLO uniform, strolling the streets in easy authority. One of them stops to speak his few words of English. 'Hallo good morning, I was a policeman in Palestine. English police very good,' he says good-humouredly. In the Second World War, he helped the British to fight the Nazis. Now he is fighting 'imperialism'. What is imperialism? 'Imperialism is what is bad for the Palestinians.'

A man of sixty or so sits outside a narrow entrance leading into a dim store which sells flour, vegetables, oils, sugar and beans. He is evidently prosperous, wishing to make it clear that the Palestinians are a talented people.

'Many of the companies in Hamra [Beirut's most expensive shopping area] are Palestinians. You could say that we have helped build this country for the Lebanese. That is why the Arabs are afraid of us. You take Kuwait – we are the engineers and the lawyers. We run the country. Likewise in Libya, the Emirates and Saudi Arabia. We are a successful people and there are a lot of us.'

He walks through the underground passages from one cavern to another, showing off his wares.

'In Palestine I had a hotel, and the family owned two farms near Jaffa.'

After two years in tents in Gaza, his family moved to Sidon, and then to Beirut, where they built up the business.

'I have two children, a boy and a girl. My daughter is thirty-two and she lives in the United States. You know, there are PLO committees even there. My son is also a lawyer, and he helps me trading in clothes. He lives just outside the camp and he works for the PLO as a lawyer in their security courts.'

An older man owns the shop next door. It is much smaller and the shelves are half bare. He sells toothpaste, biscuits, nappies and flowers. He once owned a flour mill in Jaffa. Now he barely makes a living. His face is sad, overwhelmed.

'If I could leave this place and go home . . . If

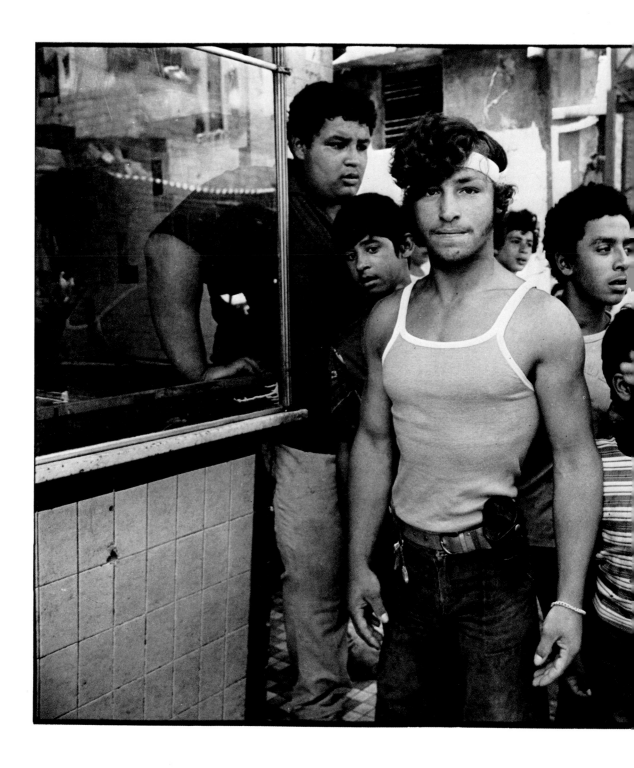

. . .'He shakes his head, not wishing to talk.

The camp is a warren of winding alleys, nondescript concrete. Palestinian peasant faces stare incuriously – black hair, brown eyes, dark, roughened skin. They wear simple flowered skirts or cotton trousers, and shoes made of old leather or cheap plastic. For a decade these people have been portrayed as abject, pitiable refugees, deserving of charity – so long as they abjure the gun. But there is order here. It is clean. These are not slums. The people are not sick. Nor are they downtrodden. They do not abase themselves by begging, they do not seek charity. They resent pity. Their manner is self-possessed. They are refugees, yes, but they have demolished the psychological walls of their prison. There is frustration and overcrowding, yes, but there is also vibrant energy, disconcerting fervour and fierce determination.

Um Emad is distrustful, although courteous enough to say, 'Whoever you may be, enter this

house as a friend.' She sends a child out to buy Coca-Cola and offers tea. The room takes shape out of the gloom: a double bed with mattresses piled on it, an old fridge, a primus stove, a broken washing machine, a photograph of a young man with black hair to his shoulders in a neat fedayeen uniform. (It is her brother, who was killed in a Fatah raid against Israel in 1970.) She is persuaded that the intruders are not hostile.

'I stay at home in the morning, preparing the children for school, giving them their food, and then cleaning the house. I also have to prepare food for when they return. My husband is a commando. He is working now. Sometimes he's away for eighteen hours a day, and sometimes for days on end. When I've done my work I go and meet other women in the camp. I work in the committees which the women need. I am trying to be a good revolutionary.'

The child returns, laden with Coca-Cola. Um

Emad offers a bottle, saying, 'We hope that we will drink again with you in our house in our own country.' She was five years old when she left.

'I remember Palestine. To me it is like a living dream. The courtyards where I played, the trees, the hills. I remember my father watering the trees in the orchard. We had a diesel machine for pumping the water, and I can hear now the sound of it quite clearly. My father owned the land, producing oranges, lemons, apples, bananas and grapes. We had a good life. No one said to us, "You are refugees." '

She picks up the photograph of her brother.

'It is my conviction that my brother is not dead, that his spirit lives in my family, that he will fight until we return.'

Children burst into the house, young, unformed features, laughing, curious, filthy from playing in the street, innocent. Um Emad has five of them. What is their future?

An old man from Haifa with his family : 'I am waiting to die, but I want to die in Palestine'

over
Their memories are hostile

'I hope that they will hold arms to fight and that this fight will be the basis upon which they build a future for themselves in Palestine. There is no future for them anywhere else. We want to live in peace where no one can tell us that we do not belong.'

A fat old man and his wife are standing outside the door of their shack. They came from Haifa in 1948, where he had been a butcher, working in the port. He speaks in monosyllables.

'How was it to live in Palestine? My spirit died.'

'And living in the camp?'

'Dead, alive, upside down. I am waiting for death. I am waiting to die, but I want to die in Palestine.'

The words are spoken not in self-pity but with impatience because it is obvious. Occasionally Palestinians project an image to meet the expectations that others have of them. If the stereotype is

downtrodden, then so is the image; if the stereo-type is ruthless, the image is murderous. Not so this old man. The revolution has unleashed in men like him, whose degradation has been acute, a violent, wild resolution. He has found himself through the symbol of the gun. It is the wildfire passion of such individuals, stoked up by the revo-lution, that it is now the awesome task of the PLO to direct and contain.

'I would have liked to make an operation myself.

A Mylot or a Munich. The men who did these things are heroes of our people.'

He points down to his small son with a fierce assertive gesture.

'When my son is able to carry a machine-gun, then he will be able to give his life for Palestine. I want to teach my son to use a gun and tell him, "Go to Palestine and die there." I hope that like me all Palestinians teach their children to fight.'

162

The young led the resurgence. Fatah
commanders are trained to endure privation in
the mountains and to overcome physical fears

The liberation of the Palestinian camps in Lebanon began as young Palestinians, enthused by the Karameh battle, found the courage to defy the authorities, openly challenging the petty and humiliating restrictions imposed upon them. The government responded with even more repression. There was confrontation in the camps and in the streets of Beirut. But, for the first time, the Palestinians were joined by the left, the nationalists, the intellectuals, and many thousands of Moslems, who found common cause with the revolution and turned upon the régime. Their demonstrations were met by soldiers and policemen, firing at first above, and later into, the angry crowds. There were dead and wounded. But the government was unable to withstand the pressure of the new militancy. Already in south Lebanon the authorities had decided to withdraw from open confrontation with the Fatah commandos who had established bases in the remote mountainous region bordering Israel, from where they launched 'ter-rorist' raids into that northern part of Galilee from where so many of them had been expelled twenty years before. The Palestinians now posed a threat to the Lebanese ruling élite. Indeed, the urge to imprison their aspirations in the camps was stronger than ever, but it was no longer possible. The resurgence of the Palestinians was irrepressible. It had developed a momentum which no mere bundle of legislation could withstand, and no army could reverse without committing a scale of military atrocity from which the government shrank, knowing well that such action would have brought about the very disaster that it would have been designed to prevent, the collapse of the fragile pillars of the Lebanese state.

The uprising against the authorities was spontaneous. In clashes between the refugees and the army in the camps, the Palestinians stood their ground and fought, those who did not have guns arming themselves with sticks and knives against the threat of tanks and machine-guns. It was too much for the Lebanese.

One by one the Lebanese formally handed over the camps to the Palestinians. It was the beginning of a new era. Free to assert their identity, the Palestinians flew their national flags from their own administrative buildings; sheikhs in the mosques spoke openly of 'the homeland'; national traditions were revived – folklore, dances, stories and songs; their leaders met openly to discuss national politics at large rallies; their radios blared forth a revolutionary blend of music and speeches designed to draw the people into a National Resistance. And, the most obvious sign of their new status – they carried guns, not furtively, but as a public assertion of their will.

Haj Talal was one of those responsible for the reorganization of the camps under PLO control.

'Until this moment the camps had been stagnating. The population of most of them had more than doubled since 1948 and the conditions were dreadful. We were overcrowded, we had no social or sporting facilities, our education and our health care were inadequate. Moreover, we were under severe restrictions. We had to be in our homes every night by six o'clock. We were forbidden to organize, only four or five people were allowed to meet together at any one time. It was necessary to obtain special permission even to form a gathering for a marriage. And on those occasions like 15 May [the date of the establishment of the state of Israel] when we defied the authorities, there were violent clashes between us. The end of the suppression was the start of the revolution.'

The poverty in the camps is still acute : families

Children are reared in homes which still lack water, sewerage and electricity

without men to work, workers without skills, skills without jobs. Jobs that pay £(L)300 a month for a day labourer, a nightwatchman or a concièrge, and which must keep perhaps a wife, ten children and two aged grandparents. Even those whose men are plumbers or carpenters, or shopkeepers and traders, or who have even managed to make a business by repairing radios or bicycles, or by making clothes or washing them, are still impoverished – their horizons blocked out by the invisible walls which always imprison the refugee.

The children are reared in small rooms, sharing beds with two, three or even more other children, in houses without running water, perhaps without lavatories or electricity. Almost all of them – 65 per cent of the Palestinian population is under the age of twenty-one – will grow up with no means of escape except by emigration or through the PLO. The revolution begins with education. As soon as they can speak, they learn songs about Palestine; and when they can read, they discover politics.

The PLO publishes a small illustrated book which is known to all Palestinian children. It is called, simply, Home.

A hen has a home
Its home is
The chicken coop.

A rabbit has a home
Its home is
The barrow.

A horse has a home
Its home is
The stable.

A fish has a home
Its home is
The sea and
The ocean.

A cat loves
Prowling
In the streets
But even the cat
Possesses a home
That it loves
And is proud of.

A bird has a home
And the bird's home
Is called a nest.

Everyone has a
Home.
For a home is
Where one finds
Peace and
Happiness.

A Palestinian has
No home
The tents and
Houses
He lives in are
Not his home.

Where is the home
Of the Palestinian?
A Palestinian's
Home is in
Palestine but he
Does not live in
His home today.

The Palestinian's
Home is usurped by
His foe.

Who is the foe
Of the Palestinian?
The Palestinian's
Foe is the one who
Usurped his home.

How can the
Palestinian regain
His home?

By arms alone a
Palestinian can
Regain his home.

A Palestinian will
Return home.
For the Palestinian
Home belongs to
The Palestinians.

The book is illustrated by bright drawings of contented hens, rabbits, horses and so forth; little children happy in little houses; and one of a bleak Palestinian boy under the stars beside his tent. There is a picture which depicts an Israeli tank with an ogre of a soldier in the gun turret; and another – intended to inspire – shows the rifle of the revolution which is to return the Palestinian child to his home.

On some wasteland by a block of houses bombed in an air-raid, a group of children is training. They are seven- or eight-year-olds, boys and girls, learning how to fire a rifle, or run for cover, or to remain cool when an unexpected explosion – a land-mine or hand-grenade – rattles the eardrums and invites blind panic. They are dressed in the uniform of the fedayeen, and they do not smile, and they carry guns. They belong to the Ashbel, a children's militia, the next generation of fighters. Who joins the Ashbel? One of their leaders explains.

'Even a four-year-old can join to watch what happens. He sees what is happening, and he is attracted because his friends are there and his older brothers. We watch him, and see how he reacts. If he is suitable then we suggest to his father that he is ready to join. There is no compulsion at all. That would be disastrous. Nor is the Ashbel a substitute for the home or the school. It complements both. We give social and political and military training. We play all sorts of sports, we teach carpentry, music and drawing. We teach history and geography of Palestine, and the principles and purposes of the Ashbel – which means Fatah.'

Some parents are reluctant for their offspring to join the Ashbel – 'those who are not yet revolutionary, whose mother might fear for her child, or whose father might want his help at work' – but children flock to join and few are turned away. In the summer they go on a six-week camp, the best being sent to summer camps abroad, usually in Eastern Europe.

'Remember that although it may seem like Boy Scouts, we are fighting a war. Remember that at Sidon a fourteen-year-old destroyed one of the tanks with an RPG. Remember that children participated in the war in south Lebanon, acting as runners, helping with supplies and communications, looking after officers, and they were under fire.'

'How many children are in the Ashbel?'

'It is a military secret.

'An Ashbel child when he reaches the age of twelve years is a commando, a fighter. We know what the response to this is in the West. You think it is terrible that children should fight. But our children are fighting for their homeland. Your anxieties are incomprehensible to us. Our children are always suffering; how can they suffer less, when they are fighting to liberate themselves?

'When we were in camp in East Germany, there were children from forty-two other countries, including Western nations. Our children in the Ashbel were very well behaved, very disciplined. And everyone wanted to know, "How do they manage to behave like this?" And for us, the PLO, it was a great advance – because they realized that we were a proper organization, that these children

were ordinary, decent and civilized young people. That they were not "terrorists".'

Nevertheless, the gun holds sway. It is by the gun that the PLO says it will 'liberate' Palestine; and it is by the gun that their children are inspired. The PLO may be right, but it has the advantage of perspective: it can distinguish the weapon from the goal. Not so some of the children for whom means and ends are merged so that the gun and the Return become one.

Although the revolution has broken through the old political structures, removing much authority from the hands of the elders and placing it in the barrel of the commando guns, the old social hierarchies persist. The camps are still built about the villages from which the refugees fled. The families in those villages still wield authority, a fact from which men like Salah Tamari derive considerable satisfaction.

'We still have strong sanctions. It is still possible

for us to turn someone out of the family, to say, "He is no longer one of us, we are no longer responsible for him." The family is most important to us. Family groups stay together like they did in Palestine. There are streets named after villages. Our tradition is deeply rooted.

'And still, despite the revolution, we respect age. The younger brother respects the older. The older honours his father. Age is the link between the past and the future. You cannot uproot our traditions. This is why the communists are so mistaken. If there is an offence in a camp, even now we try to solve it in the old ways through the village court. Even today a serious offence, perhaps a murder, is sometimes solved in this way.'

Salah, who happens to be the oldest male in his family, expects his brothers and sisters to offer him respect, which they do, and intends, perhaps implausibly, to approve his sisters' choices of husband. His appreciation of women's liberation,

167

'You think it terrible that children should fight. But our children are fighting for their homeland'

which has a strong following among the Palestinian intelligentsia, is distinctly limited. He likes women to be modest, and to obey the traditions.

Yet the dilemmas are real. A teacher in one of the camps for which Salah is responsible is caught between his commitment to the revolution and the traditions in which he has been brought up. He is a sensitive and serious man.

'We have a deep gulf now between the old and the young, particularly on social behaviour. And, naturally, the issue on which they are most divided is the role of women. The parents of most of the children I teach are illiterates. They cannot escape their past. But we have to lead our own lives according to our own values.

'In some families the young are suppressed by the older generation.

'For instance, if there were to be a film with sex in it, a young man might want to go and take his sister with him even. But the father forbids it. It is a slow process. We have to win step by step, by argument and conflict, by persuasion – and by deception. Girls are now finding their way to the cinema, but in secret.

'Likewise it is still forbidden for a girl to kiss a man. To be seduced by him is prohibited entirely. It is Islamic tradition that women should not sit with men in public. It will take time to break through this prejudice.

'The illusion is always preserved that the young have no sex. But if the knowledge of an affair becomes public, it is a terrible scandal. Sometimes a boy and a girl are obliged to get married although under these circumstances the girl is always considered to be in the wrong. Indeed, she may still be put to death by her family, and if so those who perpetrate that crime would be judged innocent.

'Of course, the revolution is changing this fast. The young are now less deferential. I have a girl friend whom I see openly (though she is still frightened in case her family witness us together in public). And some girls are now fighters in the revolution, behaving as equals – though you should notice that some of their fathers order them home before the fighting, even against their will. The more educated the girls the more openly they rebel.

'I made my father treat my sister according to the principles in which I believe. I argued with him and fought with him. I forced him to let her

decide on her choice of male friends. But if I had not been able to persuade him, then I would not have argued, the decision would have been his. We respect our parents greatly. We have to try and show them that our ways must be different from theirs. They yield only with great difficulty. And if they are stubborn we rarely resist to the end, because the bond between us is so strong. The future depends on education.'

There are few Palestinians who are not obsessed with education. It is the only means to rise out of the camps. Parents are prepared to make enormous sacrifices to provide their children with a university education. In the last thirty years the Palestinians have, as a result, emerged to become one of the most educated and disciplined people in the Middle East.

The teachers' conditions in the UNRWA school are hardly ideal.

'In my school there are twenty-two classes; each ranges in size from thirty-five to fifty-five pupils. I teach English and drawing, twenty English classes a week, using the Longman Direct Method English Course. We teach grammar and comprehen-sion. And because the numbers are so great and the resources so limited, all the schools are on double shifts. From 7.30 to 11.50, and then from 12.00 to 4.20. It is hardly ideal.

'But we depend on our teaching. The future generations depend on it. If we don't learn, we don't progress. We must progress.'

The camps are vital and volatile, the conflict is of past and future, between old and young, of rigid order *versus* spiritual anarchy, between Islam and revolution. Who rules? The elders? The muk-tars? The doctors, teachers and lawyers who are the educated rational élite, the protectors of the community? Or the fedayeen, the commandos, the men who have picked up the gun and who run the committees, who do not compromise but whose fathers are still revered? There is conflict but no contradiction. No fragmentation. The people are energized by their own divisions, driven towards the one uniting certainty: that in one way or another they are approaching the Return.

When Ibrahim Ghannan, the Palestinian painter, looks at the young around him, he does not perceive the infant machismo, only the future fighters.

He teaches the Ashbel in Lebanon, travelling the camps in his wheelchair, because he is crippled by arthritis.

'I am proud of our children because they are growing up to prepare for the battle. They leave their homes, often despite their parents. They are under military orders all day. It is a real sacrifice and sometimes they are killed.

'I try to pass on to them what I know. All my life is painting, handiwork, carpet-making, carpen-try, poetry, music and song. I try to keep alive the Palestinian traditions and to pass them on to the children. I teach the young ones to dance by show-ing them with my fingers how we used to dance.

'We now have to follow them. We can only offer them what we have. I'm always haunted by Palestine. I live there still. When I awake from my dreams, I am sad. And when I live in the past, I am content.

'When I seek enjoyment, I go to the camp and

find the old men and hear their stories and their songs and their poems. I am searching for the past. It is my job to transmit this to the next generation.

'Sometimes Abu Ammar [Yasser Arafat] comes to see me because he likes my paintings. My son who is only four years old gets very excited and likes to take his hero's machine-gun and try it for himself. So I asked my son, what does he prefer, water melons or the Palestinian leadership. He answers, "Water melons, except for Abu Ammar."

"Why do you like Abu Ammar?" I ask him. "Because he is fighting Zionism," he answers. "Aren't you ashamed of someone like that, killing people?" I ask. "No," he replies, "because they killed my people and took my home." You see, the children know already.'

The commandos are ubiquitous in Lebanon. They hurry through Beirut in jeeps wearing casual uniforms, heads half-hidden in kaffirs or flak jackets. They guard offices, scrutinizing visitors, sitting at

A commando off duty

The camps are the recruiting ground for commandos

desks surrounded by posters and coffee cups and yesterday's papers discarded on grubby floors stained with old cigarette butts, talking, filling long hours. They are bodyguards, fierce and anxious, moving fast through crowds, protecting leaders from Fatah, or the Popular Front, or the Popular Democratic Front, or Sa'iqa, or a host of other small groups, eyeing each other with distrust, fingers on triggers, in times of inner turmoil. They are at the front line, haggard, hoarse, on the edge, dangerous, not to be crossed. They are in the training camps, up in the mountains, cooking on spirit stoves, relaxed, friendly, wondering what the British or the Americans think of them and why. At road-blocks they are stern, wondering who is on this road so far from Beirut and why. Then they relax, offering or demanding cigarettes. Terrorists or freedom fighters?

They want outsiders to understand. The group of commandos in Shattila, all teenagers, have open faces, laughing but offering great courtesy. They rush to find chairs and dispatch one of their number in search of Coca-Cola. He returns almost at once with some ice-cold bottles. They compete to open one, it slips and spills on their guests. They are mortified, search for cloths and mop up with solicitous apologies. Then one of them picks up an RPG to demonstrate how it is held. He points it playfully at a friend, and everyone laughs because the RPGs are for tanks not people. They say that they are happy to talk about anything, especially 'terrorism'. 'Don't worry,' they say.

This group fought against the Phalange in the Lebanese civil war. They did not enjoy the bloodshed. But they had to fight. Some of them are still at school. There is one who speaks good English.

'When I finish school – I am now seventeen – I want to go to university, but there is no money. I would like to be a doctor but it's not possible. So I will continue to work for the revolution.'

He has three brothers and two sisters, the oldest being twenty-one, the youngest six. One of his sisters is at university in Romania, sent there on a scholarship by the PLO to study economics. His father used to be a clerk at the port, but since the war he has had to sell cigarettes for a living. The family is poor.

'My main ambition in life is to study hard and find ways of helping my family in the future.'

He speaks with great seriousness and some of his friends tease him for it.

Hassan is also seventeen, but he left school two

'We are oppressed, but we have our self-respect. That is the revolution'

years ago to become a commando. He's one of five children, his twin having been killed in a clash with the Syrians in 1976. His father is also a clerk. Hassan wants to become a teacher, although he will remain a fighter 'until Palestine is recovered'. A few months earlier, Israeli jets bombed his home in a suburb on the edge of Beirut Airport, destroying more than twenty houses. His father was killed in the attack.

'When the shelling started it was too quick for us. I went for my own gun in my room, but the roof fell in on me. It took six hours for them to get me out. I'm lucky to be alive. My father didn't escape.'

They ask why there is not moral outrage in the West when the Israelis behave in this way. The question is unanswerable. They do not wish to cause embarrassment. Seramin begins to talk. He is bigger and much rougher. His father is blind, so he has been working ever since he could fend for himself.

'I never went to school at all. I was a labourer from the beginning. I am good at repairing water pipes. What is my future? It is obvious, it is in the PLO as a fighter.'

Another is at the Arab University, studying business administration.

'I was sent by the revolution. It is very important for us to understand finance. When I finish at the university I hope to go to the Soviet Union for further training. Meanwhile I shall remain a commando. Commandos can fight in many ways, they can go into battle and they can teach. I was fighting in the south against the Israelis.'

Do they have qualms about killing innocents?

'I have been into Palestine. I've seen women and children, who are Jewish, but I didn't kill them though it would have been easy. I planted a bomb only where the military officers are.'

But civilians can still die. Bombs are indiscriminate.

'The civilians who get killed are soldiers in ordinary clothes, and like everyone else in Israel they are spies against us. All the men are soldiers, that is well known. In one of my operations I saw a camp, a military camp, with women in it as well as men. The women are with the soldiers, they are in the war against us.'

Are they not a little casual about their responsibilities? Is that not why they're called 'terrorists'?

'We are not terrorists. We do not bomb women and children. The world should know this. We are

175

against Israel and imperialism. Nor are we against the Jews. We do not understand anti-Semitism. That is European. We want our land back. When a commando goes into Israel he puts a bomb into a place which is defended by Israelis; he attacks offices and public places which are the centres of imperialism. The bombs are for the soldiers. If we place a bomb in a bus, it is a bus carrying soldiers, a military target. They are not civilians. If women and children are killed it is by mistake and we regret it, but we have no alternative.'

Another group explains that it is important to understand why they are fighters, and why their struggle is so difficult. They want a democratic Palestine, a secular state. It is for this reason that Zionism must be destroyed. Then, they say, the Arabs and Jews would live together. But Israel is an outpost of imperialism, and imperialism, the United States, is strong and puts pressure on the Arab régimes. So, for a long time, they were treated with contempt by everyone. Their defeat began in the 1930s.

'Our parents did their best, but the difference in power was vast. They sold their gold to buy guns to oppose the British. They bought rifles and cheap ammunition that used to explode inside the barrel. They had no choice.

'Until the revolution the old had the authority. After the gun, they lost it. Many of the young say to them, even now, "You are the generation of the Catastrophe." The young are still bitter and the old become their victims. Yes, we were refugees, but why did we not have the basic necessities, light, electricity, sewerage, water, houses? Why did we have to wait until the revolution? Why could we not travel? Our parents were humiliated. We are oppressed, but we have our self-respect. That is the revolution.'

Ten

Building the Nation

To the intense irritation of those Palestinians who are employed in the institutions created since 1969 by the PLO, their work is virtually ignored by the outside world. Although everyone is welcome to visit the schools, hospitals and workshops which offer, to their mind, convincing testimony to the honourable purpose of the revolution, few take up the invitation. It is true that official delegates from socialist states and revolutionaries from capitalist ones make the dutiful pilgrimage and probably record their experiences in long fraternal articles, but Western man is not apparently so easily captivated.

He is excited into horror by a massacre in a bus on the road to Tel Aviv, but he does not, so it appears, wish to hear about the 'baby factory' in the PLO's main hospital in Beirut; or of the family in Damur on PLO social security; or the PLO factory which makes blankets for the commandos and has workers sitting on the Board; or the orphanage which has space only for those children who have lost both parents; or the PLO radio station; or the PLO film centre; or the students on PLO scholarships at universities throughout the world; or even the summer camps where the teenage boys and girls learn to live rough and to shoot to kill.

In effect, the PLO is the provisional government of the Palestinian people, to which the overwhelming majority of Palestinians in exile and under occupation look – occasionally because there is no other alternative – for leadership. It is so recognized by the Arab world and by the General Assembly of the United Nations. Those who would challenge the 'revolution', find themselves at odds with perhaps 30,000 well-trained and proven guerrilla fighters, who have secured the political and diplomatic pre-eminence of the PLO. To say 'Bye-bye PLO' is not merely to denounce a political and military fact of life, but to ridicule a network of social and economic institutions which provide a glimpse into the PLO's vision of the democratic state in Palestine.

In 1969, the refugee camps were dependent exclusively upon the United Nations Relief Works Agency (UNRWA), which had been set up to provide services 'to persons or the descendants of persons whose normal residence was Palestine for a minimum of two years preceding the Arab–Israeli conflict in 1948 and who, as a result of that conflict, lost both their homes and their means of livelihood'. At the moment there are approximately one and three quarter million refugees registered with UNRWA, either in exile or under occupation. In the words of the UNRWA report for 1977, the 'services' are,

not in the nature of a dole for the permanently destitute. But on the contrary, they are directed

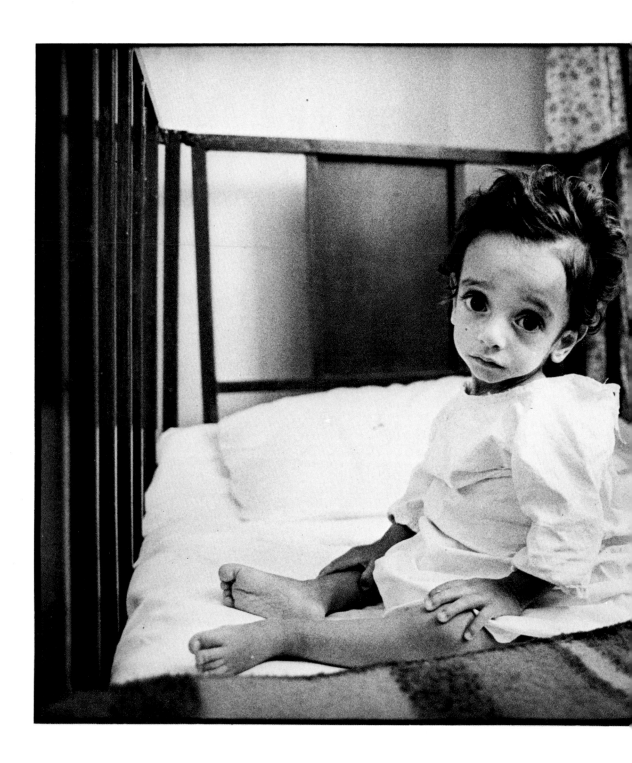

towards establishing and maintaining levels of health, education, and relief for a large part of the Palestinian people that help to make them productive, socially useful human beings who contribute to society rather than impose a burden on it.

In practice, UNRWA has been as worthy as it sounds. It has fed the hungry, it has clothed the impoverished, it has offered medicine to the sick, it has schooled the young. Moreover, it has done this under the most difficult circumstances, in conditions of permanent insecurity or often of full-scale war. Its staff are accustomed to all manner of bloodshed: air-raids, rocket attacks, tank bombardments, civil war, fratricidal shoot-outs and – in Lebanon – the horrors of an endless succession of hideous murders.

In the face of these persistent traumas, UNRWA staff are not unnaturally aware of the limitations

'The people are so poor that the children are malnourished'

of their operations. Its commissioners-general repeatedly remind the United Nations (in the most restrained language) that,

the refugee problem has dimensions that go far beyond the purely humanitarian . . . the political significance of the mass displacement of human beings is obvious, particularly when the right of return and the right to restoration of their property are acknowledged by the international community.

Meanwhile UNRWA's attempts to provide the basic necessities of social life to the dispossessed are harassed by the very governments who established it in the first place. Ninety-five per cent of its income is derived from voluntary contributions by governments. So low does UNRWA now stand upon the hierarchical rungs of international goodwill, that it has – shamefully – an annual budget of less than $(US)100 million, or about $(US)60 per refugee per year, which is less than it costs to meet

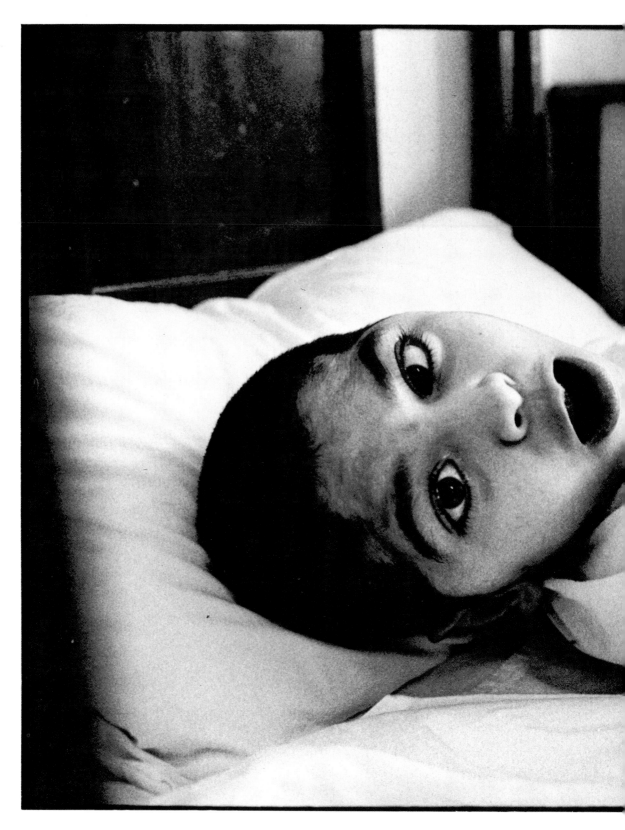

'We are at war, even when we seem to be at peace'

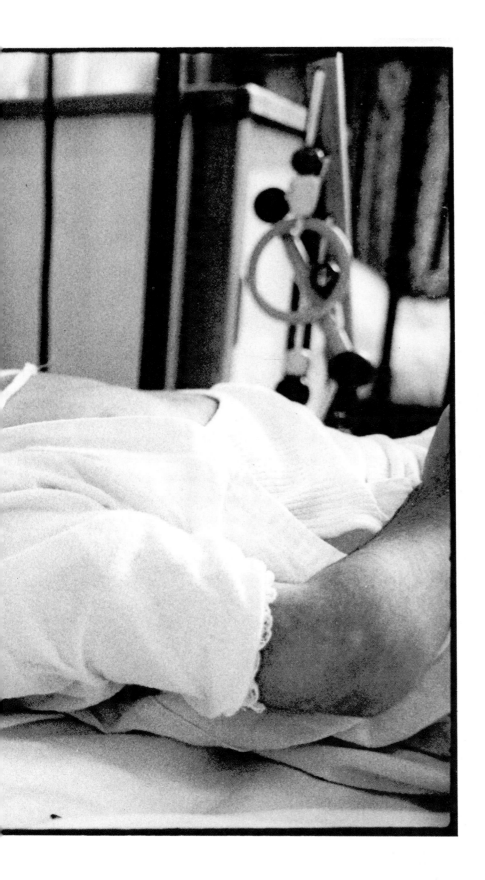

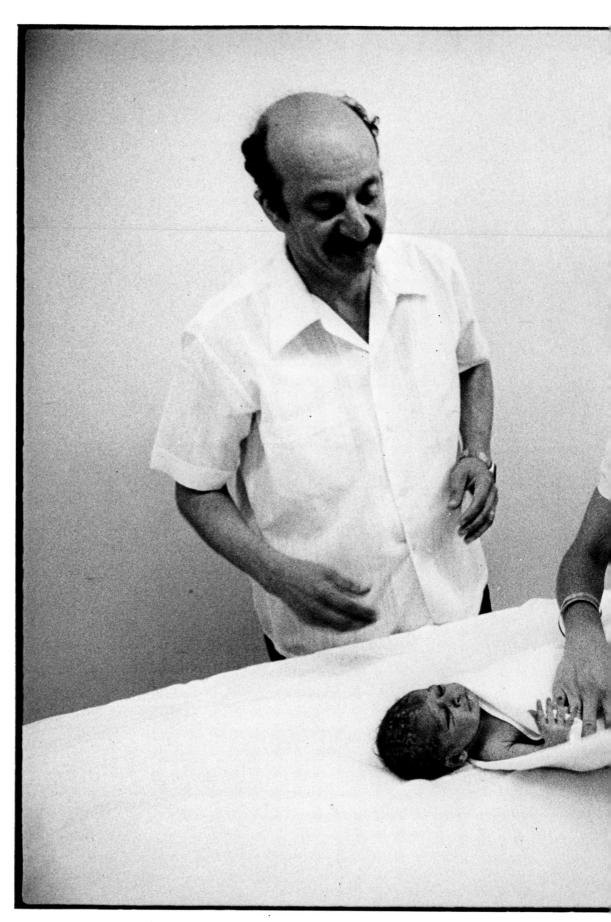

Dr Arafat, chairman of the Palestinian Red Crescent, in his 'baby factory'

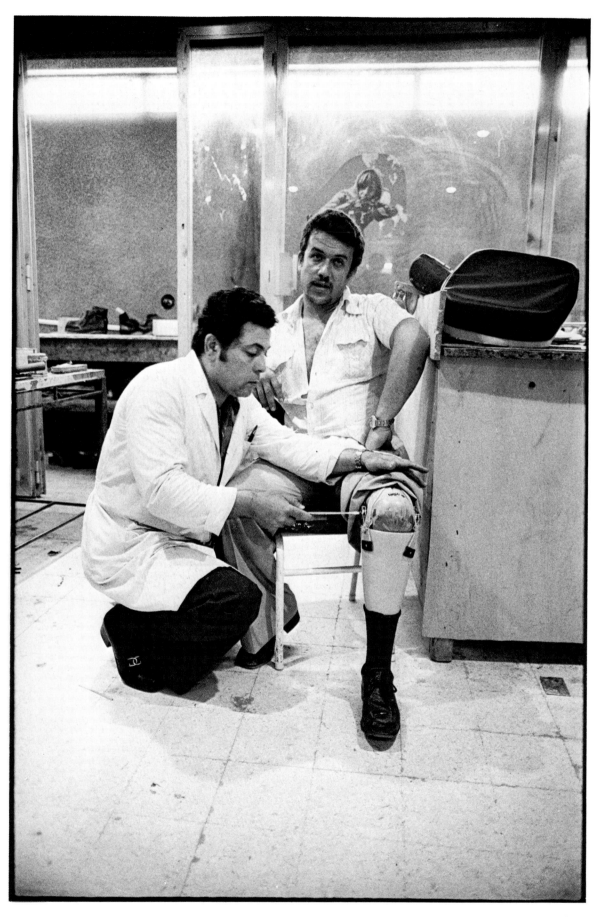

A technician adjusts the artificial leg of a Palestinian fighter

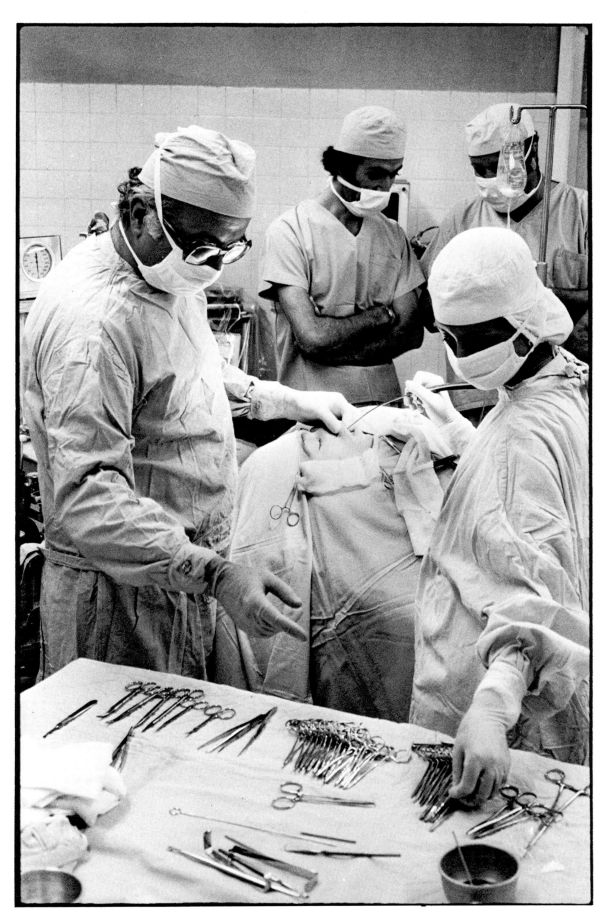

'Our hospitals are always in danger, we always have to be ready to evacuate'

the basic needs which, under its constitution, it is obliged to provide. UNRWA stumbles from one financial crisis to the next, closing schools here, suspending rations there, postponing long-term programmes and accelerating the decline of services which it says 'are already at a minimum'.

None the less it is uncertain whether the Palestinians could have survived as a people without the assistance they received from UNRWA. This has not stopped them turning upon their protector.

Thirty years of crises have made the Palestinians in the camps cautious and suspicious – sometimes to the point of paranoia – of outsiders. Nor has the PLO been unduly sensitive to UNRWA's predicament, preferring to feed the doubts of the refugees that the disruption of their schools, their feeding programmes and their clinics is part of an international conspiracy to destroy the revolution. The distrust of UNRWA runs deep. Though almost all its staff are refugees, it is commonly believed that they are reluctant advocates of the revolution, and even agents of Western imperialism: if a school is closed, it is because the West is fearful of educated Palestinians; if a teacher is fired, it is because he belongs to Fatah; if a clinic is without supplies, it is because the only good Palestinian is a dead one.

For this reason, the services offered by the PLO, although on a much smaller scale than those of UNRWA, and in no way a substitute for them, are a source of the most profound pride to Palestinians in the camps.

It is not merely that the hospitals and clinics, the schools and workshops, are 'theirs', it is that in them they sense a national purpose, a direction which UNRWA is unable to provide.

Dr Arafat looks uncommonly like his brother: the same protruding deep brown eyes, always darting, the same voice, the same gestures, the same energy, the same diplomatic charm, the same reticence, and the same sense that he is not without significance in the world.

For twelve years he has run the Palestinian Red Crescent Organization, which now has thirty-five hospitals and more than a hundred clinics scattered through the Arab world. His office is in the Acre Hospital on the edge of the Sabra refugee camp in Beirut. The building has been battered by the Lebanese war, by mortar and machine-gun fire. Breezeblocks fill empty window-frames that face over the camp towards the Christian positions three quarters of a mile away. Outside this fortress there is a Syrian road-block, and up the hill, beside the embassy of Kuwait, the Syrians have anti-aircraft guns ready to fire in most directions – at Israelis, Phalangists or – if necessary – Palestinian guerrillas, dug into the hill. During the civil war

in 1976, the operating theatres in the basement of this hospital were at work twenty-four hours a day, the floor was awash with blood, the wards were filled with broken bodies and grieving relations. Outside, the sound of gunfire intermingled with the wail of ambulance sirens.

Now, for the moment at least, it is quiet and orderly. The corridors smell of disinfectant. The operating theatres today are empty, though later a heart surgeon will fit a pacemaker, and a refugee, his face horribly contorted by an old shrapnel wound, will have a skin graft. In each of the theatres, surgeons perform upwards of twenty operations a week during a quiet period. As elsewhere, medical enthusiasts, who are Palestinian, explain the incomprehensible workings of a renal dialysis unit, or discuss the cardiovascular case waiting wanly for his operation:
'He came in here with a pain in the lower limbs. He couldn't walk. Occlusion of the arteries. Thrombosis.'

There is an intensive-care unit as complete as any, with artificial respirators and cardiac monitors. A little girl is lying in the recovery room, breathing with difficulty. Her mother has her hand in the child's, and stares fixedly at the wall, her face tense, frightened. The girl had come in for a standard tonsillectomy, only to suffer a cardiac arrest in the middle of the operation.

In another part of the hospital, skilled technicians sit under bright lights in a workshop, carving individual legs, arms, hands and feet out of wood for the victims of the Israeli invasion of south Lebanon a few months earlier. Opposite them, iron-faced young men, ashen with pain, try out their new limbs, or endure in silence as a physiotherapist pummels their bodies, pulls on cramped muscles and eases stiffened joints, trying to restore flexibility to reluctant arms and legs. In here there are a hundred patients each day. They sit in long queues, patiently.

Dr Arafat recounts his responsibilities as the Red Crescent's senior administrator with that barely restrained delight of a bureaucrat who has fathered an empire. He is dedicated to the expansion of what is, in effect, an embryo Palestinian National Health Service. He works seven days a week from seven o'clock in the morning until late at night, being driven between his home and the office by a devoted commando who has worked for him since 1969. He rarely sees his two children, who live in Cairo, where his wife is a dentist specializing in maxillafacial surgery. He pays them occasional visits, finding it difficult to leave his responsibilities.

'Since 1948, I have had only one thing in my

life, that is to return. I took up medicine, intending to use that when I returned. My entire life is in the movement. My responsibility is to the Red Crescent. I have no time to read, no time to listen to music, no relaxation.

'We face very special problems. Our hospitals are always in danger, we always have to be ready to evacuate. We are always closing down and starting up again. We are permanent nowhere.

'We exist in states which have their own laws, which are often hostile to us or, at least, have laws devised especially for us, which limit our freedom. For instance, no Palestinian can enter this country without Lebanese government approval.

'So it can be a real problem for me finding Palestinian doctors a visa. Well, I might have a visa for a short time, and then, when I need it, the authorities won't renew it.

'In Kuwait there are perhaps five hundred Palestinian doctors. I might agree with one that he should come here for a year's contract, only to find that he is forbidden by the authorities, without explanation.

'We have problems too with money. We have to compete with petro-dollars. Many of our doctors look after large families. We are not a state which can require them to work for the people for perhaps two years before going elsewhere. How can I compete when I offer only £(L)1,000 a month, and they can get ten times as much in Kuwait or Saudia Arabia?

'Then, although we are more than three and a half million people, we have no university. So we cannot plan, we cannot train doctors efficiently. We have to send them to Europe, to London, to America, to Cairo on scholarships which we, ourselves, fund.

'But we have problems with speciality. It's no good training a hundred heart surgeons and not having an anaesthetist, or having a radiologist, and being unable to provide him with the rest of the team that he needs.

'It seems to be difficult for you in the West to understand this. We are a people. It is because of this that we needed a revolution. UNWRA provides a minimum service: the clinics only open three hours a day, they are under-equipped. We needed a plan for the future. They said it was impossible: "You can't do it," they said. When they said that, we said: "We need the Red Crescent."

'We are a revolution, not because we are fighters but because we need to provide a future for our people. In our hospitals, our clinics, our convalescent homes, our rehabilitation centres, our obstetric hospital, we are answering their needs and their hopes at the same time. But I have no illusions.

Our services cannot operate adequately until we return home. Until then we are providing sedation.'

Dr Arafat speaks at speed and with clarity, anxious that no point should be omitted, recalling that the conditions of the camps are still deplorable by civilized standards.

'Remember that most of them are the same size as they were in 1948, but the population has doubled. The services are still primitive. We're still short of lavatories, the sewage system is collapsing. We are prone to diseases like rheumatic fever and diarrhoeas. Because the people are so poor, because there's no work, their children are still malnourished. Our social life is very limited, and for much of the life there is tension, so there are psychological problems. We are never free from the prospect of war. Bombing is a permanent hazard. All this makes for a state of medical alert. We are at war, even when we seem to be at peace.'

The new obstetric unit in Beirut is understandably a source of great delight for Dr Arafat. It is here, in conditions that any Western maternity hospital would envy, that he has his 'baby factory'. In neat cots, in neat rows, in neat wards, tiny heads with eyes screwed shut against the future lie on clean white sheets, motionless. They are pink and healthy. Dr Arafat picks up a new-born baby, telling the mother that he will be a fine fighter, and she laughs, delighted. He explains that the revolution needs as many babies as possible – 'babies for Fatah'. He smiles at the joke.

In the mountains overlooking the Mediterranean just outside Beirut, there is a factory. It is unimpressive from the outside: a concrete structure with a corrugated roof, cold and dreary. Inside, forty men and women are working at high speed, making blankets for the fighters. The noise and dust would have a Western trade union demanding mufflers and sprinklers. But here there is no complaint since this is work, and work for the revolution. It is one of thirty-two factories at present run by the PLO in Lebanon, which provide, apart from blankets, clothes, furniture, ornaments and leather goods, and a host of other consumer durables for the Palestinian and Lebanese market. Altogether they employ more than 3,000 people, and the number is expected to double within the next two years.

In the blanket factory, the workers regularly exceed their production targets. On the wall there are slogans. One of them asserts that the revolution will be won not just by the gun but by the worker as well. The fighters are short of winter protection. Each day the eighteen weaving machines produce 300 blankets.

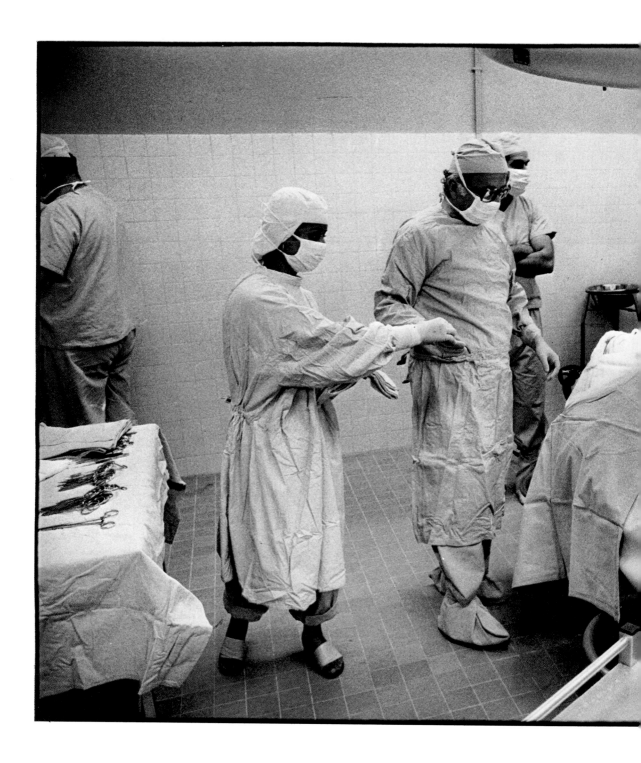

The senior engineer on this shift is called Amin Izar. He is twenty-seven years old and has a degree from Cairo University. In a few months he hopes to go to Manchester University, where he will study higher technology. For him the factory is a blueprint for the Palestinian state:

'The workshops, the factories are the nucleus for a liberated Palestine. We do not work here for the sake of work. These machines are the arms of the Palestinian people.

'SAMED [the PLO department which runs the factories] is something of ourselves. We want SAMED to grow and grow so that after our liberation it will form part of our independent economy.'

He has to yell above the noise of the machines to say in excitement:

'Our production here is to build the human being, not profit. Our production reveals us to ourselves as people.'

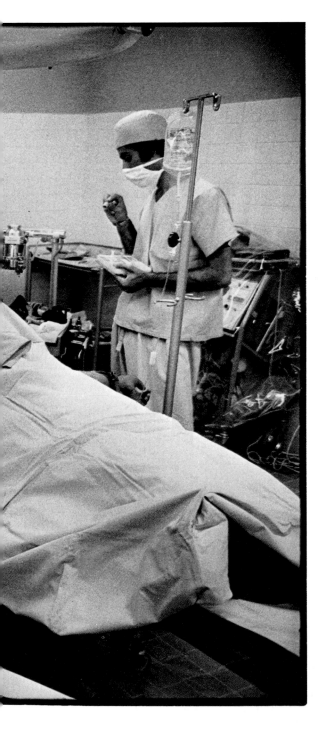

Palestinian doctors perform plastic surgery in the Red Crescent Hospital, Beirut

over

The babies for Fatah grow up to become martyrs for the Revolution. There is a cemetery in Beirut reserved for Palestinians who are killed in war. In the thirty years since the exodus, the Revolution has claimed many thousands of martyrs

SAMED has been in operation for eight years. It began by providing work for families of the 'martyrs', those who had been killed in battle against the Israeli enemy or the Arab brothers.

SAMED is the embryo industrial arm of the revolution, a government department-in-waiting, for industry, trade and employment. At the moment the director is travelling Europe. His deputy sits behind a large civil service desk, explaining the purpose. He is an articulate and talented administrator who returned three years ago from West Germany, where he had a senior post in an international bank. He has been a member of Fatah since 1965, and came back to fight against the Syrians, when they quarrelled with the PLO in the summer of 1976. He was one of a group of émigré professionals who stood in the path of the tanks in the mountains at Bamdoun, trying to slow the impervious advance of the Syrians with machine-guns and small-arms fire.

He decided to stay, convinced that his experience and expertise were needed by the revolution – here, rather than in Europe, where so many Palestinians preach the cause in comfortable isolation from the front line. His enthusiasm for the new job is unbounded. He says that he's surrounded by good men : the head of production used to run his own business, the sales manager also worked in private industry and gave up his senior position for SAMED. His account of the history and future of SAMED is precise. At first the factories were opened simply to provide work for the otherwise destitute. A bureaucracy sprang up to serve the growing demand for jobs. Soon SAMED had become an economic institution with a sales department, marketing and production divisions, staffed by a nucleus of skilled administrators and technicians. It is, however, the social potential of SAMED which most excites the vice-chairman.

'It is in an early stage as yet. But the worker is a member of the organization. He is on an equal footing with the manager. Each factory is run by its own production team. The workers also sit on the central planning, financing and marketing committees. Once a year SAMED will have a general congress in which the delegates from the shop floor outnumber the managers and technicians so that they will be responsible for the overall policy of SAMED.'

The enthusiasm, it must be said, is tempered by a sense of reality. The workers in the factories have either been unemployed or used to private industry in Lebanon, which is an industrial jungle. It has taken them time to adjust to their new rights and responsibilities. At first they were suspicious. But, according to the vice-chairman, the system is working.

'Our salary scales vary according to the needs and qualifications of each individual. The salary is determined by the worker in question with the manager and the revolutionary committee of the factory, depending upon his experience, his family responsibilities and his skills. Salaries range between £(L)600 a month and £(L)1,300 for the highest grade – a salary far less than many of our managers could earn in private industry in Lebanon.

'The industrial relations within our enterprise are drawn up on socialist lines, but we believe that they could fit into an overall capitalist society. We have been influenced by Cuba, but we have also been influenced by the situation in Yugoslavia, France, England and West Germany. We avoid ideological conflict. We have concrete problems which must be solved in concrete ways. If we permitted ourselves to indulge in ideological rows, it would limit our revolution. So we don't.'

SAMED barely touches the level of unemployment in the Palestinian camps where – among men – it runs at 20 per cent. Yet even those without work look upon SAMED as a symbol of their national potential. According to one of the workers there :

'SAMED is a demonstration of what we can do under the most difficult circumstances. We are a committed people. Imagine what we could do if we were liberated.'

The vision is intoxicating and unlimited : hundreds upon hundreds of SAMED factories, thousands upon thousands of men and women at work, driving clattering monsters of production, at sewing machines, behind lathes, before furnaces – a generation of frustration harnessed to the national cause, producing in Palestine.

Only occasionally does the deputy director permit himself such dreams. For the moment he must plan for the Lebanon, for the hundreds of Palestinians who trudge the Middle Eastern job market without success and who might, through SAMED, both find work and join the revolution.

Eleven
A Wedding Reception

There is a ceasefire in Beirut. The occasional crunch of a distant shell followed by a desultory exchange of machine-gun fire breaks the silence of the evening. The Syrians and the Phalange are each testing the nerve of the other, but in Beirut it is too hot and too humid to care who fired first.

At the wedding reception the guests shiver at the sudden air-conditioned cold draught which greets them in the hotel's banqueting suite. Elegant, remote women, brown from seeking the sun, sweep across the floor, expensive dresses shimmering under the chandeliers. Their men, greyer, pouchy and paunchy, greet each other with jovial formality, their too-tight bow ties unbending as they embrace. It is one of those occasions that will appear in *Monday Morning*, the Beirut magazine which bravely fills its front half with news of Lebanon's latest disaster, and the back with photographs of the young socialites who have managed to survive to produce rich young smiles for the camera.

Some of the guests have flown in from other countries: from Kuwait, Syria and Britain. Most of the men travel much of the time. They are lawyers, bankers and diplomats; they belong to the international élite of the Middle East. They are at home in first-class aeroplanes and first-class hotels. They know New York and Frankfurt, Riyadh and Lagos. They deal in the dollar markets,

they advise on the price of oil, they plan new cities in Arab deserts and finance the projects. They work in embassies, preparing subtle position papers for not-so-subtle politicians. They are a pervasive influence, greatly respected as advisers and planners in the raw world of commerce, finance and diplomacy in which the new rich of the Middle East have to find their uncertain way.

They are all – or almost all – Palestinians. It does not signify so in their passports, which record that they are citizens of Jordan or Syria or Lebanon or Britain or the United States. But these precious *laissez-passers* are no more than that. To the question, 'Where do you come from?' they answer, invariably, 'Palestine.'

The reception is in honour of the daughter of Badr S. Fahoum, the deputy chairman and general manager of one of the most powerful insurance companies in the Arab world. His headquarters are in down-town Beirut, on Phoenicia Street, a few hundred yards away from the Holiday Inn, where some of the fiercest fighting of the Lebanese war took place. Lebanese journalists, in search of good news amid the misery, made much of his tenacity in refusing to emulate most other large finance companies by transferring his business outside Lebanon. Fahoum told them why he had stayed:

'We decided not to desert Lebanon in this difficult period, as an expression of our recognition

and gratitude to the country which opened its doors to the company in 1948, when it had to transfer its head office from Jerusalem to Beirut. We felt it would be ungrateful on our part to walk out on Lebanon in times of crisis.'

Badr Fahoum is not given to self-doubt. His success is worn easily and without undue modesty. At his home the walls of his study are covered with the record of past achievements: BAs and diplomas from London University, one of which,

he points out, is 'With Distinction'; a photograph taken in the Vatican, where he is shaking hands with a red-robed cardinal and the Mayor of the City of Rome; another, at a luncheon held in his honour in California. In a corner on a stand he has a bust of himself, which was sculpted in London, and now stares down at his desk, smoking a Churchillian cigar. His apartment is cool and expansive. Through french windows at the back, two women – his wife and daughter – can be glimpsed in white cane

chairs, sipping at iced drinks under an awning in a formal garden.

A painting of Acre, with its white houses clinging together above the sea wall, is the only reminder that Mr Fahoum comes from Palestine. He is not given to introspection, and seeks to protect himself from the intrusion of outsiders with bluff courtesy.

'Being a Palestinian? Of course it makes a difference. We know how to run things because we have to. The Palestinian has to work to exist, and he has to work hard and honestly. If any government decides it doesn't like us, it can kick us out just like that. That is why we need our education, the best education possible. We have had to fight to survive. All of us. Do you know that the Palestinians must cut back on their food so that their sons can study?'

He is distressed, however, at the drive of the conversation, interrupting himself to issue an

Badr Fahoum is not given to self-doubt

instruction through the intercom, at which a secretary promptly appears with the company balance sheet.

'You know that my company operated at full speed throughout the crisis in Lebanon. I work all the time. Ten or eleven hours a day. And I'm making a success of this business. Look at the balance sheet. Net profit up 150 per cent. I distributed 50 per cent free shares this year, and our shareholders come from all over the Arab world and further afield.'

The conversation gently returns to Palestine.

'Other difficulties for the Palestinian, Mr Fahoum? Which is your home, Palestine or Lebanon?'

Mr Fahoum is too courteous to show his irritation, but is evidently uneasy. The composure fades a little. He begins to play with his glasses, moving them up and down uncertainly, and then drums on the table with his fingers as he answers:

'I live here in the Lebanon. I'm a Lebanese citizen, so I do my best to serve Lebanon like any good Lebanese. But I am not Lebanese so I keep out of local affairs.

'I wasn't born here so I mustn't interfere.'

He begins to speak more openly, as if relieved that he has unburdened himself of an uncomfortable truth.

'I feel that something is missing and it is something essential. Yes, we have our cars, we have the good life, but we don't have what we need. I have no home. My home is Palestine. I would be strong there. It is where I belong. It is not a question of base – that I have here – it is a question of home.'

Badr Fahoum was born in Nazareth, went to school in Jerusalem, and won a government scholarship (awarded by the British Mandate) to the American University in Beirut. Thereafter he went to the Institute of Education in London, where, in 1939, he managed to embarrass the University Senate by addressing a public meeting, at which he likened the British High Commission in Palestine to a combination of Hitler and Mussolini. The speech was reported in the *Evening Standard* under the headline: 'Sheikh Alleges British Atrocities in Palestine'. He was summoned for an explanation. The young student explained to the authorities:

'I came to learn about democracy here. I can't open my mouth in Palestine. I thought I could here. I wasn't at Hyde Park Corner but in the university. I want to tell those of your people who will run your empire, your students, what the truth is. If this upsets you then you must instruct me to keep silent, and explain that you wish nothing to threaten the grant-in-aid that you have from the government which is doing these things to our people.'

In 1942, Badr Fahoum went to work for the British as a district officer in Palestine.

'You should differentiate between the British government and the civil servants who were driven mad by the policy they had to carry out. They knew that it was disastrous, but they had no choice in the matter. I had the highest esteem for them.'

In 1948 he became a refugee, caught on the border when Acre fell, unable to return at the end of the Mandate. His wife escaped with him to Lebanon. They are now forbidden to return.

'I haven't seen my family since that date. I don't know where they are, how many they are, who has died or who has been born.'

In Lebanon he met up with other Palestinian friends. They rented four rooms, bought four steel desks and two typewriters, and founded a trading company, calling it Intra. Within five years it had become the largest financial institution in the Middle East. Intra-bank, as it became known, had offices in Syria, Liberia, Nigeria, Frankfurt, Rio and New York. With the Royal Families of Saudi Arabia, Kuwait and Qatar as shareholders, it expanded rapidly, taking over Middle East Airlines, the Phoenicia Hotel, Radio Orient in Lebanon. According to Badr Fahoum, who recalls the details with great bitterness, it was precisely this power that was Intra-bank's downfall.

'We had thought that if we became strong in the economic field, then, as Palestinians, we would later become strong politically. We believed that the Lebanese did not like Palestinians having such control in their economy, and we know that the United States didn't want us to invest elsewhere in the world. We felt they were frightened of us – because we were Palestinians. So they got together to fight an economic war against us. They knew that the Kuwaitis and Saudis were behind us, and we were handling their investments. They knew how rich these countries were, and that if they left their monies with us, we could even be in a position to buy up General Motors. And quite simply they didn't want this money coming into America through a powerful bank run by Palestinians. So they said to themselves: "Why don't we blow them up?" So, between them, the Americans and the Lebanese began to spread rumours against us. The Central Bank of Lebanon here, and the Zionist banking lobby in the United States, with whose financial interests we were at war, and who

liked to think of us in terms of "the tent, the camel and the desert", fought us – resisting the arrival of our flag on Sixth Avenue, which was for them an inconvenient demonstration that we were civilized.'

The rumours were effective. There was a run on Intra-bank's reserves, and within a few days the empire which Badr Fahoum and his colleagues had built was in ruins. The Lebanese charged the bank with fraudulent practice. Intra fought the case and won, bearing out the view which is now almost universal in the financial world, that Intra-bank was brought down because its economic and political enemies feared its power.

Surviving the crash without damage to his reputation, Badr Fahoum emerged from the rubble to lay the foundation stone of the Arabic Insurance Company, but he is no nearer home.

The conversation edges towards politics, in which, like so many Palestinian businessmen, he affects to take no interest. The revolution? He is guarded, insisting that he is not a politician. Yet he acknowledges without prompting that the PLO has the support of the mass of the Palestinian people, that there is no other organization which could possibly take its place. He is irritated, too, by accusations that the PLO forces funds out of rich Palestinians. For the first time in the conversation he becomes incensed by the suggestion that he would in any way dissociate himself from the struggle to return. It is an issue which frequently arises when members from various Western establishments discover that he is not only highly educated, but a rich and dedicated capitalist. They understand when he asserts the Palestinian case, but are bemused by his apparent support for the struggle to return, which they have led themselves to believe is a communist plot guided by fanatics. He is frustrated by their ignorance.

'They call the Palestinians terrorists. By what right? What do they mean? They are not terrorists. All other means have been tried. But the decisions of the UN have been thrown in the basket. How else do they force the world to listen except by using violence? You can call them terrorists if you like. They are not. They are freedom fighters.

'Do you think that I enjoy seeing innocent women and children killed? And yet look what the Jews do. They bomb our camps. It is outrageous. They are bombing civilians, yet no one ever calls them terrorists. They behave like savages and the world remains silent.

'There can be no doubt that we have the right to return. I tried to explain it this way once to the Chairman of *Time* magazine when he came to see me. "Suppose," I said to him, "that someone came to your home on Long Island and told you to get out, to find somewhere else, that you no longer had the right to live there. What would you do?" He said, "I'd call you a son-of-a-bitch and tell you to get out." I said, "You said it." I think he understood.

'If only we could have justice, then there would be room for Jews in the Arab world. We are not against the Europeans, we are not against the Jews, we are against Zionism. If they were not in our home, I would have nothing against them whatsoever.'

The guests at the reception include also the professionals, the consultants, the engineers, the lawyers and doctors. Not all of them are committed.

'My parents told me that politics and religion should never be discussed in public. I do not think about politics.'

An overweight young man has said this, turning away with his mouth full and his fork deep into the food which he had heaped upon his plate from the buffet trolley. Another is more anxious to discuss the achievements of her offspring, who – she seems to think – have escaped the stigma of being 'Palestinian':

'They have the best jobs, one of them works in senior management, another teaches at a business school.'

Indeed, a very great number of Palestinian students pursue courses in commerce and business at university. Badr Fahoum, for example, has four children, two of whom have degrees in economics and two in business administration. A broker, whose office is in London, understands the struggle against Israel: 'We must fight, those who fight have nothing to lose, no home, no land.' But he is relieved that his son prefers to remain in London.

'He wants to be peacefully there, out of the way of the struggle. He feels sympathy with the cause but frankly it is not a particularly strong feeling. I think he hates politics.'

Although the PLO, and Fatah particularly, rely heavily on contributions from rich Palestinians (who would like to see the democratic state in Palestine devote itself to capitalism, where they could be secure in business), those of the élite who are indifferent to the cause are held in disdain by the militants. Unlike the refugees who huddled in the tents, many of these well-rounded, well-polished and well-groomed exiles were sheltered in second houses, acquired long before the Catastrophe. Insulated by money, they side-stepped the misery and drove the images of humiliation out of their mind. To keep their self-respect intact, they chose to forget that they were Palestinians, embracing the cause of 'Arabism' with the fervour of those who suspected that it would come to very little. In exile they prospered. They had talent and skills to lay out in the market-place.

Nor did they suffer at the hands of the Lebanese secret police. They had work-permits, and were quickly offered passports by backward states, anxious for their skills. Nor were they threatened for asserting their identity, for saying, 'I am Palestinian,' because they never wished to say it, slipping instead into the disguise of modern 'international' man. But their hatred of Zionism, and sometimes (because they failed to make the distinction) of Jewry, festered. Their exile rankled. The thought had to be suppressed that perhaps they had a duty themselves to the people to whom they belonged, and over whom once they had held some sway. The camps were an embarrassment, a persistent reminder to them of obligations not fulfilled. When young men, of a different, fierce determination managed to escape from that incarceration to fight their way into university, and from there into the jobs provided for professionals, making them the peers of the élite, but retained their passion, determining to put their talent at the service of the Resistance, the members of *haute-bourgeoisie* found themselves face-to-face with their own muddled and long-suppressed identity, confronting the choice they had hoped to escape. Were they Palestinian? If so, should they serve the revolution?

Although they managed to resolve these questions into ambiguities like 'What is a Palestinian?' and 'How do we serve?' the responsibility could not be escaped. The revolution insisted that the Palestinian cause could no longer be ignored. The resurgence of the camps had to be answered in the boardroom and executive suites: are you for us or against us? In the end there was no real choice. Once the élite faced up to their national identity, they found themselves no longer embarrassed by the camps, which instead became a source of pride. At the same time, the PLO, growing in wealth and stature, needed expertise and went in search of the élite.

The élite then became curious, seeing that the PLO was not simply a military organization, an army of desperados whose excesses they deplored, but that it was a financial and economic institution as powerful as many multinationals. They saw the schools, the hospitals and the workshops. They counted the bureaucrats needed to run them. They saw the pension schemes and the scholarships, the radio stations, the research centre with its books, magazines, newspapers, pamphlets and growing library; the diplomatic corps with offices around the world, the information department with its press officers, film-makers and journalists; they noticed the transport fleet, the imports and exports, the real-estate, the office blocks and apartments, the shops; they realized that the international bank virtually controlled by the PLO was becoming a significant influence in the money markets of the Middle East. They saw this, and they realized that the 'terrorists' they had tried to ignore were, in reality, the leaders of an organization which had all the elements of a provisional government, complete with an embryo civil service. And seeing this, they came to recognize that the PLO would be the star around which the future of the Palestinian people revolved; and sensing this, many of them were sucked into its orbit – albeit in the most discreet manner – dovetailing their professional ambition with their national obligation, and in the process once again influencing their people's destiny.

A crisis of identity has never afflicted Ahram Zuayter, who is also a guest at the reception. Zuayter emerged from his internment by the British to become a prominent Palestinian diplomat, representing Jordan in the Arab world and at the United Nations. He now lives in Beirut with his wife and four children. Their apartment is in the Western suburbs, and looks out towards the mountains which rise up to the east of Beirut. Below the veranda on some waste ground is a temporary barracks for the Syrian army, empty except for the jagged remains of some military trucks, bombed or burnt out in the war. Lebanon remains the battleground upon which those who compete to determine the destiny of the Palestinian people spill one another's blood. The Syrians have not shunned their part in the tragedy, intervening first upon one side and then upon the other, inflicting heavy casualties upon right and left, Christian and Moslem, Lebanese and Palestinian with indiscriminate military precision according to the dictates of their strategy.

Ahram Zuayter's home is an elegant refuge from the barbarities of the conflict. It is free of the mock Louis XIV vulgarity which disfigures so many opulent apartments in the Middle East. Instead, there is a confident display of aesthetic and intellectual discrimination. Persian rugs and ancient Chinese vases are unobtrusive but carefully placed to attract the discerning eye. A bookcase in delicately grained wood is filled with old Arabic manuscripts, letters, texts and poems, with European writings of the eighteenth and nineteenth centuries in French, German and English, well-thumbed and marked: Voltaire, Goethe and, among the historians, Arnold Toynbee, much fav-

oured by Palestinians for his drily devastating assault on British colonial policy in their country. It might be thought that, in this environment, passion and commitment would have been driven out long ago. Such is not the case.

Ahram Zuayter is reading his diaries for the memoirs upon which he is now engaged. 'See this, see this,' he says excitedly, scattering a pile of yellowing paper on his desk. 'You must see this. You remember I was telling you about the British. Here it is . . .' He reads from a tattered diary, dated 6 June 1938:

' "Today the military court sentenced Ali Khalil to death for having a pistol." You know that the most remarkable attribute of you British is your capacity to forget. How can you forget? You were the cause of our tragedy.'

Passion conflicts with courtesy, and Ahram Zuayter is quick to explain that he refers not to the British people but to the government which represented them in those dark days.

His children have been nurtured by their father's commitment, and it now inhabits their personalities with equal conviction, so that although they were born after the Catastrophe, they are as vehemently attached to Palestine as their father.

Sari, the eldest, is twenty-four, an engineering consultant who works for an Abu Dhabi construction company; Razan, who is twenty-two, is the only woman in Lebanon to have become an agricultural engineer; Ayman, who is a year younger, is an architectural student at the American University; and the youngest, Aroub, is nineteen, at the same university, studying public health.

Their skills, which are in great demand in the Middle East, command high salaries and offer a life far removed from the rigours of the Palestinian struggle. They could deny their past, and assert that fashionable internationality which owes no allegiance to either man or place. They would slip easily into that future, lacking neither talent nor charm, and being gifted with the air of confident modesty upon which the practice of diplomacy depends. But they are not free of Palestine.

Sari believes that he has no choice in the matter; it is a question of identity.

'I am a Palestinian. To me life is not only a comfortable flat and a lot of money. I prefer to live in any small house in Nablos than to live here in elegance as the son of an ambassador. It is very hard to live away from your roots.'

He speaks gently, in precise English, using words with care.

'I believe that there is a contradiction between us and Zionism. The only way in which the world can be reminded of our existence is by force. We

cannot be without our identity. Our identity is Palestinian and we can only assert this by struggle. And that means the PLO. If I want to go back, I must struggle. If I want to go back, I must stand by the PLO.'

Sari is an active socialist, and dreams of a socialist Palestine – though like most Palestinians he is reluctant to define the nature of that socialist state.

'The Palestinians don't have a distinct ideology. This is the era of national liberation. The threat from Zionism is against all Palestinians, whether they belong to the bourgeoisie or the peasantry. We are together against the enemy.'

Sari's father is evidently ill at ease with such ideological clarity, but he is tolerant of his son's political commitment.

'How can I interfere? My children know my history. If I want to stop them, they tell me that they are only following in my footsteps. I might want them to be a bit more moderate, but they are

young. When I was their age I was perhaps more radical – no, not radical, I don't like that word – I was less moderate than I am now.'

When Ahram Zuayter uses words like 'moderate' and 'radical', he refers only to the political persuasion of his offspring, not to their unswerving anti-Zionism. When Sari explains that his hope in the future will be 'to give more time to the struggle; I think the time must soon come when the struggle will take up the major part of my life', Ahram is approving; nor is the father chilled by the son's cool rationale of terror.

'I regret killing innocents. But you must be aware that the Zionists survive there only by fighting the Palestinians whose land they occupy. Those who enjoy life there are settlers and occupiers. And therefore they are soldiers and we treat them as soldiers. When they took our land they didn't think of us as "civilians". They drove us out and kept us out.

'I don't think that in itself killing benefits any-one, but the only way of letting the settlers know that there won't be an easy life for those who have taken our land is to fight them. And therefore even Munich, however horrible, was necessary.'

It is not fanaticism which drives Sari to this conclusion, but that clinical sense of political necessity which invariably defines men and women, in terms which deprive them of their humanity, as 'the enemy' – a distortion of perspective which has frequently afflicted the 'civilized' world, and from which Israelis, no less than Palestinians, are prone to suffer.

Sari's brother and sisters do not dissent from their elder brother's conclusions, though none of them is as rigorous in their analysis. Ayman is an architectural student in his second year at the American University. He's been working on a project to build prefabricated houses for the refugees from Lebanon's upheaval.

'You know that architecture is an expression of the civilization which produced it. I hope one day to build my country. I will work as an architect for my people. I don't yet know how I will devote my time when I finish, but I think I will work fully for the PLO if they want me.'

Until that choice has to be made, Ayman spends much of his spare time working with the refugees. When the Israelis invaded south Lebanon, driving a quarter of a million civilians out of their towns and villages, he went south to work among the victims.

'We collected food and tents. We brought medicine. We never stopped. But I am proud of the battle we fought. It showed that the Palestinians are strong. For eight days we stood in front of the Israeli army: 30,000 Israelis and we, our guerrilla fighters.'

Aroub is working in the dining room preparing for her exams, anxious to do well. She lacks that air of certainty which her brothers have cultivated, but her mind is no less active, and her personality is strong enough to reach its own conclusions. She speaks diffidently but with enthusiasm about problems of public health in the Middle East, and particularly among her own people in the over-crowded and often insanitary camps.

'I want to help my people in the best way I can. I don't want to sit and draw all the time like Ayman; I don't like business like Sari, and I don't want to live in the fields like Razan. I just like people and I want to help.'

At school she was a member of the New Citizen Clubs which met to discuss 'what makes a good citizen'. She now belongs to a Social Services Club to help 'our people'. It is obvious that – under normal circumstances – the intricacies of inter-national politics would not greatly interest her, that by choice she would ask no more than to work for the community by caring for those weaker than herself. But she is unable to escape politics.

'I am a Palestinian. I have no place here. My home is in Palestine. I can never be at peace in Lebanon.'

The moral seriousness which distinguishes the Zuayters occasionally causes friction between the generations, and more especially between the parents and the daughters. Only the supine are left untouched by the tension between the teachings of Islam and the secular faith of the Western world. The Zuayters are unusually emancipated and remain resolutely undismayed by their off-springs' addiction to Western music (The Who and Supertramp are a pervasive presence). Nor is it simply 'men' that are the problem. Aroub has a boy friend at the university whom she sees every day, although she does not set out to test the limits of parental tolerance. But Aroub's sister, Razan, is left in no doubt that her parents would frown upon a lasting involvement with any man but a Moslem. It causes her anxiety :

'Ninety per cent of my friends are Christian. I look differently at religion from my parents. They want me to know what someone's religion is like before I decide if I like him. For me this is im-possible. And I am stubborn about it. So they sometimes get angry.

'But I must be fair – my father is also highly intelligent. He does not only rage at me, he tries to explain. He says it will be better for the children, that logically it is better if the parents are of the same religion.

'Now I am a strong believer and it is therefore difficult for me to disagree with him. But I cannot accept that he is right. So it does cause problems.'

Razan is a woman of independent mind who is not given to overmuch introspection. Like Sari, she exhibits little self-doubt, speaking in forthright language, though, in her more extrovert nature, the emotion of fierce beliefs is less skilfully suppressed.

'Why agriculture? This is the nearest job to the earth there is. Farmers are simple people and so am I. And you know how generous the earth is. Even if people abandon the soil, it remains as the only source of life. This may sound philosophical, but it is practical too. In my opinion, if you don't ad-vance in agriculture you won't advance in any-thing else.

'The first thing I do when I return is to help develop our agriculture. You know that I think of our land, of our orchards at Nablos, every day,

The Zuayter family: Sari, Ayman, Aroub, Razan, Zeena, Ahram

though I have not seen them since 1967. You might think that I will be satisfied with my standard of life here in Lebanon. But I don't have an identity here. I'm not a Jew. I'm not an Israeli, I'm a Palestinian. It is true that we don't suffer material discomfort, but we need more than that. We need our pride and our dignity.'

She becomes insistent, almost beseeching.

'I know that my people were kicked out. I know that my people are suffering in prisons in the West Bank, and I know that they are calling me. I hear Palestine calling all Palestinians whoever they are or wherever they might be. You are torn apart by the suffering of your brothers in the camps. When a person knows about Palestine, the "holy hatred", as my father calls it, becomes deeper. It is not a real hatred but a complete rejection. I refuse Israel. They want it for the Jews alone. I am telling you my personal feelings. I do not think that one religion is better than another. But how can people find a logic in Israel? I can't understand it – setting up a state for a religion. This destroys me.

'They tell me that because Jews were tortured in Germany, then we must be tortured in exile. But why must we be tortured?

'I am with the PLO. It is our only hope. I think that anyone who is Palestinian and not partici-

pating in the revolution is a . . .' – she pauses – '. . . a traitor . . .' – and she smiles, abashed at finding herself driven to use so fierce a term. It is easy to see the father in the daughter: the outrage at the knowledge of injustice, and the frustration at the sense of impotence before her perception of the world's indifference.

Razan's room is a feminine retreat. Pretty dresses on the bed, the smell of powder, bottles and jars, a blow-dryer and a tape-recorder in higgledy-piggledy array. But on the wall, among the photographs, is one of a young man, looking out impenetrably. He is a cousin, a Fatah representative in Italy, who was assassinated in 1973.

'He never held a gun in his life. He was a vegetarian, he loved poetry and music – which is why he chose to live in Italy. He spoke three languages. And they – the Israelis – put twelve bullets through him. Why? He was a civilian, a civilian. Why? Because he was fighting for our cause.'

Razan also had a diploma from an Illinois high school where she was an exchange student three years ago.

In appreciation for your contribution to world understanding.

Razan's warmth and charm were evidently a diplomatic advantage in Illinois, where she made twenty-five speeches altogether about the Palestinian cause, to audiences which were usually ignorant, sometimes suspicious, and occasionally hostile.

'I was asked to talk to the classes, and most of them really wanted to know. I would say at the beginning, "What shall I talk about? Politics or social affairs?" They always wanted to talk about politics. Then it became very difficult. The Americans had been brought up in ignorance of us. Once or twice they even booed when I attacked Zionism. Once there was a girl who asked some very fierce questions: "Why do you want to kick the Jews out of Israel?" – things like that.

'I tried to explain that we didn't want to kick them out, but that Palestine is ours and it must be a democratic state in which we live together, not a racialist state as it is now.

'Afterwards this girl came up to me and I was very touched. She said that she was a Jew and had tried to put me down, but she understood a little more now. After that we became real friends.'

There is also a poster on Razan's wall, in which the dove of peace and the guerrilla gun are depicted in juxtaposition, offering the alternatives posed by Yasser Arafat at the United Nations. Another shows the Palestinians – fighters, peasants, workers, women and children – as the branches of a tree whose roots are in Palestine: a symbol of the unity upon which, Razan believes, victory will depend.

'I help in the camps, in the hospitals, I am always ready to serve the cause. Sometimes we go to the south, to the poor villages. It is like a work camp.

We empty garbage, dig drains and help repair the damage that was done by the Israelis. My mother is always very worried. And she always tells me that I shouldn't sleep out. Occasionally she can get very angry – especially with me because I'm very stubborn.

'It is difficult for her and for my father. They think a great deal about Palestine and it makes them nervous and angry very quickly. Sometimes, when my father disagrees with me he will point his finger and talk about "your army" – meaning Fatah. But he understands really. He is a real friend of ours. But it is natural for our parents to worry.'

Zeena Zuayter is torn between pride and fear at her children's commitments. She is a cultivated woman whose life has been circumscribed by the diplomatic circuit which she has trodden for most of her adult life. Her life is a permanent preparation for the cocktail parties and formal receptions which the ambassadorial wife is obliged to attend. Zeena Zuayter can be as glitteringly elegant as protocol requires, though she is rarely able to disguise the volatility of a woman who loves her homeland and children with conflicting intensity.

'I am a mother and I feel as a mother. But if they go for the sake of Palestine, they must go. It is our land. We come from Nablos, where we had orange groves. They took our land. We feel anger about this. And my children must do their duty.

'I hope that they do not need to fight. But if they must fight, then . . .' – she gestures, as if to say that, under the circumstances, she would have neither the power nor the will to prevent them.

Twelve
Voices in Art

An oboe concerto by Albinoni is playing in the background. A cat with a white collar is curled up on a sofa. The walls are covered with paintings: minor masters of European art from the late nineteenth century, an abstract of the Manhattan skyline, poppies in the Bekka Valley. A light but carefully chosen lunch, with fragrant white wine, is served by the housekeeper. The apartment is in the centre of Beirut, and Afif Bulos, its owner, is quietly, fastidiously and elegantly at ease in his domain.

Afif Bulos is a prominent member of the city's intelligentsia. He teaches English at the Beirut University College, and has taught at the American University and in the United States, at Princeton and Harvard. He founded the Orpheus Choir, which is renowned in Lebanon for its performances of Gilbert and Sullivan, whose works have not yet fallen out of fashion in the Middle East. In 1974, he was awarded the Order of the Cedars for the distinction which he brought to Lebanese music; and a year later, he received the MBE for his services to British culture.

His main concern at the moment is with the choir. Before the civil war it had sixty-five members. Now there are twenty-eight because the rest have left the country or become casualties of the fighting. When UNRWA moves its headquarters from Beirut to Vienna, he will lose two more singers. He fears that it will be a long time before his choir will be able to perform to its former high standard.

Although he managed to insulate himself from the worst of the war's ravages by remaining at home, he found that the conflict had most disagreeable aspects.

'I remember arguing with Edward Said [the distinguished Palestinian intellectual who lives in the United States]. He is a friend of mine. He told me that the war was between "left" and "right", but while he was in America I lived through the horrors here. What I saw was a good-for-nothing fellow, a fourteen-year-old boy, asking me for my identity card or a little twerp in a shop almost killing me because I was trying to buy cat food. That was thuggery.

'Edward says that I'm a reactionary. Why then do we have any identity? Because we are both intellectuals, we both love music, and most of all, because we both come from the same town, from Palestine.'

The Bulos family had owned land in Palestine. His father was a prominent surgeon and his uncle owned a factory which was famous for the oils and soaps it produced from olives, for export to Europe. Afif was in England at the moment when the Catastrophe hit his people, studying at the Royal College of Music, unaware of how 'un-

Afif Bulos

pleasant' the situation had become in Palestine.

'I used to belong to a crowd in Jerusalem which I suppose you would describe as lotus-eaters. We wanted to read, write, sing, and *vivere in pace*. I had several Jewish friends, especially German Jews. We were all intellectuals together, and we were extremely sensitive to the atmosphere. As it deteriorated, I remember the young violinist, Franz Rozner, saying, "I can't stand this hatred, I must go." Myself, I took little interest in politics, although I had some British friends – among them the ADC to General Barker, who was the British commander in Palestine after the war. He would tell me that the politicians in London had tied the military's hands; that whenever they wanted to stop the Zionists, there was an outcry from Washington.'

The collapse of Palestine came as a shock to the young musician, who suddenly found himself without funds and out of contact with his parents. He had no means to return and, in any case, nowhere to go. A year spent teaching English, Arabic and music to schoolboys at Millfield paid for his music lessons, but the strain became severe. Although he had found a place in the chorus at Glyndebourne, and had sung for the BBC, he was – by the Christmas of 1948 – in despair. His deso-

lation is delicately recalled in a short story, 'The Bells of Bethlehem', whose hero, George, is stranded in England, alone in a flat on Christmas Eve, suffering from 'the homesickness which filled his soul and mind'.

His home town, as he knew it, had ceased to exist – a fact which filled him with bitterness so deep that he could hardly feel it. All the friends had been dispersed, all the little haunts had disappeared. The little villas and houses built of beautiful pink and cream stone were still standing; the garden suburbs were still there, but they were inhabited by a strange motley of people, of a different faith, speaking foreign tongues, and filled with blind hatred and fanatical aggressiveness . . . His heart ached with longing to hold in his hands some of the earth from those well-remembered hills and drink their exhilarating air . . .

George sat with closed eyes . . . then the voice of the BBC announcer said that in a minute the bells of the Church of the Nativity in Bethlehem would be heard. George sat up, alert. When the first peal rang clearly through, he shivered as though touched by a live electric wire. He sat without motion until the last peal had faded

210

away, then he turned off the wireless, his feet felt cold and numb. He drew his chair nearer to the fire, then he wept bitterly.

Afif Bulos returned to the Middle East, to Beirut, where he had been accustomed to spend his summer holidays as a child, and where his family had now taken up residence. His life seems ordered, far away in time from the Catastrophe, and detached and cushioned from the miseries of the camps. He acknowledges the observation.

'If I were in my twenties, then I might feel the urge to fight for the Return. But frankly now I would not wish to go back. In 1948 I entered a new life. What would I do in Palestine? I have a niche here, my friends are here, my relations, my possessions.

'It is too late to start again.

'But do not misunderstand me. No, I am not in the camps, but I believe absolutely in the justice of the Palestinian cause. I have deep emotional ties with Palestine. I am committed. There has been a terrible injustice. I believe, too, that although time is against us in the short run, in the long run it is on our side. Israel is doomed.'

In the foreword to Afif Bulos's volume of short stories, Edward Said notes that the writer 'not only encourages awareness – he positively creates it'. The anguish of the Catastrophe produced an outpouring of poetry and literature which remains almost unknown in the West. Unlike Bulos, most Palestinian writers are militantly committed to the revolution. Much of their work was produced in 'occupied territory'. It is bitter, angry and defiant, giving violent artistic expression to the outrage of the Arabs in Israel at the occupation of their land and the violation of their rights under Israeli rule.

The most famous Palestinian poet is probably Mahmoud Darwish, whose most popular poem is called *Investigation*. It was written in 1964, in anguished protest at the condition of the Palestinians under Israeli rule. It is directed at an Israeli interrogator in jail, but it speaks to the outside world.

Write Down,
I am an Arab,
My card number is 50,000,
I have eight children,
The ninth will come next summer.
Are you angry?

Write Down,
I am an Arab,
I cut stone with comrade labourers,
I squeeze the rock,
To get a loaf,
To get a loaf,
To get a book,
For my eight children.
But I do not plead charity,
And I do not cringe
Under your sway.
Are you angry?

Write Down,
I am an Arab,
I am a name without a title,
Steadfast in a frenzied world.

My roots sink deep
Beyond the ages,
Beyond time.

I am the son of the plough.
Of humble peasant stock.
I live in a hut
Of reed and stalk.
The hair : Jet black.
The eyes : Brown.
My Arab headdress
Scratches intruding hands,
And I prefer a dip of oil and thyme.

And please write down
On top of all,
I hate nobody,
But when I starve
I eat the flesh of my marauders.
Beware,
Beware my hunger,
Beware my wrath.

When Mahmoud Darwish was released from detention in Israel into exile, he was much in demand as an authentic and potent voice of the Resistance, asserting the will of the Palestinian people to emerge from the long night of oppression.

> We will come out of our camps
> We will come out of our exile
> We will come out of our shelters
> We will have no more shame
> If the enemy insults us.
> We will blush no more,
> We know how to manage our arms
> And we know the art of unarmed
>   self-defence
> We also know how to build
> A modern factory
> A house
> A hospital
> A school
> A bomb
> A missile
> And we know how to write the most
>   beautiful poems.

A similar defiance strides through the poetry of Samir Al-Qassem. In the penultimate stanza of his *Report of a Bankrupt*, he confronts Israel with the prospect of undying resistance:

> If you blow out the candles in my eyes,
> If you freeze all the kisses on my lips,
> If you fill my native air with lisping curses,
> Or silence my anguish,
> Forge my coin,
> Uproot the smile from my children's faces.
> If you raise a thousand walls,
> And nail my eyes to humiliation,
> Enemy of man,
> I shall not compromise
> And to the end
> I shall fight.

The Israelis were not too disposed to ignore the Resistance poets, nor did they underestimate their power. It is said that General Dayan once remarked of a poem by Fadwa Tuqan, 'This is equal to twenty commandos.' The revolt through literature against the conditions endured by Arabs under Israeli rule was as intolerable to the authorities as outright rebellion. Poets and writers were placed under house arrest, imprisoned and driven into exile. They were forced to write in secret and their poems were banned. Their pens, however, were not stilled.

> They shut me in a dark cell,
> My heart glowed with sunny torches.
> They wrote my number on the walls,
> The walls transformed to green pastures,
> They drew the face of my executioner,
> The face was soon dispersed
> With luminous braids.
> I carved your map with my teeth upon
>   the walls
> And wrote the song of fleeting night.
> I hurled defeat to obscurity
> And plunged my hands
> Into rays of light.
> They conquered nothing,
> Nothing,
> They only kindled earthquakes.

The poems smuggled out of 'occupied territory' reached the PLO, and then the Palestinians. Yahya Rabah, the boy who grew up among the Gaza tents to become a Fatah commander, is also a broadcaster who has helped to spread the clandestine message of the Palestinian poets through the PLO's radio stations throughout the Arab world.

'Our poetry is both political and patriotic. Our poets have revolutionized poetry. Traditionally Arab poems spoke to the ear, not to the mind or to the imagination. They took the narrative form, portraying romantic visions, using repetitive words and rhymes. They recounted the exploits of warriors and lovers. But the Palestinian poets have been greatly influenced by modern trends: the interior monologue, the philosophical stream of consciousness in poets like T. S. Eliot, as well as the Romantics, like Wordsworth, Shelley and Coleridge. But they have retained the power of the Arabic tongue, its variety, its ambiguity, its resonance. The combination of the modern and the ancient in Palestinian poetry gives it vitality and power so that it touches our people greatly.'

The PLO's radio stations are devoted to Palestinian propaganda, directed at the Arab world and into Israel and the occupied territories. Yahya Rabah is a sophisticated and dedicated communicator, concerned to use the limited hours of broadcasting that their transmitters relay to the greatest effect. Like the poets, broadcasters such as Yahya try to break away from the Arab traditions.

'There is a conflict between the oral tradition and modern communication. If I am writing a "Words to Palestine" [a ten-minute daily talk], I try to write to the mind and the heart, not to the ear. So many Arab broadcasters speak only to the ear, assuming that the audience is lethargic and only capable of absorbing a series of disconnected and separate ideas. I believe that there is a conflict between the sensitivity and feelings of the audience and the crude propaganda that is thrust at them. So we try to mix the oral tradition, using the imagery, symbolism and narrative style, while at the same time avoiding rhetoric, so that we can better convey a unified, coherent idea.'

PLO broadcasters operate within tight constraints. They are obliged by the leadership to avoid serious debate and argument, to hide internal dissension and dutifully to echo the united voice of the Revolution. In this self-strangulation, however, they at least copy the rest of the Arab world, although their propaganda is often in direct conflict with other Arab states. During Black September, for instance, Yahya was in Algiers, directing four short-wave stations, urging on the fedayeen against the Jordanians. In 1976, despite Arafat's conciliatory public stance, the Beirut PLO station was outspokenly critical of the Syrian assault on the fedayeen – dismaying some senior officials, who murmured presciently that it was not wise 'to attack those who will soon be our friends again'. In Cairo, Palestinian broadcasters turned upon the Egyptian authorities, an irritation that was dealt with summarily by President Sadat's decision to close down their radio station. Indeed, only in Algeria, South Yemen, Iraq, Lebanon and – jostling with scores of rivals – in San Francisco is the PLO still free to broadcast the untrammelled message of the Resistance to the world.

Those of the Arab masses who listen, hear at length about the conditions of the Palestinians in 'occupied territory'. They are reminded of hideous atrocities, like Deir Yassin and Kafr Qasim. The massacre at the village of Kafr Qasim, which occurred in 1956, and in which forty-seven innocent people were shot down in cold blood by squads of Israeli soldiers in an hour of careful and premeditated mass murder, never received great attention in the West. Yet the facts are undisputed. Palestinian exiles have learnt of them largely through the writings of the famous Palestinian author and broadcaster, Sabri Jiryis, whose account of this atrocity is compiled exclusively from official Israeli sources and appeared in his carefully compiled history, *The Arabs in Israel*, which had to be smuggled out of the country, before he too was forced to leave. Although the Israeli courts convicted eight soldiers of murder, after Kafr Qasim, they were all released within two years of their trial, and within three years one of them who had been convicted of killing forty-three Arabs in an hour was engaged by the municipality of Ramleh as the 'officer responsible for Arab affairs in the city'.

But the Palestinian radio does not only recall the past. Its leaders hear about today: about prisons and torture; detentions and deportations; students arrested and beaten; schoolchildren terrorized; land confiscated and houses blown up – about a state in which the Jews are treated to democracy and the 'non-Jews' endure a tyranny. Although this view of Israel is unrecognizable to the West, it is held, by the PLO, to be responsible in no small measure for the overwhelming support that the 1.2 million Arabs under Israeli occupation in the West Bank and Gaza Strip gave to the Resistance when they were offered their first opportunity to express their will in the ballot box.

The news from 'Palestine' is merged with legends, images and memories to become one endless, fervent statement of Palestinian intent, distilled, refined and repeated by the poets.

> Enemy of man
> The signals are raised at the forts,
> The air
> Is thronged with beckonings,
> I see them everywhere.
> I see the sails at the horizon
> Striving,
> Defying,
> The sails of Ulysses are veering home
> From the seas of the lost
> The sun is rising,
> Man is advancing,
> And for his sake,
> I swear
> I shall not compromise
> And to the end
> I shall fight
> I shall fight.

There is a tiger, assertive and outsize, straddling the rooftops of a village, claiming possession. The image states silently 'this is ours'. The painting is by Jammana Al-Husseini, one of the most successful of Palestinian artists, whose works sell on the international circuit for upwards of £(L)7,000 each. She has exhibited at the Woodstock Gallery in London, in Paris, where she has just bought a studio, in Brussels, in West and East Germany, and all over the United States. She works in Beirut in an apartment which looks out over the Mediterranean, where the sun sinks into the evening sea. You would hardly know that it belonged to a Palestinian. Its taste could be found in any one of the countries in which her paintings are on display: a zebra-skin carpet, Persian rugs, a deep-brown leather sofa, a low smoked-glass table, John

Jammana Al-Husseini

The Western Wall: liberated? Or occupied?

Barry's *The Deep* on the hi-fi. The beautiful mirrors, inlaid with mother-of-pearl and ivory, from the old Souk in the city, and the ancient headdress from Hebron, lavishly embroidered and hung about with long chains made from Ottoman coins, might have been bought to grace a Manhattan or a Paris home. Jammana Al-Husseini's identity, like her preoccupation, is not on vulgar display. She prefers to speak of herself through her paintings and will not talk of them at length. Her manner is gentle, her voice soft, her personality understated, reticent. Her face is delicate, pale, fragile. Only in the certainty of her expression is there a hint of the fierce and stubborn commitment for which her family is renowned; and of the sudden, withering anger before which even the toughest PLO man is said to blanch.

The Husseinis belong to one of Palestine's most famous families. They were the aristocrats of the Resistance. Jammana's father, Jamal, sat on the

214

Higher Committee, which organized the general strike and negotiated so disastrously to preserve Palestine, with her uncle Moussa and Haj Amin, the Mufti of Jerusalem. Jammana's earliest memories are of conflict.

'I do not remember a happy childhood. Our life was sad. My first memory is of being asleep in our home in Jerusalem and then waking up to a banging and shouting at the gate. I looked out of the window. A voice said in Arabic, "Young girl, open the door!" It was a group of British soldiers coming to take my father.'

In fact, Jamal had been forewarned and had escaped to Lebanon, disguising himself as a Bedouin. His family followed soon after, to be met on the border by an Arab who told them, 'Your father sends you his regards,' and then whipped off his headdress – 'And suddenly we saw that it was him, and that he was safe.'

Jammana lived in Lebanon and then in Iraq until

her father fled to Persia, before being captured and exiled to Rhodesia, where he remained for the duration of the Second World War, because of his persistent and active opposition to Zionism. When her father was released, he returned to Palestine, being sent to the United Nations to plead the case against partition in the autumn of 1947.

'I do not like to remember that time. It was so bad, so sad, like a nightmare. My home was bombed. My mother was alone in the house and

someone threw a hand-grenade into it. It was decided that we should leave for Beirut. We left. And we stayed for ever.

'When I am working I live in the past, with images of how it might have been. The present is sad too. I've been a refugee since I was born. You do not have to live in a tent to be a refugee. The memory of the past can be an inspiration. It makes me forget the ugliness that is present all over the Middle East today. It is getting worse and worse.

An Israeli teacher and his pupils tour occupied territory

And it all concerns the Palestinians. There is nothing but this truth, and the ugliness of this truth.'

Influenced by Mahmoud Darwish, whose work she reveres, Jammana's paintings are metaphors for the Return: the tiger, the horse, a flight of birds, butterflies – all representing 'the force which is the people' that will never surrender their claim to the homeland.

In *The Return of the Palestinians*, a white horse is poised, floating over the roofs of Jerusalem, as vast as the city, not menacing but innocent, protective, permanent. It is a vision or a dream. Only the Dome of the Rock is awake. Otherwise the old city is sombre, dark brown, at peace. In another, Jerusalem is like a fairy castle in silver; a hotch-potch of houses, vaulted arches, and a myriad pricks of yellow light, beckoning the traveller from Jericho, warm, welcoming home.

Jammana has returned to the West Bank several

217

'If you freeze all the kisses on my lips . . .'
Young Israelis by the Western Wall

times since the 1967 war. It is a miserable experience. She has in her mind the reports from the first days after the Israeli occupation. The flight of the refugees; the Arab villages blown up by dynamite or swept aside with bulldozers; the shame of some Israelis:

> We were ordered to block the entrances of the village and prevent inhabitants returning to the village from their hideouts, after they heard Israeli broadcasts urging them to go back to their homes. The order was to shoot over their heads . . . At noon the first bulldozer arrived and pulled down the first house on the edge of the village. After the destruction of three houses, the first column arrived from the direction of Ramallah . . . There were old people who could hardly walk, murmuring old women, mothers carrying babies, small children. The children asked us for water. They all carried white flags . . . They told us that they were driven out everywhere, forbidden to enter any village, that they were wandering like this for four days, without food, without water, some dying in the road . . .[41]

Others were unyielding. General Dayan addressed the kibbutz youth on the newly occupied Golan Heights, reminding them of the achievements of the early pioneers:

> Jewish villages were built in the place of Arab villages. You don't even know the names of these Arab villages, and I don't blame you, because those geography books no longer exist, not only do the books not exist, the Arab villages are not there either.

His vision of the future was equally unrelenting:

> We are doomed to live in a constant state of war with the Arabs and there is no escape from sacrifice and bloodshed. This is perhaps an undesirable situation, but it is a fact. If we are to proceed with our work against the wishes of the Arabs, we shall have to expect such sacrifices.[42]

General Dayan urged Israel's young men to perceive the Zionist vision and not to flinch in their duty.

> Twenty years ago we were 600,000; today we are near three million. There should be no Jew who says, 'That's enough' . . . Your duty is not to stop: it is to keep your sword unsheathed, to have faith, to keep the flag flying. You must not call a halt . . .[43]

Jammana Al-Husseini finds it hard to understand why rational Western men cannot detect that Zionism is – as the PLO claims – both 'racist' and 'expansionist'. On her return to 'occupied territory', she was appalled by the destruction in and around Jerusalem, as the Arab past was obliterated to make way for the Zionist future.

'Really my heart was bleeding. Palestine was being destroyed. The damage to Jerusalem, the most beautiful city in the world. The horror of the ugliness they are creating. And they are still doing it. They go on stabbing at the heart of the city. It is unforgivable. In human terms, in terms of culture, beauty and civilization, it is unforgivable. And the villages, where we the Palestinians had lived, where there are now the remains of houses, overrun with cactus. I paint to capture what was there before they destroyed it all.'

The violence of her feelings is restrained. The voice soft. She prefers, usually, not even to discuss Palestine, finding it too painful.

'This house, this studio, is my temple. I stay here. I only go out for food or to go to the bank or to buy paints. I work all the time. If I do go out, I always find myself drawn into argument, always about the Palestinians. I hate arguing, but I find I get angry and lose control. The Lebanese are always blaming us for their problems, for every little thing, and we're not always at fault.

'My uncle Moussa wants me to return to the West Bank. He is sad that I stay away. "Why don't you return?" he says. "No one should have left. If we'd all stayed they couldn't have beaten us." But if I went back, and in theory I could, I would be separated from my children. They are Palestinian, but they are not permitted to return to their country. If I went back they would remain here. We would be cut off from each other completely. I have to stay with my children.'

Her children, like the Zuayters, are militants. And so is Jammana – but discreetly. She does not work for the PLO, nor is she greatly attracted to the bulging bureaucracy that the revolution has acquired, the offices and the fast cars:

'I don't like the show. I suppose it is necessary, but it destroys the purity of the revolution.

'The revolution has restored our pride in ourselves. We were suppressed, we felt we had lost our cause. But with the Resistance, we have new hope, new horizons.

'Foreigners can never understand because they can never put themselves in our place. To see how we feel, to see that we are a people. Whether in a beautiful apartment or in a camp we are one and we help each other.'

But it is true, is it not, that some Palestinians are rather less committed than others?

'It is true, but it is rare now to find someone who is ashamed of the cause. I travel for my work and I've only once come across such a thing. There was a conference in Paris. I was with a group of Lebanese and they did not know who I was. One of them, a rather handsome young man, said jokingly, "Oh yes, we know the Palestinians all right . . ." and he gestured disdainfully as if to push us away with his hands. I said, "There is no need to push us, we want to go." There was an embarrassed silence. And then one of them said, referring to the man who had just spoken, "He was originally Palestinian, you know." I said to him, "What do you mean, 'originally'?" He said, "I'm a brother of so-and-so," naming a prominent Palestinian. So I said, "Then you're a Palestinian." "I've a Lebanese passport." "That makes no difference." "Well, I have no intention of returning to Palestine." "All right, don't go back to Palestine, but you are Palestinian, and you can never ever forget it."

'I'm afraid that I argued very severely, more than I have before. This man is ambitious. He thinks he will do well in his job if he makes a point of turning upon the Palestinians, disowning his identity. It was terrible. If I'd heard of it happening, I could never have believed it.

'I am working for my country, I sell my paintings abroad and it is for my country. I try to help Palestinians in difficulties. I do not like to say what or how much I do, but I help in many ways. It is in my blood. I have no choice.

'What are my thoughts about the "armed struggle"? It is natural. The south of Lebanon is not our home, not our land. We know that we are not really wanted there. But we have no choice. We have to fight to preserve our existence. When a fighter goes into Israel, he feels his identity, he becomes himself, he is at home.'

Thirteen
The Long Struggle

Of the poor, Damour is the poorest. Of the wretched, Damour is the most wretched. The town is a ruin, gutted. The houses that still stand – that have not been pounded into rubble – are pockmarked by bullets and scorched by flames. There are no doors, no windows, no glass. Sacks and plastic sheeting ineffectively challenge the wind and rain which drives in from the Mediterranean. Inside, the houses are barren: rickety chairs, perhaps a table, broken doors or planks serving as beds, and upturned orange boxes in which are stowed neat, frugal piles of clothes. There are no fridges, few televisions, rarely a cooker.

It is the people, however, that best express Damour. The men who are not there, the women who sit listlessly in doorways, the children unnaturally subdued, incurious. It is two years after Tal-Al-Zaater, but it might be two months.

Damour was once a pleasant and prosperous small town in the Beirut commuter belt. Its houses were built of stone, conforming to unusually high standards of architectural aesthetics. The people were Christians. In so far as they owed allegiance, it was to the antiquated leadership of Camille Chamoun and Pierre Gemayel, whose militia vied with each other for control of the town. In the civil war, Damour occupied a strategic position on the coast road linking Sidon to Beirut, a crucial

route between the secure Palestinian bases in the south and the front line in the capital. The military argument for the seizure of Damour was compelling, although for some months the Palestinians and their leftist allies stayed their hand.

The sack of Damour was, in the end, not so much a military operation as an act of revenge for the hideous slaughter in Karantina and Maslakh, in which the rightist militia 'cleansed' west Beirut of a few thousand of its most vulnerable and impoverished inhabitants.

In reflex, the left and the Palestinians drove the people of Damour out of their houses, down to the edge of the sea, and into the boats which carried them to the security of a partially purified west Beirut. But there still remained Tal-Al-Zaater, the fortress in which upwards of 30,000 Palestinian refugees came under siege in the late spring of 1976. Unlike Karantina, Tal-Al-Zaater was defended by an array of sophisticated weaponry, which had originally been intended to protect its inhabitants from Israeli – not Lebanese – attack. The horror of Tal-Al-Zaater has been well documented and widely reported: the fifty days of unremitting shellfire, directed indiscriminately into the camp, forcing the population into underground shelters where they stayed until they started to die of starvation and thirst, and the PLO finally ordered

their exhausted fighters to surrender. After the siege there were the atrocities: the innocents who had not already perished were now exterminated with a ferocious brutality that appalled even those who had become accustomed to the barbarism by which the Lebanon had been held in thrall for so many months.

By now it had become clear, even to the most naïve observer, that the 'civil' war was not merely a confrontation between competing religions and classes. It no longer required a conspiracy theorist to perceive that, besides the Lebanese themselves, the principal participants in the 'civil' war had come to include, among others, the Syrians, the Iraqis, the Egyptians, the Saudis, the Israelis and the United States.

And why, it was now asked, were so many states manoeuvring upon this battleground, albeit in dif-

The people of Karantina fled en masse to escape the rightist onslaught. Those who did not escape were massacred. The homes of 10,000 people were razed to the ground

fering ways and to differing degrees? For Palestinians, the explanation begins with the Balfour Declaration, continues through the Arab rebellion, via the Catastrophe, to the wars of 1956 and 1967, to the Black September of 1970, on to the war of 1973, until it reaches the Lebanon, where in 1976 the Palestinians were fighting not only to preserve their last stronghold in the Middle East, but for their survival, and with it the right to insist that no 'settlement' in the Middle East that was engineered over their heads or against their will could be worth the treacherous paper upon which it was written.

The survivors of Tal-Al-Zaater shambled out of the carnage eventually, to find shelter in the ruins of Damour, where, despite the best efforts of clinics and workshops, the trauma persists. Those who have seen a baby garrotted, a husband tied between

Damour: a refugee from Tal-Al-Zaater whose entire family perished in the massacre

'The heroism of Tal-Al-Zaater had come to symbolize the Resistance itself'

Her mother and father were both killed

The father is dead, the family live in the ruins of Damour

A survivor

two vehicles facing in opposite directions, and then torn in half as they accelerate away, or teenage boys lined up and 'executed' by a firing squad, and little girls suffocated under the press of panic-stricken bodies which filled the trucks that drove them to safety, do not quickly recover. In the summer of 1978, two years after Tal-Al-Zaater, Damour's wounds had yet to heal.

In Palestinian mythology, the heroism of Tal-Al-Zaater had come to symbolize the Resistance itself. But in Damour the survivors remembered the horror, and some of them still recalled with bitterness the 'failure' of the PLO to counter-attack, to descend from the mountains to lift the siege. And these people were not satisfied with the PLO's explanation that it was impossible to spare fighters from the front line to engage the Syrians (whose 'peace-keeping role' at this time was still devoted primarily to securing the submission of the PLO to the diktat of Damascus). These dissidents had grouped themselves around Ali Salim, whose courageous leadership in Tal-Al-Zaater had made him a hero in the refugee camps of Lebanon, and who had become openly critical of the PLO leadership.

In August 1978, on the personal instruction of Yasser Arafat, Ali Salim was executed.

To extract the truth from the maze of rumours which followed was not simple. He was variously accused of intimidating the people of Damour, running a brothel and raping a girl. It was on these grounds that Abu Jihad insists, in the most vehement and agitated manner, that the 'extreme action' taken against Ali Salim was justified.

'When our resistance began, even in 1936, the men would say, "You see the families of the martyrs, the women and children, they are begging in the market-place and you expect us to become fighters?" This is a most sensitive issue for us. The fighters have to know that we will care for their families. At the moment we do this, protecting financially and in other ways no less than 25,000 families, 250,000 people. This is the social security that we provide for our fighters. But if for a moment they thought that they could be killed and then something like this could happen to their families, it would be very serious indeed for the revolution. That is why we acted in this way.'

Nevertheless, none of these charges was put to the test in a PLO court: there was no trial, no

conviction; only execution. Since the PLO has a reputation among Palestinians for operating a meticulous – albeit unofficial – judicial system, it was obvious that the execution of Ali Salim was of greater significance than the unproven charges suggested. It did not take long to discover that he had been a friend of the 'renegade' Fatah leader, Abu Nidal, who from his refuge in Baghdad had been organizing a campaign directed against the PLO, with the avowed purpose of unseating if not eliminating Yasser Arafat.

Those who recalled this remembered, too, that members of Group 17, Yasser Arafat's personal security service, had been sent into Damour to investigate not the moral frailties of its leaders but their political affiliations. Their task, to put it as crudely as they have the reputation for fulfilling it, was to root out friends and sympathizers of

Damour's wounds have yet to heal

Abu Nidal. By all accounts, these security officers imposed the equivalent of martial law upon Damour, over-ruling the unhappy Fatah officials who were in nominal control of the town, and subjecting its inhabitants to a brief but disconcerting reign of terror.

The execution of Ali Salim exposed a raw nerve in the Resistance. Whether or not the hero of Tal-Al-Zaater was in league with Abu Nidal, the un-precedented manner by which he was silenced provoked bitter debate within the PLO, and more particularly within Fatah itself. Why had there been no trial? Was this an act of revenge against Abu Nidal? Was it a warning to other such friends? Was this a precedent? Was it a symptom of the new despotism which some feared threatened to cloud Arafat's judgement? Or was it an isolated incident to be explained by the extreme pressures

The survivors do not forget

of the moment? However they answered, normally discreet Palestinians were unable to conceal their dismay at the sudden erosion of the moral and political principles upon which they had believed the Resistance to be based. Within the limitations imposed upon them by a state of permanent emergency, the Palestinians are fiercely protective of the democratic rules which govern their institutions, and by which the delicate coalition of competing interests which forms the PLO is preserved from disintegration. Yasser Arafat, for once, departed from the guidelines he himself established. One of his critics, who had turned away from him in rage a few days after the incident, reflected the Palestinian anguish:

'I don't for a moment doubt Abu Ammar. I doubt neither his aims, nor his motives, nor his leadership for one moment. But we become the losers if we are driven to such measures. We must retain our humanity, otherwise we will lose our revolution.'

The debate gradually faded under the press of new developments: the dangerous confrontation in Beirut between the Syrians and, by way of the proxy force of the Phalange, the Israelis; the Camp David summit; the Baghdad counter-summit;

the rapprochement between Iraq and Syria; the crisis surrounding the Begin/Sadat settlement and their subsequent peace treaty. Soon Palestinians were inclined to look upon the Damour incident as a disturbing but not critical symptom of the stresses to which the PLO is perennially subject. If Arafat could be autocratic – even sometimes dictatorial – it was because he had been driven into a corner from which there was no other diplomatic escape.

In public, the PLO speaks with a united voice, and in so far as it expresses the minimum position that the confrontation with Israel must be unremitting, its spokesmen express a consensus. But they also hide basic questions. Do the West Bankers really feel as fiercely about the right of return as the exiles from Galilee, from Acre, Jaffa and Haifa? And how deep is the unity between rich and poor? Or between those who receive their political education (and sometimes their orders) from opposing Arab states with conflicting designs? And what is the advice that they tender? And what influence do they exert? And how can these differences be reconciled?

These social and political cracks are interlaced by ideological chasms. On the one extreme there are those who reject any compromise; who counsel against dealings not only with Israel and the United States, but also with every 'reactionary' régime in the Arab world. On the other, there are those who sit in the inner councils of Fatah, urging an end to the military struggle and the acceptance of a West Bank 'entity' under the tutelage of King Hussein. Both these minorities have influence, if only to the extent that they anchor the majority within the PLO – which will not, in the words of one of its leading members, 'deviate from the ultimate objective of the destruction of the Zionist state in Palestine and its replacement by a secular democracy', but does not object to the tactical manoeuvres for which Yasser Arafat is renowned.

Within the majority, there are numerous minorities who differ about strategy, about the style of Arafat's leadership, about the role of their institutions, about the degree of influence that should be permitted to competing factions – but the whole is more united than the sum of its parts.

Yasser Arafat's diplomacy is conditioned by his need to retain this unity as well as to lead the Palestinians towards the Return. He must preserve his position in the quasi-democratic institution which he leads and ensure that his freedom of tactical manoeuvre is not unduly restricted by minds that are not as free of naïvety as is his own. In public he is therefore careful to sidestep the basic issues, reiterating instead a series of ringing but ambiguous declarations of Palestinian resolve. Rarely does he permit himself to let slip an unequivocal statement of policy on the most delicate issues that face the Resistance. Instead, he hammers a variety of fiercely expressed but predictable themes: that the Palestinians seek to establish a democratic, secular, progressive state in Palestine; that Zionism and imperialism are in league to thwart this just aspiration; that the Resistance will continue until a just peace is achieved; that President Sadat's initiative is an act of treachery; that the Palestinians will accept a state in any part of 'liberated' Palestine, but that the future relations of this state, either with Israel or other Arab states, will be determined by the Palestinians themselves – all of which, in the Arab world, is tantamount to asserting that you are against sin and in favour of righteousness.

The respect in which Arafat is held by other Arab leaders – grudging though it occasionally is – springs from their recognition of his enormous talent. Again and again he has reconciled conflicting trends within the PLO while out-manoeuvring Arab régimes bent upon his imprisonment to their will – securing the Resistance from disintegration on the one hand and dismemberment on the other.

He has led the PLO first to the Rabat Summit in 1974, where it was recognized as the sole legitimate representative of the Palestinian people, and thence to the United Nations, where, to the outrage of Israel, he was greeted with all the deference reserved for a visiting head of state. Under his leadership, it has slowly been impressed upon the West that the PLO is not simply a gang of desperados; that the conflict with Israel, however dreadful the methods sometimes adopted, is no less honourable than any other national liberation struggle; and that without the PLO there is little prospect of lasting peace in the Middle East.

And yet this awareness has made little discernible impact upon Western strategy. To the irritation of Palestinians, Western diplomats persist in behaving as if the PLO can be sidestepped; as if a treaty between Israel and Egypt, under the direction of the United States, could bring a settlement to the Middle East – which, they assume, most of the Arab world would secretly welcome. Such 'optimism' reminds Palestinians of the imperial arrogance which originally initiated the tragedy fifty years ago. They conclude that the Western world is still purblind: that it still fails to realize that no people can be managed, manipulated or driven into accepting the intolerable; that the Palestinians will not meekly surrender themselves to a 'homeland' in the West Bank – a bantustan under the tutelage of outside powers, either under continued occupation or the threat of assault from Israel, created in violation of the normal rules governing international relations, without real self-determination, in defiance of those two thirds of the Palestinian people who still remain in exile, and who (while their compatriots were silenced by the Israeli occupation) led the resurgence which propelled their nation back into the argument. Such a 'settlement', they argued vehemently, will merely provoke increasingly bitter confrontation and even greater upheaval.

For Abu Jihad, the co-founder of Fatah with Yasser Arafat, that brand of diplomacy which seeks to heal the festering wound of the Middle East by the application of a sticking plaster is a dangerous and foolish waste of time, perpetuating the self-delusion that those things which are hidden are not there.

'Of course we dream of peace. I want to be with my family in peace. But our dreams are destroyed by reality. We are obliged to fight and to remind the world that we exist. If we were to wait for the world's conscience, we would never return.

'Surely it is now understood that we are at war with the Israelis. The Israelis are at war with the Palestinian revolution. This war will continue until

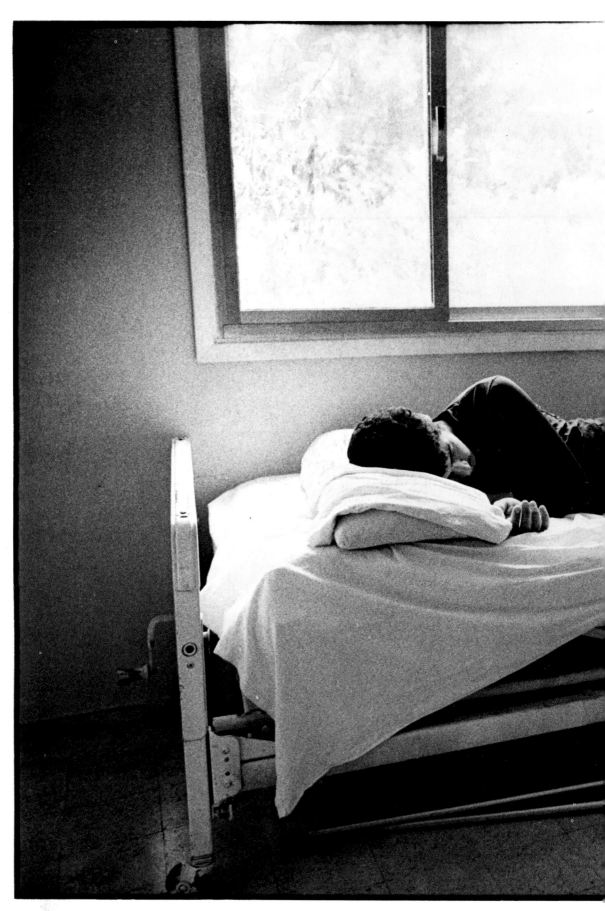

One of the 100.000 casualties of the Lebanese war. A Palestinian with his leg amputated

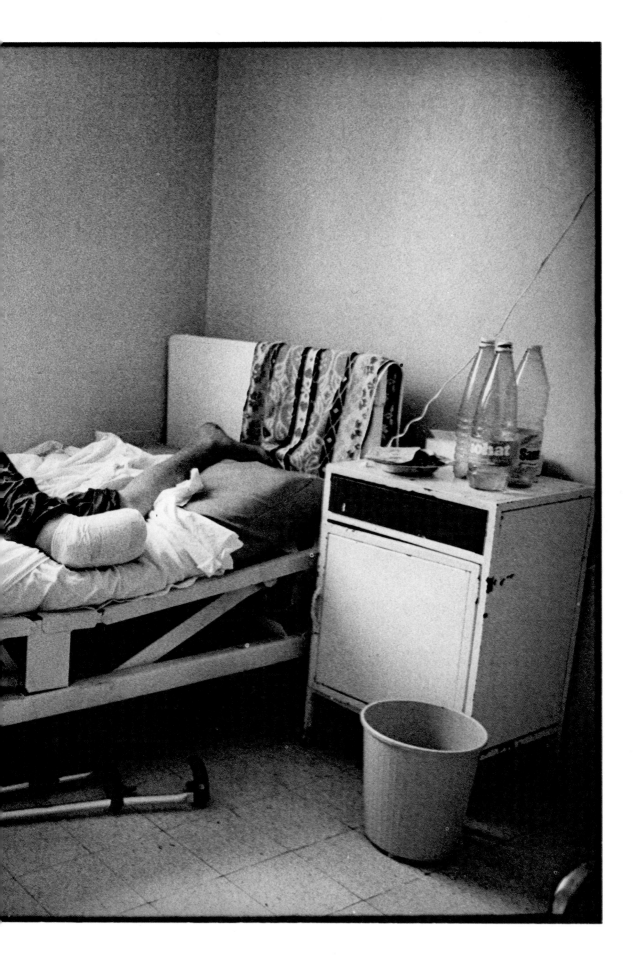

there is a just peace.

'I want my home, I want my passport. I want my national flag. I want to live like a human being. And for this I have to fight.'

At the United Nations, Yasser Arafat stood before the world 'bearing an olive branch and a freedom fighter's gun'. He held out the vision of a secular, democratic state in which Jew and Arab could live together as equals in brotherhood. But the olive branch soon withered. The PLO was still refused admittance to the negotiating chamber. The guns did not fall silent. The bitter alternative – terror and counter-terror – still held sway. Nor is the majority now optimistic, believing rather that the Israelis will remain intransigent until they are forced to concede. Until that time, most of them believe, any discussion of the 'Palestinian state' is a waste of their energy. As articulated by Salah Tamari, their reasoning is bleak.

'We believe that the creation of a Palestinian state would be a very great step towards the establishment of a secular state in Palestine. Why? The conflict between the Palestinians and the Zionists is between two wills, two existences. One of the pillars of the Israeli state is the ideology which asserts that Palestine was a country without people; that there is no Palestinian people.

'Therefore, for them to accept a Palestinian state is to retreat a very great deal. If we get that we will have initiated the decline of the state of Israel. I do not see their leaders permitting such a thing of their own free will.

'So I believe that we should not waste time arguing about the new state lest it breed the illusion that we are about to have it. We cannot lay our heads upon the soft pillow of a settlement arranged by others. We cannot afford to allow a crack in our unity. There will be no state offered us. We must fight.'

Yasser Arafat, chairman of the PLO

Fourteen
In Salah's House

In Salah Tamari's house, two men are playing chess. One of them, his nephew, is young, neatly dressed, with close-cropped hair, relaxed. The other, his brother, is dishevelled, tense, irritated by the little boy and girl, the children of his opponent who keep interrupting the game, distracting their father from his imminent victory, and him from his embattled queen. There could hardly be two men so different in appearance. Salah is in a corner, smoking, watching them. It is Sunday; the phone is silent for once and the parade through the house of Fatah officials in search of instructions, advice or conversation has ceased for the afternoon. This is a family occasion.

Salah talks softly about his brother, who is called Said.

'I feel guilty about him. He carries the burden of our family. He lives in Kuwait and comes here once a year just to take his exams at the Arab University. His life is barely tolerable. He's a clever man but he is under terrible pressure all the time.

'If I could help him, I would go on ten suicide missions to spare him.'

Said is about to lose the game. He is out of practice, upset at losing, at the noise, at the exams which begin tomorrow. He is perspiring in the heat, his brow wrinkled. His face is open and honest, but his expression is unendurably sad. He is only thirty-four but he looks at least ten years older. Once he was a body-builder, a champion. Now his physique has collapsed; he is pasty and slackly overweight. He is a trapped man. There is no self-pity in his manner, however. He speaks fast, impatiently, his thoughts tumbling out, but more detached than his words might suggest.

'I am an accountant in Kuwait. I have my brothers and sisters to care for, so I need to do well. I have to advance as much as possible so that I can force my employers to recognize that they need me. They have to know that if I go, they would need two men to replace me. As a Palestinian we have no security anywhere, my situation is not uncommon.

'I think only of the rent, of keeping my job, and of feeding the family. I am killing myself, I feel it. But the rest of the family must study. I have two sisters at university in Alexandria, and two living with me.

'I must pay for their learning. If you know things, you're safe from danger. If you have another language, you have another possible personality. Two languages is two personalities. Weapons are not our only way out. It is not like ten years ago. Our brains are weapons now also. It is this that will guide us to a solution. Thirty years ago we were ignorant, poor and hungry. We thought

Salah Tamari and his wife Dina

only of survival. If we had been educated, we would have found a way out. Now we will.

'I am like 90 per cent of the Palestinians. My life is reading and writing and working. After the war of 1967, I gave up all pleasures, I stopped sport, I stopped singing. I have no joy.

'Tomorrow I start my exams. From 1 July to 20 July, every day; thirty-four exams. I've not been able to give enough time to the preparation. I don't know enough. I work alone at night for an hour or two only and it is a full-time course. But my work takes up fourteen hours of my day. So I use the Canadian, quick-reading method to help. It is not the right way to study, but I have no choice.

'There are thousands in the same state. After the exams I have to return to Kuwait with next year's work. I will come back again next summer for the next lot of exams, if I pass. I am tired.

'I know Salah worries about me. I tell him it is unnecessary. We have to unite as a people if we are to survive. We can only survive if we have our land back. Only the PLO is capable of mobilizing our scattered people. The PLO is Salah's life. His love is the land, the land, the land. He lives with ideas. His work is not a job, it is his life. And I

never burden him with my problems if I can help it. I am responsible for the family. He is responsible for the revolution. Like lots of Palestinians, we depend on each other.'

Salah's cousin has driven from Tyre, about forty-five minutes away, where his children live with his wife. He is the youngest officer in Fatah, and is frequently away from home for six months at a time. At the moment he is based near Tibe, in south Lebanon, and he has the weekend off. He has brought his two children, Basan who is nearly four, and Dina (named after Salah's wife) who is two and a half, to see their Uncle Salah, who adores them. Conversation with him is punctuated by his attempts to dissuade his daughter from eating an ivory bishop, and his son from pinning Salah to the ground in hand-to-hand combat. He is matter-of-fact, soldierly about his job.

'I have been into Israel. It is very difficult. They not only have barbed wire, it is electrified. There are mines, sensory devices, anti-personnel bombs, hidden trenches. All kinds of alarm systems. We go at night, cutting our way through the wire. We have shoes with hooked nails on the bottom so that we can climb up to eight metres high. And we take mattresses to throw them over so that we have a soft landing. If we have to cut the wire, we tighten it with ropes so that there is no sudden reflex.

'It is now almost impossible in the Jordan Valley because you have to clear such a distance between the river and the mountains before it gets light. In the north it is easier because the terrain is rougher.'

Salah interrupts his game with the children, who are trying to drag him out of the front door and whose smart Sunday uniforms are now in complete disarray.

'Whenever I went across I used to consider myself as a dead man. That is why we can carry out suicide missions. There is no mission that is not likely to end in death.'

His cousin continues:

'Before you go you wonder if you'll come back. You think about your land, about the occupier, about the job, about how best to do it, and, of course, about my family, about my wife and children. But when you are there, you are very cool, your head is very clear. You are not happy but confident.

'What are my hopes for my children? I do not think of them apart from their land. The best I can do for them is to help them return. If not in my life, then perhaps in their life.'

He pauses and quite unselfconsciously lifts both of his children on to his lap, and cuddles them. He is still quite matter-of-fact.

'My son is now too small to teach. However, he already knows where our land is, why we are in exile, why he can't see me often and why he never sees my mother and father who are still in occupied territory. But I have much to teach him. If I die before we return, well . . .'

He shrugs, and Salah picks up the thread:

'Our motive is love, love for our country, not hatred for our enemy. Hate leads to despair. And it must be admitted that there are some Palestinians who concentrate on the hatred. They are the first to despair, the first to behave in an extreme fashion, to take drastic action.'

Salah is never at ease with violence. His friends say that he is always 'beating his head against the wall', wondering whether this or that is right or wrong. When a few Palestinians joined the Lebanese leftists in looting the town of Damour after it was seized from the Chamounists in 1976, following a fierce struggle, he was horrified by the indiscipline. It is said that he alone saved more than a hundred women and children by barricading them in a church and arranging for the Red Cross to ferry them out to safety. Now he speaks about 'terrorism'.

'Why are we terrorists if we want to liberate our country? We know the nature of our enemy. The governments of the West don't lack the same knowledge. They know the history. When we hear James Callaghan denounce us as terrorists, we think that he must be making a particularly silly joke. Who is saying that? The Prime Minister of the state which sentenced Begin to prison for terrorism. Why should we judge a people by an act of terror and ignore the general will? How can the West do that? They know that "terror" or force is the only way we have to escape from our predicament, otherwise we would be ignored. How can they do that? Do they have no conscience?'

Salah's voice is not raised but scornful. The children ignore him, still playing, and no one has noticed that Yahya Rabah has come in. There are greetings. He sits down. Salah's nephew wants to continue the thought, explaining, not pleading.

'When we see women and children killed, do you not think that we also believe it is terrible? But why should Western governments be so blind, seeing what we do and ignoring what they do?

'When we hijacked the bus near Tel Aviv, the entire Western world attacked us, but no government in the West made any comment about what Israel did in south Lebanon. Not one word. Why not? They killed 1,000 innocents. They made 200,000 people homeless. And not one word. Thirty Israelis get killed, and it matters to the West more than if an entire Palestinian community is wiped out. We are less human than the Israelis to the West. It fills me with pity.

'We have no choice but to fight. It is the only way that the world can be made to listen. Sometimes we are asked: "Why not recognize the facts? Israel exists, it is there." Yet no European state makes compromise for its land. They don't even compromise their interests.'

Yahya wants, quietly, to analyse the notion of terrorism more fully.

'It is extremely painful for us to be called "terrorists". We do not really know what is meant by this. But we return to the suffering of our people. Every Palestinian, not only the fighters, has a film in the mind's eye which goes back to the 1930s and before. In this film we are being repressed, and people are always telling us that we are terrorists. And we ask, how can they not understand that we were driven to the gun?

'I am a writer, I'm not a lover of fighting or hardship. It is against human nature which loves contentment and security. Do you think that I like to write under great stress, in wars, without leisure, without seclusion or calm? You know *The Power and the Glory*? It is my favourite Graham

Salah's cousin and his children

An Israeli at the Western Wall. 'We do not hate the Jews. It was the highly civilized nations who persecuted the Jews'

Greene. He believes in the human spirit, in the strength of humanity. He knows that men are driven to do the most impossible things. And Dostoyevsky, and André Malraux also. William Faulkner, especially, understood homesickness, the sense of loss. Do you think that we do not think about our case, and about how we behave?

'Why am I driven to fight when I could have another life? I can't escape my history. In our history, the fedayeen is the saviour, not the ter-

rorist. It is deep, deep in our consciousness. I've seen my people die of sorrow. The beginning of our life has been deferred until we return to our homeland.

'I have been fighting now for ten years. I think that one of the reasons that the West wants to dismiss our problem is that you have endured two great wars and you want to keep war at arm's length, you don't want to think about war. I sympathize with that. But someone with a conscience

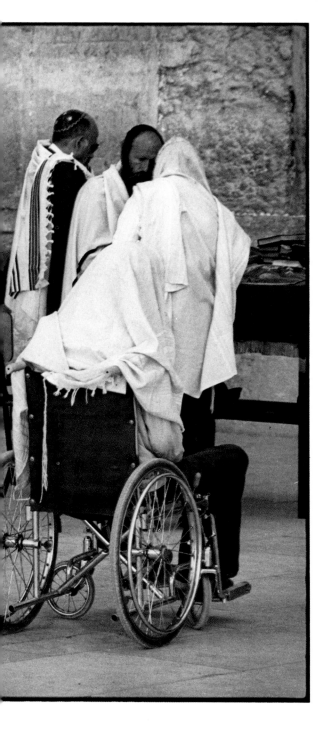

'We forget that Jews are Jews. All we feel is that they have taken our homes, and they must return them to us'

ought to appreciate the crisis which we endure, and the choice which it gives us.

'We are not fanatics. There is a line of poetry which says, "O my enemy, the victim must be one of us. I live to kill, or you kill me. There is nothing between us but the sword and the rifle and that is the judge." In the conflict for survival, when you are face-to-face with the enemy, he loses his humanity. But we do not hate the Jews. It was the highly civilized nations who persecuted the Jews,

the history of the persecution of the Jews is focused in Europe. Indeed, the West is doubly guilty for they both created the problem and then solved it by using the Jews as a pawn in their strategic game, using Israel as a stepping-stone into the Middle East.

'Fanaticism springs from fear and we are not afraid. We are the majority. We even forget that Jews are Jews. All that we feel is that they have taken our homes, and they must return them to us.

'I want to add something which is most important for me. If you ask a well-educated liberal Jew, "Are there Palestinians?" he'll say, "Yes, of course." He will also acknowledge that we have lived in Palestine for many hundreds of years. And if we ask, "Do they have the right to live in freedom?" he'd of course say, "Yes." "Should they not be permitted to return to their homes then?" At this point his loyalty to the state (the Jews are brought up in the Germanic tradition of greater loyalty to the state than to the individual) conflicts with his sense of justice, and he will say, "No." That is why we have to fight.

'A professor at the Hebrew University wrote a study likening Israel to a new-born child whose womb is thousands of years old. The new-born child is always in danger and therefore needs protection. But this is an over-simplification and it

fails to solve the problem. The Jews have had a very painful experience, and because of the great influence of their religion and the impact of Zionism, they have led themselves to believe that they are only safe inside the Zionist state. Outside that state they believe they will meet persecution.

'The Jews inside Israel are riddled with fears. They're afraid of the Arab population growing in Palestine and outnumbering them; they are afraid

of the inevitable progress of the Arab states which encircle them; of the growing might of their armies. So they gamble on the weakness of the Palestinians, on disarray in the Arab world, on the influence of America, and on the guilt complex of the West. And they recognize that all this is a dangerous gamble because these are all temporary factors.

'If only they could understand that our conflict is not with them, not with the Jews, but with the

Jewish state. It may seem unrealistic but we believe that, as the conflict continues, the Jews in Israel will cease to believe in the sanctity of their state. We believe that their mentality will change, that they will begin to accept that the future cannot lie in an artificial, racist state, but in a new natural state in which Jews and Arabs live together in equality. But we can only persuade them of this if we are strong. We are obliged to fight.'

It is becoming dark. The children are tired. There are sticky young fingers to be wiped, kisses and good-byes to be made. Then it is quiet. Salah goes into the garden, where there are exotic plants from India and Vietnam which he tends with care. There is an olive orchard, a few goats. Cicadas. It seems right – for a moment – to be at ease. But Salah breaks the silence.

'Sometimes I say to myself when I am working here, "If only this garden were in my own country." You cannot understand. I am here yet I am not here. I feel sometimes like volunteering for the suicide squad. This is no place for my old age, not for my death, here. I want my body to be buried in Palestine.'

He goes inside and shuts the door. Silence, no peace.

References

1 *The Origin and Development of the Palestinian Problem (1897–1948)*, Kuwaiti Graduate Society, p. 6

2 *Sunday Times*, London, 15 June 1969

3 Chaim Weizmann, *Trial and Error*, London, 1950, p. 115

4 *Chaim Weizmann: Excerpts from his Historical Statements, Writings and Addresses*, The Jewish Agency for Palestine, New York, 1952, p. 48. Cited in David Hirst, *The Gun and the Olive Branch*, p. 40

5 A Zionist immigrant cited in Yuri Avneri, *Israel without Zionism: A Plea for Peace in the Middle East*, New York, Collier Macmillan, 1968

6 Sir Alec Kirkbride, *A Crackle of Thorns: Experiences in the Middle East*, London, John Murray, 1956, pp. 109–12. Cited in Walid al-Khalidi (Ed.) *From Haven to Conquest*, Institute of Palestinian Studies, 1971, pp. 353–6

7 *Ibid.*

8 Frances E. Newton, *Searchlight on Palestine: Fair-play or Terrorist Methods?*, London, Arab Centre, 1938, pp. 15–18. Cited in Walid al-Khalidi, *op. cit.*, pp. 361–2

9 *Ibid.*

10 Jacques de Reynier, *A Jerusalem un Drapeau flottait sur la ligne de feu*, Editions de la Baionnière Neuchâtel, 1950, pp. 71–6. Cited in Walid al-Khalidi, *op. cit.*, p. 764

11 *Ibid.*

12 *Ha-Mashkif*, 11 April 1948. From Menachim Begin, *The Revolt*, London, W. H. Allen, 1951, p. 220. Cited in David Hirst, *op. cit.*, p. 124

13 Menachim Begin, *op. cit.*, p. 164

14 Written in 1940. Cited in David Hirst, *op. cit.*, p. 130

15 *Ibid.*

16 A. Granott, *Agrarian Reform and the Record of Israel*, London, Eyre and Spottiswoode, 1956, pp. 30–9. Cited in Walid al-Khalidi, *op. cit.*, pp. 381–98

17 *Ibid.*

18 *Ibid.*

19 Chaim Arlosoroff, *Jewish Frontier*, October 1948. Cited in Walid al-Khalidi, *op. cit.*, p. 253

20 Schechtman, *Fighter and Prophet, The Vladimir Jabotinsky Story*, p. 449. Cited in David Hirst, *op. cit.*, p. 103

21 Schechtman, *op. cit.*, p. 485

22 David Ben Gurion, *Jewish Observer and Middle East Review*, 27 September 1963

23 Leonard Moseley, *Gideon Goes to War*, London, Arthur Baker, 1955, pp. 55–64

24 *Ibid.*

25 Morris Ernst, *So Far So Good*, New York, Harper and Brothers, pp. 170–7

26 President Truman at the White House in 1945 speaking to diplomatic representatives of various Arab countries. Cited in William A. Eddy, *F.D.R. Meets Ibn Saud*, New York, 1954, p. 37

27 *The Origins and Development of the Palestinian Problem (1897–1947)*, Kuwaiti Graduate Society, pp. 52–3

28 Yit Zhaqi in *Yediot Aharonot*, 14 April 1972. Cited in David Hirst, *op. cit.*, p. 140

29 David Hirst, *op. cit.*, p. 140

30 *Ibid.*, p. 141

31 *The Book of Palmbach (Ha Sophar ha Palmach)* Vol. 2, p. 286. Cited in *The ABC of the Palestinian Problem*, Part I, *1896–1941*, Beirut, Arab Woman's Information Committee

32 *Ibid.*

33 Michal Bar-Zohar, *The Armed Prophet: A Biography of Ben Gurion*, London, 1967, pp. 139–40

34 *The Book of Palmbach*, Vol. 2, p. 286. Cited in *The ABC of the Palestine Problem*

35 *Jewish Newsletter*, New York, 9 February 1959. Cited in Erskine Childers, 'The Other Exodus' in *Spectator*, London, 12 May 1961

36 Jon and David Kimshe, *Both Sides of the Hill*, London, Secker and Warburg, 1960, pp. 227–8

37 Yuri Avneri, *op. cit.*, p. 134

38 *Ibid.*

39 *Maariv*, 24 March 1972. Cited in David Hirst, *op. cit.*, pp. 210–11

40 Conversation with Nabil Shaath, July 1970. Cited in John Cooley, *Green March, Black September, The Story of the Palestinian Arabs*, London, Frank Cass, 1973

41 Amos Kenan, Israeli journalist writing about Beit Miba in *Israel Imperial News*, London, March 1968. Cited in David Hirst, *op. cit.*, pp. 226–7

42 Words to a student of Haifa Techmin, quoted in *Haretz*, 4 April 1969. Cited in David Hirst, *op. cit.*, p. 221

43 *Haalan Hazeh*, 8 July 1968. Cited in David Hirst, *op. cit.*, p. 221